The Right to Read

The Right to Read

Beating Dyslexia and
Other Learning Disabilities

Dr. Jan Strydom
Susan du Plessis

Important Notes

Part two of this book contains a practical program. The following conditions apply:

See authors' contact details on page 169.

Published by Remedium CC, Pretoria, South Africa.
Cover design by Nico Grobler.
Printed by V & R Printing Works (Pty.) Ltd.

ISBN 1-919751-01-7

Meet the Authors

Jan Strydom has been involved in consultation and research on learning and behavior problems for twenty-five years. He is a man of many talents. He holds a doctoral degree in education and an M.A. in philosophy, speaks several languages, is a trained opera singer and is internationally recognized as a chess problem composer. He is father of three and grandfather of two. He coauthored *The Myth of ADHD and Other Learning Disabilities. Parenting without Ritalin.*

Susan du Plessis has been coresearcher of Jan Strydom for more than ten years. She holds B.Div. and an honors degree in psychology. She is author of three books on learning disabilities and coauthored *The Myth of ADHD and Other Learning Disabilities. Parenting without Ritalin.*

Acknowledgement

The authors wish to acknowledge the contribution of Benetta Strydom in compiling the *Audiblox* 2000 program.

Index

Part Two—Practice

Introduction

by Susan du Plessis

> He who ne'er learns his A,B,C,
> Forever will a Blockhead be;
> But he who to his Book's inclin'd,
> Will soon a golden Treasure find.

This verse from an American colonial schoolbook shows that from the earliest days of Western society, the importance of mastering the written word was understood and stressed. The ability to read does not only enable a person to get a job and then to advance in a career, but it is also necessary for many everyday tasks. The nonreader, for example, cannot read and understand the bank statements he receives from his bank. He is also forced to learn how to use the new TV set that he has just bought through trial and error, because the instruction booklet of the manufacturer remains a closed book to him. The variety and universality of experience that are offered by fictional and nonfictional literature are also not at the disposal of the nonreader.

There will probably be widespread agreement that, if a dog is man's best friend, a book must be a close second. The importance of reading cannot be denied. However, judging from available statistics, it seems that reading ability is on a steady and seemingly inexorable decline. Mysteriously, more and more children seem to battle with problems like reversing words when reading, writing back to front, not being able to remember the sequence of letters in a word or sometimes reading slowly and with poor comprehension. Even more mysterious is the fact that those, who are saddled with these problems, seem to be unable ever to get rid of these difficulties. Many simply fail ever to master the art of reading at all; many more fail ever to adequately master the art of reading. For millions of people this is a reality. The statistics depict a grim picture indeed. According to the New Jersey Council on Adult Education and Literacy, for example, out of six million adults in New Jersey three million (50 percent) have literacy problems, i.e. they cannot use a bus schedule or write a complaint letter; 1.4 million (23 percent) are functionally illiterate, i.e. they cannot locate information on a map or total a bank deposit slip.[1] In our world of high-tech communications this can only result in frustration, embarrassment and often destruction. For millions of children and adults this is a reality.

Although the inability to read, or read well, is sometimes the result of a lack of opportunities or ability, this often seems not to be the case. Many children come from good homes, go to good schools and, according to their intellectual potential, should be able to master the skill of reading at the age of six or seven. Or at least then at ten, or, at the very latest, at twelve or fifteen. Only, they don't.

For many decades scientists of many fields of endeavor have been greatly puzzled by this phenomenon, and since the 1960s millions of dollars have been poured into a search for a solution. Yet, despite these efforts the numbers of children, unable to master the written word, continue to multiply.

Why would *this* book offer light at the end of the tunnel? What makes it so special? The answer is that a philosopher has stepped in. In the big forest called "learning disabilities," many disciplines and professions are at work, each cultivating a separate set of trees. These professions include education, psychology, neuropsychology, speech and language pathology, neurology, psychiatry, ophthalmology, optometry, and occupational therapy. Each of these professions focuses on a different aspect of the child with learning disabilities, of which dyslexia is the most common. It is *not* their interest to integrate the findings of the various disciplines, to draw a map of the whole territory each department has separately investigated. It is *not* their business to concern themselves with the whole wood. That is the business of *philosophy*.

Many years ago Dr. Jan Strydom, educator and philosopher, stepped into the learning disabilities forest, trying to find answers to the many daunting questions that had been left unanswered by the various disciplines working in the forest. With his philosophy training as background, he was able not only to study the separate trees, but also the whole wood, and gradually a comprehensive picture started taking shape that more and more presented a reasonable answer to the riddle of learning disabilities, such as dyslexia.

It should be noted that a philosophical study does not equal a summary. A summary cannot explain the sometimes extremely divergent ideas, and often contentious disagreements that rage between the various disciplines at work. Rather, it entails a journey that tried to make sense of a history fraught with logical flaws and circular reasoning, and which eventually lead to the discovery of one key factor that made it possible to correctly interpret the phenomenon of a child with a learning disability. This one key factor made it possible to dispel the murkiness that had so far clouded the forest, so that it could become evident that in actual fact there is no such thing as a learning *DIS*ability, only an *IN*ability.

In this book the reader is taken along on a replay of this exciting journey of discovery. This will enable the reader to see that the answers to the questions that have so far riddled the field of "learning disabilities" are in fact quite plain—on condition that one must be willing and able to take a walk through the whole forest, and not get stuck at one or two of the trees. The journey ends with a practical program, effective to alleviate the symptoms associated with dyslexia and other learning difficulties.

If you are the parent of a child with a learning disability, or a teacher responsible for the well-being of a number of children, this program will offer new hope. It has already proved to be water in a barren desert and a shining light in the dark for thousands of children and adults.

Note:
1. Phillips, B., "Writing on the wall," *The Record*, 3 January 1994.

Part One

Theory

1.

The Keys to the Kingdom

The direction in which education starts a man will
determine his future life.[1] — Plato

Dear Sir

*Heardy I aply for any posision in your cumpany. I am ninteen years of age and
have now cumpleted grabe ten. I am interristed in people and a motivateb
person. I dont have any work ecsperience dut I am wiling to lern.*

Yours faitfuly.

Mr. R. M. White

When reading the above letter you might think that it was written by some-
one with a very low intelligence. You are wrong. This person's intelligence is
above average, but he is limited in his ability to read and spell correctly. He is
what professionals call dyslexic.

The term *dyslexia* was introduced in 1884 by the German ophthalmologist,
R. Berlin. He coined it from the Greek words *dys* meaning ill or difficult and
lexis meaning word, and used it to describe a specific disturbance of reading in
the absence of pathological conditions in the visual organs.[2] In a later publication, in 1887, Berlin stated that dyslexia, "presuming right handedness," is caused
by a left-sided cerebral lesion. He spoke of "word-blindness" and detailed his
observations with six patients with brain lesions who had full command over
verbal communications but had lost the ability to read.[3]

In the century to follow the narrow definition Berlin attached to the term
dyslexia would broaden. By the mid-1970s it was describing a condition of
epidemic proportions, and although it had no universally accepted symptoms,

it was commanding the attention of an armada of professionals, including pediatricians, neurologists and educational psychologists.

In its short history the condition would have a multiplicity of names. In 1895 James Hinshelwood, an ophthalmologist from Glasgow, established the term "congenital word-blindness," but since then it has been called strephosymbolia, word amblyopia, bradylexia, script-blindness, primary reading retardation, specific reading disability, developmental reading backwardness, analfabetia partialis, amnesia visualis, genetic dyslexia, reading disability, and learning disability.[4] Most of these have now been discarded in favor of the terms dyslexia, reading disability and learning disability, with learning disabilities (LD) as the umbrella term for a variety of learning difficulties, including dyslexia.[5]

Although there are a large number of other "disabilities" to be found within the LD field, a reading disability—or dyslexia—remains the most common. Estimates of learning-disabled students being dyslexic vary between 70 and 85 percent. Some experts are of the opinion that this percentage is even higher, so much so that labeling a child as learning disabled is understood to include a reading disability.[6] If one evaluates the importance of reading in the learning situation, this opinion probably comes close to the truth. Reading is regarded as the most important skill that a child must acquire at school,[7] because one must learn to read in order to be able to read to learn.[8] The implication of this is that the child who is a poor reader will usually also be a poor learner.

The fact that we have a label called learning disabilities at all is due to the times and the society in which we live. After all, it is a society's priorities that determine whether a particular child will be considered disabled. In every society there have always been people who could not meet the demands that were placed on them. Those who could not comply with such demands were mostly rejected or considered to be an outcast. The Spartans in the seventh century B.C., for example, set great store by physical prowess. Training to serve the state physically commenced at the age of seven years and was only concluded at the age of thirty. In cases where a newborn was very weak or severely deformed and would not be able to serve the state, he was left on a mountain to die. In order that their women might bear children who would become as strong and fierce as their fathers, the soldiers offered their wives to the strongest and most powerful warriors.[9] In the Elizabethan era, again, the focus was on musical talent, and people who could not play an instrument or could not sing, were looked upon as uneducated.

In the Anang society of Nigeria, musical talent—including bodily-kinesthetic abilities—is still looked upon as important. By the age of five, the children of that society can sing hundreds of songs, play numerous percussion instruments, and perform dozens of complex dances. In Eskimo cultures, spatial ability is a major strength because Eskimos place a high survival value on noticing subtle differences in snow and ice surfaces. They don't want to be on the wrong side of a chunk of ice when it floats off into the sea! Sixty percent of the children in Eskimo cultures score as well as the top ten percent of American schoolchildren on tests of spatial aptitude. In certain South Sea island cultures, the ability to build and steer a canoe and navigate it by the stars—requiring superior bodily-kinesthetic and spatial abilities—is very important.[10] Highly literate people from our culture with superior linguistic or logical-mathematical abilities might find their smartness to be useless in these cultures. They might find themselves labeled "dancing disabled" or "navigating disabled."[11]

In modern Western society, as it happens to be, mastery of basic academic skills—reading, writing and arithmetic—is a necessary prerequisite for success in both school and employment settings and society at large. Naturally, also in our society there are members who are unable to meet the expectations, and the seriousness of such difficulties is hard to exaggerate. It is therefore understandable that a child who cannot cope in the classroom is a source of distress to his parents. To see how one's otherwise normal child drops further and further behind in comparison to his classmates and perhaps fails year after year, is no laughing matter. Few parents are driven to tears if a child does not achieve well on the sports field. However, because reading and writing are essential in life and making a living, problems at school can lead to great anxiety in parents. Unless the child's problem is dealt with in an adequate manner, what awaits him outside the school gates is probably nothing but a hopeless future:

> Many adults with learning disabilities are underemployed, often stuck in dead-end jobs that do not tap into their true vocational potential.[12] Many others are not finding employment at all. Many are unsuccessful in their pursuit of further training, and few are accessing the adult services that have been developed to serve them. Many LD young adults have major academic . . . and vocational needs that make it hard for them to . . . live independent lives . . . [13]

The figures on the salary check, however, might not be the only concern. People who cannot read can also not read instructions on a bottle of prescription medicine, look up numbers in a telephone directory, or read the menu in a restaurant. Being unable to read traffic signs and street names, or maps on long journeys, they cannot travel freely. They cannot read the letters that their children bring home from their teachers or help them with homework. They cannot write to friends or read for pleasure. In fact, they are severely isolated in a reading world.

Choice, in all its facets, is diminished in the life of the reading-disabled person. If he votes, he is forced to cast a vote of questionable worth. Being unable to read important information in print, he can't make an informed decision. He would probably vote for a face, a smile, or a style, not for a mind or character or body of beliefs. Even the printed TV schedule, which provides people with the luxury of preselection, does not belong to the arsenal of options in the life of a nonabled reader. One consequence is that the viewer watches only what appears at moments when he happens to have time to turn on the switch. A lot more common is that the TV set remains in operation night and day. Whatever program is offered at the hour when he walks into the room will be the nutriment that he accepts and swallows.[14]

Learning or reading disabilities can have destructive emotional effects. Persistent learning failure leads to anguish, embarrassment and frustration. "There is something terrifying about sitting at the back of the class and having somebody ask you questions which you know you will never be able to answer,"[15] an adult dyslexic told British actress Susan Hampshire, who is also dyslexic.

In describing his feelings about growing up with a learning disability, Nelson Rockefeller, who served as vice president of the United States and governor of the state of New York, recalled:

> I was dyslexic...and I still have a hard time reading today. I remember vividly the pain and mortification I felt as a boy of eight when I was assigned to read a short passage of scripture at a community vesper service and did a thoroughly miserable job of it. I know what a dyslexic child goes through . . . the frustration of not being able to do what other children do easily, the humiliation of being thought not too bright when such is not the case at all.[16]

For some the humiliation becomes too much. In one study, Peck found that over 50 percent of all suicides under age fifteen in Los Angeles County had been previously diagnosed as having learning disabilities. The actual percentage of youngsters labeled "learning disabled" in most school districts in the United States is below five percent; therefore, it seems clear that youngsters with learning disabilities constitute a disproportionately large percentage of adolescent suicides compared with the general adolescent population.[17]

In another study, conducted in Ontario, Canada, the researchers analyzed all the available suicide notes (n = 27) from 267 consecutive adolescent suicides for spelling and handwriting errors. The results showed that 89 percent of the twenty-seven adolescents who committed suicide had significant deficits in spelling and handwriting that were similar to those of the adolescents with LD.[18]

Behavior problems resulting from their negative experiences are not uncommon in LD youngsters. The strain and the frustration of underachieving can cause them to be reluctant to go to school, to throw temper tantrums before school or in some cases to play truant. Cheating, stealing and experimenting with drugs can also result when children regard themselves as failures.[19]

Former U.S.A. First Lady Barbara Bush, who has a learning-disabled son, noted that "learning disabilities can destroy lives. To get a really disturbing sense of this—we need only to look at the estimates of the learning disabled among juvenile delinquents."[20] Results from a study in the U.S.A. by the National Center for State Courts demonstrated that youths with LD were 200 percent more likely to be arrested than nondisabled peers for comparable offences.[21] According to the U.S. Department of Education 60 percent of America's prison inmates are illiterate and 85 percent of all juvenile offenders have reading problems.[22]

Bob Turney is a dyslexic who turned to crime because he thought he was thick. At primary school, he sat at the back of the class looking at picture books and did not have a clue what the teachers were talking about. When they said that he was stupid, he believed them; and when they treated him as disruptive, uncooperative and lazy, he behaved accordingly. He left school at fifteen, barely able to write his own name, got involved in his first burglary, and spent the next eighteen years in and out of prison.[23]

Desperate parents, therefore, clutch at any straw in an effort to rescue their child. . . .

The tragedy is that children who receive treatment for their learning disabilities are seldom better off than children who receive no help at all.

Zigmond and Thornton sum up this sad state of affairs:

> Despite concerted efforts at early intervention and remedial teaching, learning disabilities are pervasive and persistent. Elementary school programs do not save LD students from serious academic and social problems in high school. High school programs for LD adolescents do not rescue these young adults from problems out in the world.[24]

There can be only two explanations for this inability of experts to assist the learning disabled. The first explanation may be that they are trying to solve an insolvable problem. Statements such as "learning disabilities cannot be 'fixed',"[25] "a learning disability is a lifelong condition,"[26] and "dyslexia is like alcoholism . . . it can never be cured"[27] are often found in the literature. Other statements are even more dooming. According to Professor Gerald Coles, author of *The Learning Mystique*, learning-disabled children will either not learn to read or will read so poorly and slowly that each year they will fall further behind classmates who are normal readers.[28] In other words, the poor get poorer and the rich get richer.

The only other explanation for the deplorable results obtained in the LD field, is that learning disabilities are in fact curable, but the experts in the field are still groping in the dark to find a cure.

One finds that LD experts are divided in schools or factions. They often differ so violently from each other that one sometimes wonders whether they are talking about the same thing. Their arguments are often based on illogical suppositions and circular reasoning and their research on unsupported claims. Literally thousands of research reports, articles and books on learning disabilities are published each year, more than any person can read. However, the tremendous amount of knowledge that has already accumulated is not a reflection of the progress that is made.

There is only one way in which any science can make progress: its point of departure must be based on fact. If the point of departure of any science is questionable, what follows will naturally be questionable too. Suppose Neil Armstrong and his fellow astronauts did not know that the moon was circling around the earth. All their calculations would have been wrong and they would probably still be trying to reach the big piece of cheese.

The field of interest in the science of LD is children with learning problems. Most problems can only be solved if one knows what *causes* that

20

particular problem. A disease such as pellagra, also called the disease of the four D's—dermatitis, diarrhea, dementia and death—took the lives of thousands in the Southern states of America during the early part of the twentieth century. Data is sketchy, but by 1912, the State of California alone reported 30,000 cases and a mortality rate of 40 percent. Today, pellagra is virtually unknown because we know that it is caused by a vitamin B3 deficiency.[29] A viable point of departure in the LD field would thus be: what *causes* a learning disability? To illustrate the present state of affairs on this point, we quote Hallahan, Kauffman and Lloyd: "But what actually is *known* about why children are learning disabled? The answer to this question is "very little!"[30]

If "very little" is *known* about why children are learning disabled, it implies that, whatever is regarded as the cause or causes of this problem may be based on no more than guesswork. The causes are *presumed* and as we all know, presumptions can easily be wrong. The whole science of LD could well be based on a false point of departure, which could certainly be the reason why so little—if any—progress is being made. If this were true—and the reader is soon to discover that it is—at least one possible inference could be made: Statements claiming that learning disabilities were incurable, could well be wrong. Once the *cause* of pellagra was discovered, it was no longer considered to be an incurable disease.

Note that inherently there was nothing inherently wrong with the people who died from this disease. It was caused solely by a deficiency in their diet. In the same way, as this book will show, inherently there is nothing wrong with the majority of children who struggle at school! Once the true nature of the problem afflicting these children is understood, we can disregard the idea of learning *DIS*abilities, and start solving learning *IN*abilities.

Although the supposition of "learning disabilities" is criticized in this book, it is not the intention to deny the existence of learning problems. It is a well-known and accepted fact that worldwide there are millions of children to whom school is a nightmare. However, the time has come to start thinking about learning failure in a meaningful and scientific manner. This book offers an alternative theory for the cause of the learning disabilities phenomenon, one that is based on logical, rational and scientific principles. Moreover, the practical method based on these principles holds out an answer to many prayers.

Whatever your present point of view on learning disabilities, do not allow your beliefs to overrule your scientific judgement. No stone may be left unturned to eradicate this problem, especially as it brings such devastation in the lives of so many children. As Richardson states so succinctly:

> Literacy gives us the keys to knowledge and wisdom—the keys to the Kingdom. Isn't it time now for us all to put our heads together, to work together to see to it that those keys are given to every child?[31]

Pointers to Dyslexia

Generally, the term *dyslexia* is used to describe a severe reading disability, but there has been little agreement in the literature or in practice concerning the definition of *severe* or the specific distinguishing characteristics that differentiate dyslexia from other reading problems.[32] Instead of getting involved in the wrangling over a definition, we would rather use the "symptoms" below as an indication that a person has a reading problem and therefore needs help:

- One of the most obvious—and one of the most common—telltale signs is reversals. People with this kind of problem often confuse letters like **b** and **d**, either when reading or when writing, or they sometimes read (or write) words like "rat" for "tar," or "won" for "now."

- Another sure sign, which needs no confirmation by means of any form of testing, is elisions, that is when a person sometimes reads or writes "cat" when the word is actually "cart."

- The person who reads very slowly and hesitantly, who reads without fluency, word by word, or who constantly loses his place, thereby leaving out whole chunks or reading the same passage twice, has a reading problem.

- The person may try to sound out the letters of the word, but then be unable to say the correct word. For example, he may sound the letters "c-a-t" but then say "cold."

- He may read or write the letters of a word in the wrong order, like "left" for "felt," or the syllables in the wrong order, like "emeny" for "enemy," or words in the wrong order, like "are there" for "there are."

- He may spell words as they sound, for example "rite" for "right."

- He may read with poor comprehension, or it may be that he remembers little of what he reads.

- The person may have a poor and/or slow handwriting.

Notes:

1. Bartlett, J., *Familiar Quotations* (16th ed.), (Boston: Little Brown and Company, 1992), 75.
2. Berlin, R, "Über Dyslexie," *Archiv fur Psychiatrie*, 1884, vol. 15, 276-278, cited in G. Opp, "Historical roots of the field of learning disabilities," *Journal of Learning Disabilities*, January 1994, vol. 27, 10.
3. Berlin, R., *Eine besondere Art der Wortblindheit (Dyslexie)*, (Wiesbaden, Germany: Bergmann, 1887), cited in Opp, "Historical roots of the field of learning disabilities."
4. Drew, A. L., "A neurological appraisal of familial congenital word-blindness," *Brain*, 1956, vol. 79, 440-460, cited in G. S. Coles, *The Learning Mystique* (New York: Pantheon Books, 1987), 10.
5. Coles, *The Learning Mystique*, 10.
6. Ibid., xii.
7. Blignaut, C. M., *'n Inleiding tot Leesonderrig* (Johannesburg: A. P. B., 1963).
8. Barkhuizen, B. P., *'n Psigologies-Pedagogiese Ondersoek van die Leesprobleem in Transvaalse Laerskole* (Unisa: Unpublished DEd thesis, 1963).
9. Sussman, N., " Sex and sexuality in history," in B. J. Sadock, H. I. Kaplan & A. M. Freedman (eds.), *The Sexual Experience* (Baltimore: Williams & Wilkins, 1976), cited in J. P. Dworetzky, *Introduction to Child Development* (St. Paul: West Publishing Company, 1981), 82.
10. Gardner, H., *Frames of Mind: The Theory of Multiple Intelligences* (New York: Basic Books, 1983), cited in T. Armstrong, *In Their Own Way: Discovering and Encouraging Your Child's Personal Learning Style* (Los Angeles: Jeremy P. Tarcher, Inc., 1987), 17.
11. Armstrong, *In Their Own Way*, 17-18.
12. Gerber, et al., cited in H. B. Reiff & P. J. Gerber, "Adults with learning disabilities," in N. N. Singh & I. L. Beale (eds.), *Learning Disabilities: Nature, Theory, and Treatment* (New York: Springer-Verlag, 1992), 186.

13. Zigmond, N., & Thornton, H. S., "The future of learning disabilities," in K. A. Kavale (ed.), *Learning Disabilities: State of the Art and Practice* (Boston: College-Hill Press, 1988), 199.
14. Kozol, J., *Illiterate America* (Garden City, NY: Anchor Press, 1985), 23, 26-27.
15. Hampshire, S., *Every Letter Counts: Winning in Life Despite Dyslexia* (London: Corgi Books, 1991), 220.
16. Rockefeller, N., *TV Guide*, 16 October 1976, 12-14, cited in J. Lerner, *Learning Disabilities: Theories, Diagnosis, and Teaching Strategies* (4th ed.), (Boston: Houghton Mifflin Company, 1988), 4.
17. Peck, M., "Crisis intervention treatment with chronically and acutely suicidal adolescents," in M. Peck, N. L. Farberow & R. Litman (eds.), *Youth Suicide* (New York: Springer, 1985), 112-122.
18. Hazel, E., McBride, A., & Siegel, L. S., "Learning disabilities and adolescent suicide," *Journal of Learning Disabilities*, November 1997, vol. 30.
19. Hampshire, *Every Letter Counts*, 291-292.
20. Ibid., 151.
21. Broder, P. K., et al., "Further observations on the link between learning disabilities and juvenile delinquency." *Journal of Educational Psychology*, 1981, vol. 73, 838-850.
22. http://www.hcity.com, website maintained by G. Sagmiller, author of *Dyslexia My Life.*
23. Hinds, D., "Word blind," *Independent*, 11 July 1996, E8, E9.
24. Zigmond & Thornton, "The future of learning disabilities," 199.
25. "New perspectives on teaching from successful adults with learning disabilities," *Remedial and Special Education*, 1 January 1995.
26. Reiff & Gerber, "Adults with learning disabilities," 172.
27. Clark, M., & Gosnell, M., "Dealing with dyslexia," *Newsweek*, 22 March 1982, 55-56.
28. Coles, *The Learning Mystique*, xii.
29. Kraut, A., "Dr. Joseph Goldberger and the war on pellagra," website address: www.nih.gov/od/museum/exhibits/goldberger/full-text.html, 1996.
30. Hallahan, D. P., Kauffman, J., & Lloyd, J., *Introduction to Learning Disabilities* (Englewood Cliffs, NJ: Prentice Hall, 1985), 16.
31. Richardson, S., "Specific developmental dyslexia. Retrospective and prospective views," *Annals of Dyslexia*, 1989, vol. 39, 3-24.
32. Sawyer, D. J., "Dyslexia: Introduction to the special series," *Journal of Learning Disabilities*, January 1992, vol. 25, 38-39.

2.

Birth of a Syndrome

We must take all history seriously—the history of
what we did right and the history of what we did
wrong. People learn from both their successes and
their failures.[1] — Blatt

On Saturday, April 6, 1963, a new disease was invented in Chicago, Illinois, that over the next twenty years would slowly begin to infect millions of school-children nationwide. This was no simple virus or common bacteria. Hidden deep within the neurological system, it resisted detection by medical personnel, evaded clear diagnosis through testing, and had no discernible cure. The federal government would spend billions of dollars on this affliction over the next twenty years, and yet between 1977 and 1983 the number of sufferers would double.

It was on that Saturday in April that Samuel Kirk, then a professor of special education at the University of Illinois, told a group of concerned parents about learning disabilities. He suggested that they use the term to describe "children who have disorders in development of language, speech, reading, and associated communication skills." They enthusiastically agreed and shortly thereafter established the Association for Children with Learning Disabilities.

Since that time, the learning disability (LD) movement has mushroomed, with the founding of many more organizations, the writing of hundreds of books and tens of thousands of articles. The popular media have made it a suitable subject for dramatic television shows and full-length feature films. More importantly, and devastatingly, millions of children have been labeled learning disabled, dyslexic, hyperactive, and a host of related terms, then sent to special programs to be treated for their "condition."[2]

Problems with learning and behavior in children are certainly not a new phenomenon. Long before 1963 teachers and parents were complaining that some children are difficult to teach and control, that they underachieve academically or that they can't sit still. As early as 1867, Heinrich Stotzner, a German teacher of the deaf, founded a school for slow learning children. These children did not have mental retardation but, according to Stotzner, their memories were too weak to retain letters, and due to the poor motor coordination of their fingers, they had difficulty learning to write. Stotzner understood that the learning problems of these children called for remedial teaching efforts.[3]

Even earlier, in 1845, the physician Heinrich Hoffman had written and illustrated the story *Zappelphilipp* ("Fidget Philipp") for his own son. Philipp was a hyperactive boy, rocking in his chair at the dinner table until everything fell to the ground with the tablecloth. *Zappelphilipp* at the time was probably the most popular book for the young, at least in Germany.[4] Half a century later, in 1907, the neurologist Hermann Oppenheim reported his clinical experience with children who could not sit still, could not keep their extremities calm and caused significant trouble for parents and teachers with their fidgeting and their uninhibited translation of psychic processes into motoric acts.[5]

Problems with learning and behavior have therefore always been around, although they may perhaps never before have existed in the alarming numbers that they occur now. What also did not exist until 6 April 1963, was the increasingly fashionable attribution of these problems to neurological abnormalities and to describe "these affected children" as victims of a clearly defined medical syndrome.[6] According to this medical explanation, learning disabilities has a biological cause. To be more exact, there is something wrong with the child's brain. In accordance with this view, learning is a neurological "process" which takes place inside the brain. On these grounds it is supposed that the child who struggles to learn must have a neurological "dysfunction."

The idea of a neurological dysfunction soon became more and more popular, giving rise to an armada of theories. According to one such a theory, dyslexia is the result when the link between the language, hearing and comprehension centers of the brain is somehow misconfigured during fetal development.[7] Other theories state that dyslexia is caused by "faulty wiring in the brain,"[8] or a subtle impairment of vision.[9] Dr. Harold N. Levinson blames it on a cerebellar-vestibular dysfunction,[10] while in an article in *The Economist* it was stated, "natural selection has equipped mankind with impressive spoken-language skills. But it never had a chance to prepare people for reading. The first known language in which written letters corresponded to particular sounds was developed by the Canaanites around 1700 B.C. By then the human brain had already been chiseled into its current form."[11] The list of proposed causes for reading and learning failure is endless.

It is impossible to trace any of these supposed neurological abnormalities through any form of medical examination or test. The abnormality is nevertheless inferred from observing the child's behavior. Bob Algozzine, once professor of special education at the University of Florida and contributing editor to *The Journal of Learning Disabilities*, wrote: "No . . . one has been able to demonstrate to me that a specific, distinctly unique group of behaviors differentiate LD children from many of their classmates. To build an empire on such a foundation is very dishonest."[12]

Professor Coles concurs. After decades of research, he says, it has still not been demonstrated that disabling neurological dysfunctions exist in more than a minuscule number of children. The few research studies that have made such claims, have serious methodological flaws. Through repeating these ideas and beliefs over and over, however, the theory of a neurological dysfunction has taken on the authority of proven fact.[13] And indeed, this "fact" has become the point of departure in the science of learning disabilities.

To have a better understanding of this medical fabrication it is necessary to go back in history to the time when the ideas on learning disabilities originated. The present can only be fully understood if one examines its roots in the past. In this case the key to comprehension resides in the work of James Hinshelwood, a Glasgow eye surgeon, who today is cited as the first major figure in what became the field of learning disabilities, and in the research done by two German refugees, the psychiatrist Alfred Strauss and the psychologist Heinz Werner. These two scholars were employed during the late 1930s at the Wayne County Training School in Northville, Michigan, a school for educable mentally retarded children.

In 1907, a schoolmaster in Glasgow, Scotland, mentioned to a county Medical Officer of Health that he was "greatly puzzled" about four of his students. They were the youngest brothers in a family of eleven children and, unlike their seven siblings, had "experienced the greatest difficulties in learning to read." The medical officer, a former student of James Hinshelwood, "at once recognized" the "true nature of the difficulty." He referred the boys to his former mentor to confirm the diagnosis and provide the schoolmaster with expert help.

Hinshelwood confirmed the medical officer's preliminary conclusions: the boys indeed had congenital word-blindness, a condition that "frequently assumes a family type," that probably was hereditary and that was caused by a defective language-related area of the brain. He reasoned that, because the reading problems were clustered in one family, and because the four boys had normal general intelligence, lacked visual problems, had good visual memory except for letters and words, had a family life which had not impeded their siblings' learning, but had failed to read with school instruction that had been successful with their siblings, it was "evident that their cerebral defect was a purely local one, . . . that it was strictly confined to the cerebral area for the visual memory of words and letters, the left angular gyrus, and did not extend at all beyond that."[14]

Hinshelwood concluded that the root of congenital word-blindness lay in children's brains because he had observed that dysfunctional reading symptoms found in adults with brain lesions were analogous to those of certain children with reading problems. If an inability to recognize and remember letters and words, or to unite recognizable letters into syllables or into words, was acquired word-blindness, a symptom of localized brain damage in adults, and if it was clear that sensory functioning, intellectual functioning and environmental conditions could be excluded as causes of the reading disability, and if the reading symptoms were similar to those of acquired word-blindness, it was "evident"—Hinshelwood's exact word—that the problem was caused by localized brain damage that was probably hereditary.[15]

This line of reasoning, however, comprises an invalid argument: If A then B; B; therefore A.

Hinshelwood's argument can be summarized as follows:

If an individual has brain damage, he exhibits reading problems.
This individual exhibits reading problems.
Therefore, this individual is brain damaged.

There may perhaps be some readers who are unable to see that the above argument is invalid. For their benefit, another argument, showing the same form as the above one is offered below. The invalidity of this argument, however, cannot be doubted.

If I am Superman, then I am a man.
I am a man.
Therefore, I am Superman.

Goodman used another analogy to point out the logical flaw inherent in Hinshelwood's reasoning: A drought can kill vegetation. If, however, we find dead vegetation, we cannot assume that drought was the cause. The vegetation could have been destroyed, not by drought but by any number of causes including nonbiological ones such as lumbering.[16] Consider also that, when a person is being chased by a ferocious bull, he will run. However, when we see a person running, we cannot jump to the conclusion that he is being chased by a bull. Similarly, if a brain-damaged person exhibits certain characteristics, we cannot simply jump to the conclusion that a person is brain damaged when we see him exhibiting the same characteristics. There may be many other reasons for his behavior.

In his diagnosis of the four boys, Hinshelwood rejected or ignored the role that school, family, and other environmental conditions may have played. As Coles points out, there were other plausible explanations for the boys' reading difficulties. Perhaps by the time the eighth child arrived, the parents of this large mining family were too busy and too tired to provide the nurturing they had given the others. Perhaps a large family dependent upon a small salary had become increasingly poor as the family grew, and the diminishing financial means relative to family needs had adversely affected the younger children.[17] Hinshelwood also ignored the role motivation might have played. Upon leaving school, the oldest of the four boys, motivated by his enthusiasm for football (soccer), managed to master on his own the vocabulary of football terms, and could read, "fairly well," the football reports of a sports newspaper that he religiously bought. Yet, the young man had great difficulty reading a child's first primer or an "ordinary book."[18]

At the beginning of the twentieth century the number of children that were diagnosed as cases of congenital word-blindness was still small.

However, following research that was done during the 1930s and 1940s by Strauss and Werner, this situation was to change dramatically during and after the 1960s.

While Strauss and Werner were employed at the Wayne County Training School, they came to believe that their educable mentally retarded students were of two basic types. The first group, which they referred to as the *endogenous type*, consisted of children who had a family history of mental deficiency. The second group, which they referred to as the *exogenous type*, had, on the other hand, no family history of mental deficiency. According to Strauss and Werner, their retardation was caused by brain injury— before, during or after birth. In comparing endogenous and exogenous children on perceptual and cognitive tasks, they found the endogenous group to be more successful than the brain-injured children regarding these abilities. The endogenous children had no behavioral problems, while the brain-injured children engaged in—what they described as—disturbed, unrestrained and volatile behavior. Furthermore, the endogenous children exhibited a small increase in their IQ scores during their stay at the Wayne County Training School, while the exogenous children displayed a small decrease. Strauss and Werner concluded that the IQ changes indicated that the curriculum for the mentally retarded was ineffective for the brain-damaged children.[19]

A few years later Strauss and another coworker, Newell Kephart, expanded the study of brain injury to include children of normal intelligence. They argued that the kind of perceptual-motor and cognitive problems and behavior problems, that Strauss and Werner had found among the exogenous group, were not only to be found in mentally defective children. These problems were also found in children of normal intelligence. On these grounds they concluded that children of normal intelligence, who exhibited these learning and behavior problems, were also brain damaged.[20] In this way, they committed the same logical error that Hinshelwood had committed earlier: If A then B; B; therefore A.

The research of Strauss and Werner has been criticized by many. Kenneth Kavale of the University of Iowa and Steven Forness of the University of California, for example, reanalyzed Strauss and Werner's original studies on brain-injured children. They concluded that the performance differences reported between the two groups of children—the endogenous and exogenous

—were in fact too small to justify the distinction which Strauss and Werner had made.[21]

There was, furthermore, a critical problem involved in their research. Neither Strauss and Werner in their initial research with mentally defective children nor Strauss and Kephart in their studies of children with normal intelligence provided evidence of brain damage or other neurological dysfunctions. The brain damage was inferred *only* from the children's behavior.[22]

The Learning Disabilities Scapegoat

Despite these obvious problems and the criticism, the work of Strauss and Kephart has been continued by many. Although these followers of Strauss and Kephart could also provide no proof of brain damage or neurological abnormalities in otherwise normal children, the idea became more and more popular. The term "brain damage" was, however, mitigated to a less deleterious one, namely "minimal brain dysfunction." A few years later this term also fell into disfavor in educational circles, and was replaced with the term "learning disabilities."

In spite of the inability of experts to prove any neurological dysfunction, middle-class parents, especially, accepted this idea with great relief. Before the 1960s their children were often described as "dumb," "mixed up" and "lazy," even though they were smart in some ways, were not crazy, often tried very hard, and "would learn if only they could."[23] Children were frequently misdiagnosed as mentally retarded and had to live with this stigma for the rest of their lives. One cannot but sympathize with the parents and the children of that time. "You felt like you were all alone," one parent said, "and no one could help. The educators made you feel like your child was a freak, and most of the medical people just didn't understand."[24]

Many middle-class parents thought that special-education classifications such as "mentally retarded" and "emotionally disturbed" and prevailing social science categories for explaining academic failure such as "culturally deprived" seemed appropriate for children from minority and poor communities, but not for children from the middle class:

> The variety of problems afflicting minority groups and the poor were said to affect the emotions and intellect of children in ways that explained their

difficulties in school. An applicable but *different* explanation was needed for children who had grown up in the suburbs, with the advantages of middle-class life, and who, despite their academic problems, often appeared to be good learners outside of school. The learning-disabilities explanation—that the problem was caused not by retardation or other exclusionary factors, but by a minor neurological "glitch"—made sense to many. The explanation also offered different advantages to different interests: it was less pejorative than other special-education categories and it did not consider or criticize any role schools, families, or other social influences might have had in creating the learning disabilities.[25]

Within a few years after the idea of a minimal brain dysfunction and learning disability had taken root, it was not only the cause of poor school achievement, but of nearly any physical or psychological problem, and simply any form of behavior that adults found troublesome. William Cruickshank is worth quoting at length:

> Parents attending a lecture on learning disabilities have . . . seen fit in a public forum to question me about their child who stuttered, who teased the family cat, who could not deal with geometry in the tenth grade but who otherwise was getting along well in school, who had night terrors, who was diagnosed by the family psychiatrist as depressed—all of these under the label of learning disabilities. I have had parents question me on the failure of the child of nine years of age to be able to swim, another who could type but could not write legibly, another who masturbated, and still another who did not like to go with girls. Parents in their concept of learning disability have talked with me about nail biting, poor eating habits, failure of the child to keep his room neat, unwillingness to take a bath, failure to brush teeth. . . . One parent asked me if the fact that his college-student son wore long hair and, he "suspected," lived with a girl outside his dormitory was the result of a learning disability.[26]

Even parents' problems were considered to be the result of a dysfunction inside the child's brain. Nancy Ramos, once president of the California Association for Neurologically Handicapped Children, echoes the message: "A good many LD children come from single-parent homes, but it's not the broken marriages that cause LD, it's that the learning-disabled child broke up the marriage in the first place."[27]

Keeping the Syndrome Alive

The LD enterprise soon became an enormous machine—indeed a factory—with attending cottage industries, fueled by legal, sociopolitical, educational, and entrepreneurial energy.[28] By the end of the 1960s children began to be classified as "learning disabled" and an "antidote" for the syndrome had to be found. State funds were appropriated for LD curricula. An array of tests and remedial materials were devised and published. Schools catering specifically for learning-disabled children started rising up like anthills. The number of journal articles and books on the subject multiplied. A profusion of LD research projects commenced and pharmaceutical companies promoted and profited from drugs for the learning disabled.[29]

Advocacy groups, in the rush to generate public awareness of the condition of dyslexia, with the cooperation of a compliant media, have perpetuated the belief that a host of famous individuals such as Albert Einstein, Auguste Rodin, George Patton, and Woodrow Wilson were dyslexic. The folk myth—the "affliction of the geniuses"—continues to be spread despite the fact that knowledge of the definition of dyslexia and the reading of any standard biographies would immediately reveal the inaccuracy of many such claims.[30] For example, as Coles points out, Einstein's reading of Kant and Darwin at age thirteen is hardly representative of individuals who are currently labeled dyslexic.[31] According to Moats and Lyon, parental advocacy groups have remained the strongest force in keeping alive the concept of learning disabilities. "Science has taken a back seat (and more accurately, the rumble seat.)"[32]

In spite of the obviously illogical roots of this idea, it nevertheless spread like wild fire throughout nearly the whole world. In South Africa, for example, it was taken so seriously that in 1968 a commission of enquiry was appointed by the then Minister of Education to investigate the prevalence of minimal brain dysfunction among South African schoolchildren. Following the report by this commission in 1969, a network of school psychologists was established all over the country. Remedial education for the children with supposed minimal brain dysfunction was undertaken with great fervor and a course in minimal brain dysfunction was offered to teachers at the College of Education for Further Training.[33] The large number of teachers who followed this course shows how much easier it is to swim downstream.

33

Once a sizeable number of people have started moving in a certain direction, it seems that, like with the lemmings in the Arctic regions, it is always easy for them to entice others to join them.

Professionals from different spheres of scientific endeavor started going along with the stream. Using modern techniques, screens and tests to diagnose and treat the LD child, they built a mystical aura around the field, remarked Peter Schrag and Diane Divoky in their classic book *The Myth of the Hyperactive Child*. The professionals can "see" things in the child that the layman can never see. But, upon investigating the results they achieve, we find that LD children continue to fail miserably in the classroom.[34]

"Treatment" is seldom, if ever, directed at the environment. The possibility that there may be other problems relating to the home, school or other social conditions is ignored. The teacher may be fickle, brutal and stupid, but when a child fails or cannot adjust, only the child is tested and treated. Does this perhaps imply that every teacher, school, and the schooling system are perfect? Does this further imply that all teachers are equally capable, that "if *I* cannot teach him, *nobody* can teach him?"

An interesting research study in this regard was done in a school where the children were from poor socio-economic backgrounds. The study compared the success of children of similar backgrounds, who had been randomly placed in three first-grade classrooms. Their teachers had taught in this school for many years.

The researchers found that although family status and conditions were related to academic success, the effect of teacher influence was quite strong. Using reading achievement as the primary measure of educational achievement, they found that 64 percent of the children in the class of one teacher (Miss A) were high achievers, compared to 28 percent of the other first-grade classes. Conversely, Miss A had 7 percent low achievers, while the other teachers had 28 percent low achievers. Furthermore, the average academic achievement of children from Miss A's class remained consistently higher throughout their elementary school years.

How did Miss A enable so many of her pupils to do well academically? A reporter who did an in-depth story on Miss A and her pupils found that her attitude was, "It did not matter what background or abilities the beginning pupil had; there was no way the pupil was not going to read at the end of first grade." Miss A imbued her pupils with self-confidence and an appreciation of the importance of schooling. Hard work was one of the keys to her success with students; for children who were slow learners, Miss A devoted extra hours.[35]

This study, however, reveals more than just the effect of successful teaching, but also an implicit school policy of indifference. Although the school administrators had a standard in Miss A's teaching by which they could judge teaching success, they did not intervene or take corrective measures to change less effective instruction and less favorable academic outcomes in the other classrooms. Because schools simply accept that a proportion of their pupils would fail, Miss A's colleagues appeared to have been doing an acceptable and normal job. Miss A's success remained hers alone. Had she been much less successful, less would have been just as acceptable.[36]

Teachers often underestimate the importance of their role in determining a child's future success. The story is told about a woman who attended her twenty-year high school reunion. There she encountered her freshman year art teacher. She told him that she decided to go to college as a result of his inspiration and that she was now an art professor at a large state university.

At the end of the evening's festivities, the teacher searched out his former student, shook her hand and said, "Thank you for saying those nice things about my teaching. You've really made my day."

"You're welcome," said the woman as she hugged him, "But let me thank you—you've made my life."

In 1974 Bateman recommended that the term "learning disabilities" be replaced by the term *teaching disabilities*. The focus should be on the inadequacies of teachers' skills and the teaching environment, instead of always blaming the student's inadequacies.[37] In 1987 Dr. Thomas Armstrong coined the word *dysteachia* to refer to the children suffering from "pedagogical illness" or inappropriate teaching strategies. He wrote, "if we taught children to speak the way we teach them to read, we'd have a nation of stutterers. This is just another way of saying that our schools are selling millions of kids short by putting them into remedial groups or writing them off as underachievers, when in reality they are disabled only by poor teaching methods."[38]

But let us not be too hard on teachers. Even if one considers just the two illustrations given below, it should be clear that poor pedagogical preparation must be recognized as a major reason for poor teaching. In fact, if elementary school teachers succeed in teaching at least *some* of the children in their classes to read, they deserve to be patted on the back. In 1961, in her book *The Torch Lighters*, Mary C. Austin made the shocking revelation that only seven states in the U.S.A. required a course in the teaching of reading for certification of elementary teachers. As a result, instruction in reading methods was most often imbedded in a block course, or in one in the language arts. In 60 percent of these broad courses, the actual time devoted to reading methods ranged from $4^1/_2$ to $11^1/_4$ clock hours; 30 percent of these courses gave reading even less time.[39] Three decades later, writing in the *Journal of Teacher Education*, Nolen et al. raised the same concerns. They reported that only twenty-nine states required elementary teachers in training to have course-work specific to reading instruction, and even in those states only about twelve hours of graduate training is mandated.[40]

The role that the parents might have played in creating the learning problem is also never considered—as if parents were infallible. A tragic defect of our society is the fact that we are not allowed to take upon ourselves the responsibility of doing the work of a policeman, or of a teacher, or of an attorney, or of any other work without having undergone prior training. No training, however, is provided on how to bring up children. Many parents believe that they are doing everything that can be expected from them if they provide for their children's physical needs, and then send them to nursery school or school, supposedly there to be educated.

The school has grown from the modest institution it was in the nineteenth century, with limited functions, to one that is now blamed for all the ills of society and is also seen as potentially capable of curing them. It has extended —some would say overextended—its reach and therefore is exceedingly vulnerable to criticism.[41] It is very important to note, however, that the whole of education does not take place in the school and that not only teachers are educators. Parents, in fact, are children's *primary* educators and among many other duties and responsibilities they have, it is also their task to make sure that their children are suitably equipped that they may profit from the subject instruction offered to them at school. The important role of the parents in a child's school achievement is confirmed by the famous Coleman report in the U.S.A., which stated that achievement differences in schoolchildren were accounted for mostly by what the children *brought with them to school*.[42]

The objective of this book, however, is not to fling about accusations and to create feelings of guilt. Parents need feel no more guilty about their LD child than did Dr. Samuel Johnson, the author of the first English dictionary, who was once twitted about a silly error he had made in defining a term. When asked by a lady why he had made the mistake, he looked at her and thundered, "Ignorance, Madam! Sheer ignorance!"[43] In the camera obscura that has been built by the notion of learning disabilities, the intention of this book is not to blame but to shine a ray of light. The intention is to show parents that they, like teachers, *can* make a difference, and this book will tell them how. The myth of learning disabilities has for long enough maintained its position at the top of the educational pecking order. The time has come to depose it and expose it for what it really is: a mere fabrication. The time has come that we should all take the words of Dr. Thomas Armstrong, which he wrote in the preface of his book *In Their Own Way*, to heart:

> Six years ago I quit my job as a learning disabilities specialist. I had to. I no longer believed in learning disabilities. After teaching for several years in public and parochial special education classes in the United States and Canada, I realized I was going nowhere with a concept that labeled children from the outset as handicapped learners. I also began to see how this notion of learning disabilities was handicapping all of our children by placing the blame for a child's learning failure on mysterious neurological deficiencies in the brain . . .[44]

Notes:

1. Blatt, B., "Bandwagons also go to funerals," *Journal of Learning Disabilities*, 1979, vol. 12(4), 222-224.
2. Armstrong, T., *In Their Own Way: Discovering and Encouraging Your Child's Personal Learning Style* (Los Angeles: Jeremy P. Tarcher, Inc., 1987), 6-7.
3. Stotzner, H. E., *Schulen für schwachbefähigte Kinder* (Berlin, Germany: Marhold, 1864), cited in G. Opp, "Historical roots of the field of learning disabilities," *Journal of Learning Disabilities*, January 1994, vol. 27, 10.
4. Opp, "Historical roots of the field of learning disabilities."
5. Oppenheim, H., *Nervenleiden und Erziehung* (Berlin: Karger, 1907), cited Opp, "Historical roots of the field of learning disabilities."
6. Schrag, P., & Divoky, D., *The Myth of the Hyperactive Child and Other Means of Child Control* (Middlesex: Penguin Books, 1975).
7. Turner, R. D., "Beating dyslexia: The reading and language disorder is often misdiag-

nosed," *Emerge*, 31 March 1994.

8. Kantrowitz, B., Underwood, A., & Wingert, P., "Dyslexia and the new science of reading," *Newsweek*, 22 November 1999, 72.

9. Yee, K., "Dyslexia may be caused by visual impairment," *University Wire*, 15 January 1998.

10. Coles, G. S., *The Learning Mystique* (New York: Pantheon Books, 1987).

11. "The cat sat on the tam," *The Economist*, 6 December 1997, vol. 345.

12. Tucker, J., Stevens, L. J., & Ysseldyke, J. E., "Learning disabilities: The experts speak out," *Journal of Learning Disabilities*, January 1983, vol. 27, 9, cited in Armstrong, *In Their Own Way*, 7.

13. Coles, *The Learning Mystique*, xii.

14. Hinshelwood, J., "Four cases of congenital word-blindness occurring in the same family," *British Medical Journal*, 1907, vol. 2, 1229-1232, cited in Coles, *The Learning Mystique*, 3-5.

15. Coles, *The Learning Mystique*, 5-6.

16. Goodman, J. F., "Organicity as a construct in psychological diagnosis," in T. R. Kratochwill (ed.), *Advances in School Psychology* (Hillsdale: Lawrence Erlbaum, 1983), 101-139.

17. Coles, *The Learning Mystique*, 4.

18. Hinshelwood, "Four cases of congenital word-blindness," cited in Coles, *The Learning Mystique*, 4.

19. Franklin, B. M., "From brain injury to learning disability: Alfred Strauss, Heinz Werner and the historical development of the learning disabilities field," in B. M. Franklin (ed.), *Learning Disability: Dissenting Essays* (Philadelphia: The Falmer Press, 1987), 29-46.

20. Ibid.

21. Kavale, K. A., & Forness, S. R., "The historical foundation of learning disabilities: A quantitative synthesis assessing the validity of Strauss and Werner's exogenous versus endogenous distinction of mental retardation," *Remedial and Special Education*, 1985, vol. 65, 18-24; Kavale, K. A., & Forness, S. R., *The Science of Learning Disabilities* (San Diego: College Hill Press, 1985).

22. Franklin, "From brain injury to learning disability."

23. Smith, C. R., *Learning Disabilities. The Interaction of Learner, Task, and Setting* (Boston: Allyn and Bacon, 1991), 8.

24. Schrag & Divoky, *The Myth of the Hyperactive Child*.

25. Coles, *The Learning Mystique*, xiii.

26. Cruickshank, W., "Some issues facing the field of learning disability," *Journal of Learning Disabilities*, vol. 5, 1972, 380-388, cited in J. G. Carrier, *Learning Disability: Social Class and the Construction of Inequality in American Education* (New York: Greenwood Press, 1986), 100.

27. Schrag & Divoky, *The Myth of the Hyperactive Child*.

28. Moats, L. C., & Lyon, G. R., "Learning disabilities in the United States: Advocacy, science,

and the future of the field," *Journal of Learning Disabilities*, May 1993, vol. 26, 282-294.

29. Coles, *The Learning Mystique*, 23-24.
30. Stanovich, K. E., "Learning disabilities in broader context," *Journal of Learning Disabilities*, May 1989, vol. 22(5), 287-297.
31. Coles, *The Learning Mystique*, 124.
32. Moats & Lyon, "Learning disabilities in the United States."
33. *Verslag van die Komitee van Ondersoek na die Opvoeding van Kinders met Minimale Breindisfunksie* (Department of Higher Education, South Africa, 1969).
34. Schrag & Divoky, *The Myth of the Hyperactive Child*.
35. Pederson, E., Faucher, T. A., & Eaton, W. W., "A new perspective on the effects of first-grade teachers on children's subsequent adult status," *Harvard Business Review*, 1978, vol. 48, 1-31, cited in Coles, *The Learning Mystique*, 156-157.
36. Coles, *The Learning Mystique*, 157.
37. Bateman, B., "Educational implications of minimal brain dysfunction," *Reading Teacher*, 1974, vol. 27, 662-668.
38. Armstrong, *In Their Own Way*, 40.
39. Austin, M. C., *The Torch Lighters* (Cambridge, Mass.: Harvard University Press, 1961).
40. Nolen, P. A., McCutchen, D., & Berninger, V., "Ensuring tomorrow's literacy: A shared responsibility," *Journal of Teacher Education*, 1990, vol. 41, 63-72.
41. Schmidt, W. H. O., *Child Development: The Human, Cultural, and Educational Context* (New York: Harper & Row, 1973), 12.
42. Kerlinger, F. N., *Foundations of Behavioral Research* (New York: CBS Publishing Ltd., 1986).
43. Van Riper, C., *Teaching Your Child to Talk* (New York: Harper & Row Publishers, 1950), 75.
44. Armstrong, *In Their Own Way*, ix.

3.

Brains, Genes and Education

We are educators—we need NOT know what goes
on in the brain.[1] — Poplin.

One could probably fill a vast library if one would put together all the research studies that attempted to prove that a learning disability is caused by either a neurological dysfunction, or that it is a genetically transferred disorder. The problem faced by researchers, who try to prove that it is a brain dysfunction, is that it is impossible to directly examine the living brain of a learning-disabled person in order to discover whether there is an abnormality in the brain. They have therefore been forced to study the brain indirectly. Although many methods and measuring instruments have so far been employed—including autopsies on the brains of deceased learning-disabled people and advanced technological developments—proof of a neurological dysfunction still eludes the researchers.

It is not the intention—and it will also be impossible—to discuss all of these studies in this book. The intention is rather *first*, to demonstrate that a brain difference—the heart of the LD notion—is not necessarily the equivalent of a brain dysfuntion, and *second*, that a human being is more than the sum of his genes.

EEG

Up to the late 1970s, authoritative publications listed the EEG among the ten most frequently recommended diagnostic tests for LD.[2] An EEG, or electro-encephalogram, uses electrodes to measure electrical activity at various points near the outer surface of the brain. The electrical signals are amplified and graphed on a continuously moving paper. It had been assumed that because the EEG could detect tumors, malformations, convulsive disorders, sleep states and coma, it might also shed light on the brain functioning of the learning disabled.[3] For quite a while it appeared as though the EEG might have won the day. These hopes were, however, dashed towards the end of the 1970s.

A paper in 1949 reported an ample 75 percent of EEG abnormalities in a group of dyslexic children. Research the following year reported a dip to 59 percent, but the percentage picked up in the next decade, soaring to 88 percent in the early 1960s and peaking in the mid-1960s at an astronomical 95 percent.[4] However, the 1960s ended with a decline to 50 percent and the 1970s opened with 37 percent. By 1973, reported EEG abnormalities in the learning disabled had fallen to only 32 percent. Toward the end of the 1970s there was strong doubt that any significant EEG abnormalities could be found in the learning disabled.[5]

This decline in percentages was caused by more stringent research methods being used. One of these more stringent research methods, which seemingly caused the faith in the EEG to take a nose-dive, was the use of replication studies done "blindly." In the studies that reported a high percentage of EEG abnormalities in learning-disabled children, the research-ers knew beforehand that the children were learning disabled. Their fore-knowledge encouraged them to "find" what they were looking for in an "abnormal" group, and caused them to interpret the EEG results as abnor-mal much too easily.[6] In replication studies done blindly, EEGs of learning-disabled children were mixed with EEGs of normal or typical learners, and the researchers had to analyze whether a child is learning disabled or not according to his EEG result. Now, that was a different matter! The EEGs of the two groups proved to be indistinguishable from one another.

The following research studies compared the EEGs of typical and disabled learners, and found that there are no differences in the number of typical and disabled learners who show abnormal EEGs. In the left-hand column are the percentages of poor learners who show abnormal EEGs, and in the right-hand column the percentages of typical learners who show abnormal EEGs:

Poor learners:	Typical learners:	
41%	30%	Myklebust and Boshes 1969[7]
10%	10%	Meier 1971[8]
14%	22%	Owen et al. 1971[9]
23%	32%	Harris 1983[10]

Even when children are known to have suffered brain injury, their EEGs often are normal.[11]

A 1967 review by Freeman concluded that for detecting LD brain dysfunctions the EEG is not the outstanding diagnostic tool that people had once thought. His conclusions remain valid today:

> The EEG appears to be regarded with more awe than it deserves. It is not very reliable, and there are many technical problems in its use with children, yet our electronic age, with its admiration for gadgets and the paucity of knowledge in the behavior sciences, lends to this instrument a certain mystique. . . . The influence of the EEG among educators may possibly be due to the inundation of the literature with poorly done papers describing children with supposed minimal brain damage.[12]

Neurological Signs

One often finds that "soft neurological signs" are mentioned in clinical reports of learning-disabled children. The term "hard neurological signs" points to behavioral signs that always reflect brain injury, for example seizures, cerebral palsy, cranial nerve abnormalities leading to blindness and deafness and microcephaly.[13]

Soft neurological signs, on the other hand, point to a lag in children's gross and fine motor development, such as poor balance and coordination difficulties.[14] Studies trying to prove that the learning disabled have more neurological signs than typical learners, fared no better than EEG-studies. In one study, in fact, children with the most neurological signs actually had the fewest learning problems.[15] In the most comprehensive study of this type in the U.S.A., the so-called National Collaborative Perinatal Project, the relationship between neurological signs and learning disabilities in seven-year-olds could account for only one percent of the learning problems.[16]

Structural Brain Assymetry

Because it can create visual projections of the brain in layers and from various angles, the LD field has considered computerized axial tomography, known as the CAT scan, an excellent method of comparing the size and shape of the brains of disabled and normal readers.[17]

The brain consists of three sections, the forebrain, the midbrain and the hindbrain. The forebrain is the largest of the three sections and takes up the complete top section of the skull. The most important area of the forebrain is the cerebral cortex, which among other things is responsible for learning, memory, speech and thought, and is usually looked upon as the damaged portion of the learning-disabled person's brain. The cerebral cortex is divided into two halves—the left and the right hemispheres. Each hemisphere performs its own functions. In 90 percent of all people the left hemisphere of the cerebral cortex is responsible for language and structured thought, while the right hemisphere is responsible for visual perception, music, emotions and associated with instinctive and nonverbal responses. Damage to the left hemisphere will therefore have different effects than damage caused to the right hemisphere. For example, a person who loses his ability to talk and read after a stroke, will have damage to the left hemisphere of the cerebral cortex, while damage to the right hemisphere will result in depression or improper emotional reactions.

Some evidence of structural brain asymmetry in dyslexics has been reported. In the general population, CAT scans have found that the rear portion of the left hemisphere tends to be slightly wider than the right. In normal people there is a high percentage of asymmetry in the planum temporale, the upper surface of the posterior temporal lobe, a lobe involved in language processing, such as analyzing and synthesizing speech sounds, naming objects, and recalling words. For example, in approximately 65 percent of autopsied adults, the surface area of the planum temporale was found to be larger on the left; for 11 percent it is larger on the right; and the two areas are approximately equal in 24 percent.[18] These differences were not found in dyslexics, for whom a CAT-scan study reported a larger right-surface area in 42 percent of the dyslexics examined. Along with the reverse asymmetry, these 42 percent—or ten of twenty-four subjects—had lower verbal IQs and a greater incidence of delayed speech than the remaining fourteen dyslexics. From these findings the researchers hypothesized that brain structure differences preventing normal development of brain functioning in language-related areas might cause dyslexia.[19] Another paper two years later by two members of this study group described similar findings.[20] This research was soon cited in texts and articles as "convincing" evidence "that cerebral asymmetries may be related to functional problems in reading and learning."[21]

A year after the second paper was published, a replication study appeared. Using identical measurement procedures this study failed to find "an increased frequency of reversed occipital asymmetry with reading disability reported by others." Reversed asymmetry was found in only 12 percent of the dyslexics, a percentage similar to that found in normal readers in the first studies. Furthermore, no relationship was found between the "posterior width of the hemispheres" and either verbal IQ scores, delayed acquisition of speech, or reading problems.[22]

Many other studies followed, involving magnetic resonance (MR) imaging, functional magnetic resonance imaging (fMRI), positron emission tomography (PET), and single photon emission computerized tomography (SPECT). Yet, they also failed to demonstrate specific diagnostic abnormalities. "To date, no diagnostic conclusions have been drawn utilizing these methods in the assessment of the [supposedly] neurobiologic basis to LD," Bigler et al. stated in an article to the *Journal of Learning Disabilities*, thirty-five years after Samuel Kirk had established the term "learning disabilities."[23]

Known for conducting autopsies on the brains of deceased dyslexics, neurologist Albert Galaburda and his team of researchers seemed to have found a difference between dyslexic persons and nondyslexics in the size of nerve cells in the part of the brain that helps process sounds—the left MGN, or left medial geniculate nucleus. However, as neurobiologist Margaret Livingstone at Harvard Medical School points out, Galaburda's results are not conclusive because of the small numbers studied.[24]

Brain Differences: An Alternative Interpretation

At the time of writing it was still not conclusive that the function or structure of the dyslexic's brain is different from the brain of the normal reader. Of course the inability to find such differences can be interpreted as the *absence* of any such abnormalities. But, on the other hand, they may well exist. Should this apply, then obviously such a premise would have to be interpreted, especially in relation to the question of cause and effect. Which of the two, the different brain structure or the learning disability, is the *cause* and which one is the *effect*? This, of course, can easily be misinterpreted.

Let us, for a moment, accept the hypothesis that there are differences between the brains of dyslexics and normal readers. Because of the biological determinists' reluctance to recognize that the environment can affect brain function and structure, they will immediately and uncritically assume that these differences must be the cause and the learning disability the result. On the other hand, in order to establish their position, the antideterminists often undermine themselves by thinking they must deny any brain differences between disabled and nondisabled groups.[25] Instead of denying this, we would like to present arguments that may lead to a reversal of the cause-effect problem. In other words, we hypothesize that *dyslexia may cause differences in brain function and structure.*

A logical point of departure for such an argument would be to first establish if brain function and structure can be altered. There is ample confirmation to be found in the literature that indeed it can. In 1979, in an article in the *Journal of Learning Disabilities*, Doctors Marianne Frostig and Phyllis Maslow stated, "Neuropsychological research has demonstrated that environmental conditions, including education, affect brain structure and functioning."[26] In their book *Brain, Mind, and Behavior* Floyd E. Bloom, a neuropharmacologist, and Arlyne Lazerson, a professional writer specializing in psychology, state, "Experience [learning] can cause physical modifications in the brain."[27] This is confirmed by Michael Merzenich of the University of San Francisco. His work on brain plasticity shows that, while areas of the brain are designated for specific purposes, brain cells and cortical maps do change in response to experience (learning).[28] It seems that, while stimulation causes brain growth on the one hand, the lack of stimulation, on the other hand, causes a lack of brain growth.

A good example of brain growth, caused by stimulation, can be found in Glenn Doman's research on severely brain-damaged children. At the beginning of the twentieth century brain-damaged children were still regarded as "monsters," and the "disgrace" that this brought on parents had to be hidden at all cost. Only towards the 1930s and early 1940s did research in this field begin to make the public aware of the needs of these children. Glenn Doman of Philadelphia was one of the pioneers in this field. Thanks to the work of Doman and his colleagues, the quality of life of many severely brain-damaged children has improved—some quite drastically. We have met several of these children ourselves.

Apparently Doman later broadened his audience to include learning-disabled children of normal intelligence. In the mid-1960s, he and Carl

Delacato opened several treatment centers to which parents flocked with their children. However, their technique did not achieve sufficient results in remediating the supposedly "minimal" brain damaged, and as a result they fell into disfavor among LD practitioners: "The extravagant and rather bizarre claims made for this technique prompted a number of researchers to study it more closely, and they concluded that the program was worthless."[29] Moreover, a number of professional and parents' associations took the unusual step of denouncing the Doman and Delacato method publicly.[30]

Doman's failures seemingly caused researchers to reject his work altogether. This is unfortunate, because his successes—his work with severely brain-damaged children—certainly throws important light on brain development.

The heads of truly brain-damaged children usually grow at a slower rate than those of normal children. In one research analysis done by Doman, on 278 case histories of consecutively admitted brain-damaged children, 82.2 percent were below normal in head size at the start of treatment. All but thirty-seven of the children moved to an above-average rate of growth in head size over the fourteen-month period covered by the survey. In fact, the average rate of growth during treatment was 254 percent—between two to three times faster—of the normal for that age. As a result of the therapy, the brain started growing.[31]

An example of a lack of stimulation, causing a lack of brain growth, can be found in the work of Doctors Bruce D. Perry and Ronnie Pollard, two researchers at Baylor College of Medicine. They found that children raised in severely isolated conditions, where they had minimal exposure to language, touch and social interactions, developed brains 20 to 30 percent smaller than normal for their age.[32]

In order to find out what really happens to the brain in such cases, one would have to remove the brain from the skull. Experiments in this regard have been done on animals. Of course, no conclusions on human learning or functioning can be drawn from experiments on animals, but it is nevertheless interesting to take note of such experiments, because they seem to confirm that stimulation does indeed change brain structure.

Professor Klosovskii, a neurosurgeon in Moscow, took newborn litters of kittens and puppies and divided them into two exactly equal groups, one as the experimental group and the other as the control group. The kittens and puppies in the control group were permitted to grow in the usual way in which kittens and puppies normally grow. The experimental animals, however, were placed on a slowly revolving turntable and lived there throughout the experiment. The only difference in what happened to each of the groups was that the experimental group experienced a *moving* world while the control group experienced only as much as newborn kittens and puppies normally do. When the animals were ten days old, Klosovskii began to sacrifice matched pairs of the puppies and kittens to take their brains. The last of them were sacrificed by the nineteenth day of life. The animals on the turntable had from 22.8 percent to 35 percent (one third) more growth in the vestibular areas of their brains than did the control group animals. Just what does more growth mean? Did Klosovskii see one third larger number of brain cells in his microscope? Not at all; he saw the same number of brain cells but one third larger and one third more mature.[33]

Mark Rosenzweig and his associates have shown that the brains of rats raised in an "enriched" laboratory environment—in a large cage containing many fellow rats and playthings that could be explored and manipulated—differed markedly in a number of respects from rats raised in small, isolated cages. The rats in the enriched environment had a greater weight and thickness of cerebral cortex than the ones raised in isolation. The researchers found more spines—which often serve as receivers in synaptic contacts—on the dendrites of cortical neurons in rats from enriched environments.[34] Synaptic junctions in rats from enriched environments averaged about 50 percent larger than those in rats raised in isolation,[35] and synaptic contacts were more frequent in the rats from enriched environments.[36]

The researchers wondered which of the many stimuli in the enriched environment had the most effect on the development of the rats' brains. Further experiments brought surprising findings to light. Exercising and physical activity had no effect in terms of enriching their brains; visual stimulation wasn't necessary to create enriched brains, as demonstrated by blind rats; handling and petting had no effect; whether the rats were together or isolated didn't matter; and teaching the rats to press a lever helped only a little. The experimenters found only one aspect that helped to enrich the rats' brains—the freedom to roam a large, object-filled space. Rats appear to be able to develop a good "space-brain" (one that helps them locate points in space and objects to climb over or through) rather than a "reasoning brain." Or, as David

47

Krech, one of the experimenters put it, "For each species there exists a set of species-specific experiences that are maximally enriching and maximally efficient in developing its brain."[37]

Let us now theorize on the findings of Doman, Perry and Pollard, Klosovskii and Rosenzweig, and even compare the development of the brain with the development of the body.

The structure of a person's body, as we all know, is to a great extent determined by the *type and amount* of physical exercise it receives. By lifting weights in the gymnasium Arnold Schwarzenegger's muscles became big and strong—the structure changed. A person, whose physical activity centers on typing, or who exercises only once in a while, will certainly not have muscles like Schwarzenegger. In the same way, the *type and amount* of mental exercise a person receives, may determine the structure of the person's brain. As Dworetzky states, citing Rosenzweig's experiments, "it may well be that only a very few specific stimuli are necessary for a full neural, sensory, and perceptual development to occur. Although it remains to be demonstrated, the opportunity to engage in language, problem-solving, and thinking may be for the human child what the freedom to roam an object-filled environment is for the rat."[38] Of course, there may well be other even more important stimluli than language, problem-solving and thinking. The point is, that the dyslexic may not have received a sufficient amount of these stimuli and therefore his brain may be structurally different from that of a person who did. The structural difference is therefore not necessarily the *cause* of learning problems, but may be an *effect*.

At this point the argument of LD specialists would probably be that little Johnny would never look like Arnold Schwarzenegger, even if he spent twice as much time in the gymnasium. This, of course, is true. The basic blueprint of Johnny's body structure may to a large extent already have been determined at conception. But nobody would deny that, if Johnny spent the same amount of time in the gymnasium as Schwarzenegger, his body would look completely different after two years.

We are all born with bodies that look different. In the same way, we are all born with neurological differences. We all have different talents, aptitudes and capabilities, but it is doubtful whether a *difference* represents a *dysfunction* or a *disability*. Naturally, it will be harder for some children to learn to read and there will always be those who can read better, just as we cannot all be tennis champions. In fact, some people may even find it very hard to learn to play tennis. But by following the *correct method of instruction* and with *sustained practice* according to this method, any person will at least learn to play acceptable tennis. In the same way any child can learn to read at least acceptably if the correct method of instruction is followed and if enough practice is provided. The correct method of instruction to the LD person, however, can only be found once the *cause* of a learning disability has been determined.

Researchers in the field of LD often underestimate the wonderful potential and capacity of the human brain. Compare the idea of a "learning disability" with Chafetz's view that "the human mind can learn anything."[39] His optimism is shared by Litvak when he says that "the human brain has extensive capacities beyond those normally tapped,"[40] and by Minninger and Dugan who say, "the simplest mind today controls dazzling skills, the very same skills that put the universe itself within our grasp."[41] Such conflicting views cannot exist together —either all the supporters of the "learning disabilities" idea are wrong, or Chafetz, Litvak, Minninger and Dugan and a host of others are.

Their optimism is confirmed by cases on record in which one of the hemispheres of the brain of a person was removed surgically and then the remaining hemisphere was afterwards able to take over the functions of the removed one. Consider the case of thirteen-year-old Brandi Binder, who developed such severe epilepsy that surgeons at UCLA had to remove the entire right side of her brain when she was six. Binder lost virtually all the control she had established over muscles on the left side of her body, the side controlled by the right side of her brain. Yet today, after years of therapy ranging from leg lifts to math and music drills, Binder is an A student at the Holmes Middle School in Colorado Springs, Colorado. She loves music, math and art—skills usually associated with the right half of the brain. And while Binder's recuperation is not hundred percent—for example, she never regained the use of her left arm—it comes close.[42]

Even more astonishing than the Binder case is the story of John Lorber, a British pediatrician, who studied an individual who, due to neurological illness, had virtually no brain. Instead of the normal 4.5-centimeter thickness of cerebral cortex, this young student had just a thin layer measuring a millimeter or so. In spite of this obvious shortcoming, he was measured as having an IQ of 126, was socially competent, and gained first-class honors in mathematics.[43]

If it is possible to learn to function normally—or close to normal—with half a brain or with virtually no brain, then there must certainly be hope for the supposedly learning disabled, and even for the minuscule number of children who may truly suffer from a *minimal* brain dysfunction.

Genetics in Learning Disabilities

Some researchers blame a supposed neurological dysfunction on brain damage before, during, or after birth. Others hold that the neurological dysfunction is genetically determined and inherited from generation to generation. They support this view by referring to many studies that have indicated that there is often a family history of learning disabilities. Hornsby, for example, state that 88 percent of dyslexics had a near relative who had similar problems with reading and spelling.[44] According to an American study the risk that a child will have a reading problem is increased from four to thirteen times if one of the parents has a similar problem.[45] This tendency for dyslexia to "run in families" have been confirmed by numerous studies.

Many possible explanations have been offered for this tendency. While Dr. Toril Fagerheim of Norway has apparently identified the involvement of chromosome 2,[46] others maintain that the quantitative trait locus on the short arm of chromosome 6 is involved, and Lubs et al. say that chromosome 15 is involved too.[47]

It would be foolish to deny that genes may play a role in human capabilities and talents or even difficulties. However, to determine the relative importance of the role of genes and the role of the environment will forever be impossible. How much does the genetic make-up of a person contribute to his talents or difficulties, and how much the fact that *the family members share the same unique environment?* Take Mozart as an example. He was one of the most brilliant musicians of all time. All the members of his family were musicians and from the moment of his birth he was continually exposed to music. Suppose he had been adopted immediately after birth by other parents who played no music. Would we then have known about Mozart? It is possible, but highly unlikely.

The brilliant work done by the late Shinichi Suzuki of Japan also shows how musical talent may be developed by exposure. Suzuki trained thousands of violinists, who from a very young age took part in concerts lasting more than two hours, playing works by Mozart, Beethoven and Liszt. He started stimulating these future violinists from *before* birth. As a result of his research he concluded that what a child becomes, is totally dependent on how he is educated.[48] "Talent is not an accident of birth," he said.[49]

Research on the role of the environment in children's intellectual development has also shown that a stimulating environment can dramatically increase IQ, whereas a deprived environment can lead to a decrease in IQ. A particularly interesting project on early intellectual stimulation involved twenty-five children in an orphanage. These children were seriously environmentally deprived because the orphanage was crowded and understaffed. Thirteen babies of the average age of nineteen months were transferred to the Glenwood State School for retarded adult women and each baby was put in the personal care of a woman. Skeels, who conducted the experiment, deliberately chose the most deficient of the orphans to be placed in the Glenwood School. Their average IQ was 64, while the average IQ of the twelve who stayed behind in the orphanage was 87.[50]

In the Glenwood State School the children were placed in open, active wards with the older and relatively bright women. Their substitute mothers overwhelmed them with love and cuddling. Toys were available, they were taken on outings and they were talked to a lot. The women were taught how to stimulate the babies intellectually and how to elicit language from them.

After eighteen months, the dramatic findings were that the children who were placed with substitute mothers, and therefore received additional stimulation, on average showed an increase of 29 IQ points! A follow-up study was conducted two and a half years later. Eleven of the thirteen children originally transferred to the Glenwood home had been adopted and their average IQ was now 101. The two children who had not been adopted were reinstitutionalized and lost their initial gain. The control group, the twelve children who had not been transferred to Glenwood, had remained in institution wards and now had an average IQ of 66 (an average decrease of 21 points).[51] Although the value of IQ tests is grossly exaggerated today (see chapter four), this astounding difference between these two groups is hard to ignore.

More telling than the increase or decrease in IQ, however, is the difference in the *quality of life* these two groups enjoyed. When these children reached young adulthood, another follow-up study brought the following to light: "The experimental group had become productive, functioning adults, while the control group, for the most part, had been institutionalized as mentally retarded."[52]

From the examples above, a few more in further chapters in this book (see especially chapter seven), and many other cases in the literature, we contend that, even if it were possible to inherit a learning disability, a human being is not merely a slave to his genes, but can learn to overcome this problem. Human life can be compared to a game of cards. At birth, every person is dealt a hand of cards—his genetic make-up. Some receive a good hand, others a less good one. Success in any game, however, is almost always a matter of erudition. It is undeniably so that there are often certain innate qualities that will give one person an advantage over another in a specific game. However, without having learned the game and without regular and rigorous practice, nobody will ever become a champion at any game. In the same way the outcome of the game of life is not solely determined by the quality of a person's initial hand of cards, but also by the way in which he takes part in the game of life. His ability to take part in the game of life satisfactorily, perhaps even successfully, will be determined to a very large extent by the *quality and quantity of education* that he has enjoyed.

Perhaps it is appropriate to elaborate on Poplin's well-known dictum that we are educators and need NOT know what goes on in the brain. Perhaps we should add that we are educators of *children*—not of brains, and also not of genes.

Notes:

1. Poplin, M. "Learning disabilities at the crossroads," *46th Yearbook of the Claremont Reading Conference*, 1982, 41-52.
2. Coles, G. S. "The learning-disabilities test battery: Empirical and social issues," *Harvard Educational Review*, 1978, vol. 48, 313-340.
3. Smith, C. R., *Learning Disabilities. The Interaction of Learner, Task, and Setting* (Boston: Allyn and Bacon, 1991), 78.
4. Ayers, F. W., & Torres, F., "The incidence of EEG abnormalities in a dyslexic and a control group," *Journal of Clinical Psychology*, 1967, vol. 23, 334-336, cited in G. S. Coles, *The Learning Mystique* (New York: Pantheon Books, 1987), 76; Hughes, J. R., "Electroencephalographic and neurophysiological studies in dyslexia," in A. L. Benton & D. Pearl (eds.), *Dyslexia: An Appraisal of Current Knowledge* (N. Y.: Oxford, 1978).

5. Hughes, "Electroencephalographic and neurophysiological studies."
6. Coles, *The Learning Mystique*, 76, 84.
7. Myklebust, H. R., & Boshes, B., *Minimal Brain Damage in Children* (Washington, DC: Neurological and Sensory Disease Program, Department of Health, Education and Welfare, 1969), cited in Smith, *Learning Disabilities*, 78.
8. Meier, J. H., "Prevalence and characteristics of learning disabilities found in second grade children," *Journal of Learning Disabilities*, 1971, vol. 4, 1-16, cited in Smith, *Learning Disabilities*, 78.
9. Owen, F. W., et al., "Learning disorders in children: Sibling studies," *Monographs of the Society for Research in Child Development*, 1971, vol. 36(4), cited in Smith, *Learning Disabilities*, 78.
10. Harris, R., "Clinical neurophysiology in pediatric neurology," in E. M. Brett (ed.), *Paediatric Neurology*, (Edinburgh: Churchill Livingstone, 1983), cited in Smith, *Learning Disabilities*, 78.
11. Freeman, R. D., "Special education and the electroencephalogram: Marriage of convenience," *Journal of Special Education*, 1967, vol. 2, 61-73; Black, F. W., "Neurological dysfunction and reading disorders," *Journal of Learning Disabilities*, 1973, vol. 6, 313-316.
12. Freeman, "Special education and the electroencephalogram."
13. Smith, *Learning Disabilities*, 78.
14. Ibid.
15. Ingram, T. T. S., Mason, A. W., & Blackburn, I., "A retrospective study of 82 children with reading disability," *Developmental Medicine and Child Neurology*, 1970, vol. 12, 271-279.
16. Nichols, P., & Chen, T., *Minimal Brain Dysfunction: A Prospective Study* (Hillsdale, NJ: Lawrence Earlbaum, 1981).
17. Coles, *The Learning Mystique*, 83.
18. Hier, D. B., et al., "Developmental dyslexia: Evidence for a subgroup with a reversal of cerebral asymmetry," *Archives of Neurology*, 1978, vol. 35, 90-92, cited in Coles, *The Learning Mystique*, 83.
19. Ibid.
20. Rosenberger, P. B., & Hier, D. B., "Cerebral asymmetry and verbal intellectual deficits," *Annals of Neurology*, 1980, vol. 8, 300-304, cited in Coles, *The Learning Mystique*, 83-84.
21. Coles, *The Learning Mystique*, 84.
22. Haslam, R. H., et al., "Cerebral asymmetry in developmental dyslexia," *Archives of Neurology*, 1981, vol. 38, 679-682, cited in Coles, *The Learning Mystique*, 84.
23. Bigler, E. D., Lajiness-O'Neill, R., & Howes, N-L., "Technology in the assessment of learning disability," *Journal of Learning Disabilities*, January 1998, vol. 31.
24. Cooke, R., "Dyslexia linked to hearing defect. Size of nerve cells may be key," *Newsday*, 16 August 1994, A15.
25. Stanovich, K. E., "Learning disabilities in broader context," *Journal of Learning Disabilities*, 1989, vol. 22(5), 287-291.
26. Frostig, M., & Maslow, P., "Neuropsychological contributions to education." *Journal of Learning Disabilities*, October 1979, vol. 12(8).
27. Bloom, F. E., & Lazerson, A., *Brain, Mind, and Behavior* (2nd ed.), (New York: W. H.

Freeman and Company, 1985), 240.

28. Merzenich, M., et al., "Temporal processing deficits of language," "Learning impaired children ameliorated by training" and "Giving language skills a boost," *Science*, 5 January 1996, vol. 272.

29. Carrier, J. G., "The politics of early learning disability theory," in B. M. Franklin (ed.), *Learning Disability: Dissenting Essays* (Philadelphia: The Falmer Press, 1987), 58.

30. Carrier, J. G., *Learning Disability: Social Class and the Construction of Inequality in American Education* (New York: Greenwood Press, 1986), 111.

31. Doman, G., *What to Do About Your Brain-Injured Child* (New York: Doubleday & Company, Inc., 1982), 188.

32. Perry, B. D., & Pollard, R., "Altered brain development following global neglect in early childhood," Society for Neuroscience: Proceedings from Annual Meeting, New Orleans, 1997.

33. Doman, G., *What to Do About Your Brain-Injured Child*, 189-190.

34. Globus, A., et al., "Effects of differential experience on dendritic spine counts in rat cerebral cortex." *Journal of Comparative Physiology and Psychology*, 1973, vol. 82, 175-181, cited in Bloom & Lazerson, *Brain, Mind, and Behavior*, 265.

35. Møllgaard, K., et al., "Quantitative synaptic changes with differential experience in rat brain," *International Journal of Neuroscience*, 1971, vol. 2, 113-128, cited in Bloom & Lazerson, *Brain, Mind, and Behavior*, 265.

36. Greenough, W. T., West, R. W., & DeVoodg, T. J., "Subsynaptic plate perforations: Changes with age and experience in the rat," *Science*, 1978, vol. 202, 1096-1098, cited in Bloom & Lazerson, *Brain, Mind, and Behavior*, 265.

37. Krech, D., "Don't use the kitchen-sink approach to enrichment," *Today's Education*, 1970, vol. 59(7), 30-32, cited in J. P. Dworetzky, *Introduction to Child Development* (St. Paul: West Publishing Company, 1981), 193-194.

38. Dworetzky, *Introduction to Child Development*, 194.

39. Chafetz, M. D., *Smart for Life. How to Improve Your Brain Power at Any Age* (New York: Penguin Books, 1992).

40. Litvak, S. B., *Use Your Head. How to Develop the Other 80% of Your Brain* (Englewood Cliffs: Prentice-Hall, Inc., 1982).

41. Minninger, J., & Dugan, E., *Make Your Mind Work for You* (New York: Pocket Books, 1988).

42. Nash, J. M., "Special report: Fertile minds from birth, a baby's brain cells proliferate wildly, making connections that may shape a lifetime of experience. The first three years are crucial," *Time*, 3 February 1997.

43. Lewin, R. "Is your brain really necessary?" *Science*, 12 December 1980, vol. 210, 1232-1234, cited in T. Armstrong, *In Their Own Way: Discovering and Encouraging Your Child's Personal Learning Style* (Los Angeles: Jeremy P. Tarcher, Inc., 1987), 12.

44. Hornsby, B., *Overcoming Dyslexia* (Johannesburg: Juta and Company Ltd., 1984), 16.

45. Vogler, G. P., DeFries, J. C., & Decker, S., "Family history as an indicator of risk for reading disability," *Journal of Learning Disabilities*, 1985, vol. 7, 419-421.

46. "New gene for dyslexia located," *Journal of Medical Genetics*, 7 September 1999.

47. Brooks, L., Revised version of a paper presented at the DI Guild Symposium, November 1996.

48. Suzuki, S., *Nurtured by Love: A New Approach to Education* (New York: Exposition Press, 1969).
49. Price, B., "Dr. Shinichi Suzuki (1898-1997)," *Issue of Women Newsmagazine*, Autumn 1998.
50. Skeels, H. M., et al., "A study of environmental stimulation: An orphanage preschool project," *University of Iowa Studies in Child Welfare*, 1938, vol. 15(4), cited in Dworetzky, *Introduction to Child Development*, 211-212.
51. Ibid.
52. Clark, B., *Growing Up Gifted* (3rd ed.), (Columbus: Merrill, 1988), cited in P. Engelbrecht, S. Kriegler & M. Booysen (eds.), *Perspectives on Learning Difficulties* (Pretoria: J. L. van Schaik, 1996), 176.

4.

LD or not LD?

Current practices have led some commentators to label the situation a "diagnostic scandal."[1] — Scriven

What is a learning disability? What exactly is this phenomenon that is so hotly debated by scholars? At least in regard to this aspect there should be some agreement. That however, is not the case at all:

> No group of special educators, it seems, is less certain about the nature of their field or, for that matter, about its very existence than are those who work in the area of learning disabilities. The problem is that no one can decide precisely what a learning disability is.[2]

Twenty-five years after the LD term was first proposed, Sleeter commented that professionals were still wrestling with the question of how to define it. If they agreed on the major components of a definition and debated only the finer points, one could scarcely raise an eyebrow. But that was not the case. Major disagreements exist about what it means, exactly to whom it refers, and even whether it can be defined meaningfully:

> Does the term refer to *all* children who are underachieving, or only certain children? While Cruikshank (1983) steadfastly maintained that it refers only to children whose under achievement is the "result of perceptual processing deficits" (p. 25), Mann and colleagues (1983) suggested that "we adopt learning disabilities as a generic term for all 'mildly' handicapped as *the* label to replace other stigmatizing ones" (p. 14). Kirk and Kirk (1983) reaffirmed the claim that LD results from "intrinsic, not extrinsic" problems, and that "those mildly retarded educationally, due to extrinsic environmental conditions require something other than LD services" (p. 18); to which Sabatino (1983) replied, "And that my friends, is absolute nonsense; . . . Indeed, how can one

deny a culturally-linguistic component in a socially relevant condition?" (p. 23). While Myklebust (1983) asserted that, "Learning disabilities can be defined" (p. 15), Ysseldyke and Algozzine (1983) retorted, "To us, debate about who is LD and who is not has always been the world's closest rival for Sominex" (p. 26).[3]

Kronick commented that the LD label has become a catchall for students who do not fit the system. It is so broad a label that everyone could be and is being assessed as having LD.[4]

This dispute is still continuing—"with no apparent resolution"[5]—and therefore nobody as yet knows what this "disease" is. In spite of this, millions of children have been and are still being diagnosed as having "caught" it.

Naturally, because of the confusion and contention regarding definition, the matter of diagnosis is also in utter turmoil. In the U.S.A., whenever a child is formally classified as "learning disabled" today, he becomes the financial responsibility of the state. These children, who are provided with educational programs under federal law, are in most states distinguished from other children with learning problems on two grounds. *First*, the basis of their scholastic problems is *presumed* to be due to some neurological dysfunction. The LD category excludes children who have learning problems as a result of visual, hearing or motor handicaps, of mental retardation, of emotional disturbance, or of environmental, cultural or economic disadvantage. Needless to say, this exclusion is one of the most contentious issues in the LD field. Apart from the fact that the existence of a neurological dysfunction has never been proved, it is impossible to prove that the environment has played no role in the creation of a learning disability. *Second*, to be diagnosed as "learning disabled," there must be a discrepancy between a child's potential and his achievement.

Most other Western countries have more or less accepted the American model.

Discrepancy between Potential and Achievement

It is often said that a learning disability is an "invisible disability." Other disabilities or handicaps are usually easily visible, but the existence of a learning disability can only be deduced from the fact that there is a discrepancy between a child's expected school achievement and his real school achievement, or a discrepancy between potential and achievement.[6] Miles states that a person is dyslexic provided that there is a discrepancy between his intellectual level (potential) and his performance at reading and spelling (achievement) and that this discrepancy is accompanied by some other supporting "signs," like problems with left and right, poor sense of time, putting letters and figures the wrong way around, unusual difficulty in remembering mathematical tables, putting letters in the wrong order, et cetera.[7]

If discovering discrepancies between potential and achievement is an acceptable and valid method of diagnosing disabilities, then there must be hundreds, maybe even thousands of other disabilities that we poor human beings may suffer from. They have so far gone undiscovered, simply because we have not yet compared the relevant potentials and achievements. For example, if one calculated from a person's physique, age, weight and height that he should be able to run the 100 meters in 11 seconds and the stop watch shows that he can only do so in 14 seconds, then that person must have a running disability. Now, of course the idea of a running disability is ridiculous, but isn't a learning disability then equally ridiculous? Why can't we use the same method to diagnose other disabilities?

Another matter in dispute is how big the discrepancy must be before one can refer to a child as learning disabled. The following event illustrates the untenability of the whole idea: A few years ago New York adopted a 50 percent discrepancy formula as a criterion for identification. A 50 percent discrepancy means that a child achieves only half as well as one would expect from him when considering his potential. Following the adoption of the 50 percent discrepancy criterion, the number of pupils identified as learning disabled dropped from 28,000 to 12,167, thus miraculously "curing" almost 16,000 children of their "disability." A further implication of this new regulation was that a child of normal intelligence had to spend two years at school before a one-year discrepancy (50 percent) could be calculated and the child could receive treatment.[8]

The Birth of IQ Tests

The most important criterion to determine a child's expected achievement is his IQ. The aim of an IQ test is to measure the intelligence of a child.

Intelligence testing began in earnest in France, when in 1904 psychologist Alfred Binet was commissioned by the French government to find a method to differentiate between children who were intellectually normal and those who were inferior. The purpose was to put the latter into special schools. There they would receive more individual attention and the disruption they caused in the education of intellectually normal children could be avoided.[9]

This led to the development of the *Binet Scale,* also known as the *Simon-Binet Scale* in recognition of Theophile Simon's assistance in its development. It constituted a revolutionary approach to the assessment of individual mental ability. However, Binet himself cautioned against misuse of the scale or misunderstanding of its implications. According to Binet, the scale was designed with a single purpose in mind; it was to serve as a guide for identifying children in the schools who required special education. It was not intended to be used as "a general device for ranking all pupils according to mental worth." Binet also noted that "the scale, properly speaking, does not permit the measure of intelligence, because intellectual qualities are not superposable, and therefore cannot be measured as linear surfaces are measured."[10] Since, according to Binet, intelligence could not be described as a single score, the use of his Intelligence Quotient (IQ) as a definite statement on a child's intellectual capability would be a serious mistake. In addition, Binet feared that IQ measurement would be used to condemn a child to a permanent "condition" of stupidity, this negatively affecting his or her education and livelihood:

> Some recent thinkers . . . [have affirmed] that an individual's intelligence is a fixed quantity, a quantity that cannot be increased. We must protest and react against this brutal pessimism; we must try to demonstrate that it is founded on nothing.[11]

Binet's scale had a profound impact on educational development in the United States—and elsewhere. However, the American educators and psychologists who championed and utilized the scale and its revisions failed to heed Binet's caveats concerning its limitations. Soon intelligence testing assumed an importance and respectability out of proportion to its actual value.

H. H. Goddard, director of research at Vineland Training School in New Jersey, translated Binet's work into English and advocated a more general application of the *Simon-Binet Scale.*[12] Unlike Binet, Goddard considered intelligence a solitary, fixed and inborn entity that could be measured.[13]

While Goddard extolled the value and uses of the single IQ score, Lewis M. Terman, who also believed that intelligence was hereditary and fixed, worked on revising the *Simon-Binet Scale*. His final product, published in 1916 as the *Stanford Revision of the Binet-Simon Scale of Intelligence* (also known as the *Stanford-Binet*), became the standard intelligence test in the United States for the next several decades.[14] Convincing American educators of the need for universal intelligence testing, and the efficiency it could contribute to school programming, within a few years,

> the *Simon-Binet Scale*, originally designed for identification of children requiring special instructional attention, was transformed into an integral, far-reaching component of the American educational structure. Through Goddard's and Terman's efforts the notion that intelligence tests were accurate, scientific, and valuable tools for bringing efficiency to the schools resulted in assigning the IQ score an almost exalted position as a primary, definitive, and permanent representation of the quality of an individual. Hence, intelligence testing became entrenched in the schools over the next several decades.[15]

Few people realize that the tests being used today represent the end result of a historical process that has its origins in racial and cultural bigotry. Many of the founding fathers of the modern testing industry—including Goddard, Terman and Carl Brighan (the developer of the *Scholastic Aptitude Test*)—advocated eugenics.[16] Eugenics is a movement concerned with the selective breeding of human beings. Selected human beings would be mated with each other in an attempt to obtain certain traits in their offspring, much the same way that animal breeders work with champion stock. The eventual goal of eugenics is to create a better human race. The Nazis took this idea to the extreme. All "inferior" humans, especially Jews, retarded children or adults, and any individual with genetic defects, were to be destroyed; and so many ill and retarded people, and many Jews, were killed during World War II.[17]

The founding fathers of the testing industry saw testing as one way of achieving the eugenicist aims. Goddard's belief in the innateness and unalterability of intelligence levels, for example, was so firm that he argued for the reconstruction of society along the lines dictated by IQ scores:

> If mental level plays anything like the role it seems to, and if in each human being it is the fixed quantity that many believe it is, then it is no useless specu-

lation that tries to see what would happen if society were organized so as to recognize and make use of the doctrine of mental levels . . . It is quite possible to restate practically all of our social problems in terms of mental level . . . Testing intelligence is no longer an experiment or of doubted value. It is fast becoming an exact science . . . Greater efficiency, we are always working for. Can these new facts be used to increase our efficiency? No question! We only await the Human Engineer who will undertake the work.[18]

As a result of his views on intelligence and society, Goddard lobbied for restrictive immigration laws. Upon his "discovery" that all immigrants except those from Northern Europe were of "surprisingly low intelligence," such tight immigration laws were enacted in the 1920s.[19] According to Harvard professor Steven Jay Gould in his acclaimed book *The Mismeasure of Man*, these tests were also influential in legitimizing forced sterilization of allegedly "defective" individuals in some states.[20]

By the 1920s mass use of the *Stanford-Binet Scale* and other tests had created a multimillion-dollar testing industry.[21] By 1974, according to the *Mental Measurements Yearbook*, 2,467 tests measuring some form of intellectual ability were in print, 76 of which were identified as strict intelligence tests.[22] In one year in the 1980s, teachers gave over 500 million standardized tests to children and adults across the United States.[23] In 1989 the American Academy for the Advancement of Science listed the IQ test among the twenty most significant scientific discoveries of the century along with nuclear fission, DNA, the transistor and flight.[24] Patricia Broadfoot's dictum that "assessment, far more than religion, has become the opiate of the people,"[25] has come of age.

So What are We Actually Measuring?

If an IQ test is supposed to measure a person's intelligence, the question is: What is intelligence? Is it the ability to do well in school? Is it the ability to read well and spell correctly? Or are the following people intelligent?

- The physician who smokes three packets of cigarettes a day?
- The Nobel prize winner whose marriage and personal life are in ruins?
- The corporate executive who has ingeniously worked his way to the top and also earned a heart attack for his efforts?

- The brilliant and successful music composer who handled his money so poorly that he was always running from his creditors (incidentally, his name was Mozart)?[26]

The problem is that the term intelligence has never been defined adequately and therefore nobody knows what an IQ test is supposed to measure. In spite of this the futures of thousands of children are determined by the results of this test.

Already in the early 1920s the journalist Walter Lippmann maintained that IQ tests were nothing but a series of stunts. "We cannot measure intelligence when we have not defined it," he said.[27]

In 1962 Banesh Hoffman told a shocked America about the "tyranny of testing" in his classic book of the same name. His book and others that followed stirred up much controversy, leading the National Education Association in 1976 to recommend the elimination of group standardized intelligence, aptitude, and achievement tests.[28] Sarason quotes an advertisement that was placed by *Psychology Today* in the *New York Times* in August 1979, part of which appears below:

In the chaos of controversy, the standard IQ exam is flunking the test. Many educational psychologists feel that IQ testers have failed to answer two all-important questions: What is intelligence? What have IQ tests actually measured?

The National Education Association, with membership of almost 2 million teachers, has called for the abolition of standardized intelligence tests because they are "at best wasteful, and at worst, destructive."

Yale psychologist Robert Sternberg says in P.T. that psychologists know "almost nothing about what it is that they have been measuring. The tests have proved overall to have only low to moderate power to predict such things as future job performance, income and status, or overall happiness and adjustment."[29]

However, the dust soon settled after this uprising and the testing industry became more powerful than ever. The National Education Association has completely changed its stand and now "recognizes the need for periodic comprehensive testing for evaluation and diagnosis of student progress."[30]

This is no wonder, says Armstrong, since it would have taken a major miracle to eliminate testing.[31]

Today, voices for the elimination of standardized tests are few. One is Linda S. Siegel, professor in the Department of Educational Psychology and Special Education at the University of British Columbia in Vancouver, Canada. She proposes that we abandon the IQ test in the analysis of the LD child. According to most definitions—although they are not conclusive—intelligence is made up of the skills of logical reasoning, problem solving, critical thinking, and adaptation.[31] This scenario seems reasonable, until one examines the content of IQ tests. The definition of intelligence, as is operationalized in all IQ tests, includes virtually no skills that can be identified in terms of the definitions of intelligence. To support her statement, Siegel gives a detailed analysis of the subtests of the *Wechsler Intelligence Scale for Children-Revised* (WISC-R). This IQ test is composed of Verbal and Performance sections, and is nearly always used in LD diagnosis. In each subtest of the Verbal scale, performance is in varying degrees dependent on specific knowledge, vocabulary, expressive language and memory skills, while in the Performance scale, visual-spatial abilities, fine motor coordination, perceptual skills, and in some subtests speed, are essential for scoring.[33] As Siegel rightly points out, IQ tests measure, for the most part, what a person has *learned*, not what he or she is capable of doing in the future (his potential).[34]

There is an additional problem in the use of IQ tests with individuals with learning disabilities. According to Siegel it is a paradox that IQ scores are required of people with LD because most of these persons have deficiencies in one or more of the component skills that are part of these IQ tests—memory, language, fine motor skills, et cetera. The effect is that they may end up having a lower IQ score than a person who does not have such problems, even though they may both have identical reasoning and problem-solving skills. The lower IQ score, therefore, may be a result of the learning disability, and IQ scores may underestimate the real intelligence of the individual with a learning disability.[35]

Another assumption of the discrepancy definition is that the IQ score should predict reading, so that if you have a low IQ score you should be a poor reader and that poor reading is an *expected consequence* of low IQ. However, there are individuals who have low IQ scores and are good readers.[36]

The unreliability of IQ tests has been proved by numerous researchers.

The scores may vary by as much as 15 points from one test to another,[37] while emotional tension, anxiety, and unfamiliarity with the testing process can greatly affect test performance.[38] In addition, Gould described the biasing effect that tester attitudes, qualifications, and instructions can have on testing.[39] The same applies to other diagnostic tests.

The Final Say

In the face of this, it makes one shudder to think that far-reaching decisions are sometimes made about children, and that such decisions are often based solely on test scores:

> The best example is found in the individualized educational program (IEP) meeting. Who has the most influence at these meetings? Is it the parent who has raised a child with suspected learning problems from birth and therefore has a wealth of development experience that bears on issues at hand? Is it the child's current teacher who has spent weeks or months in daily contact with the child? Is it the school principal who is responsible for the welfare of all teachers and children in the school and who may have already been involved in seeking solutions for the child's schooling?

> Unfortunately, it is none of these. The professional with more relative influence on IEP decisions is the person who probably has spent the *least* time with the child, both directly and indirectly. It is the professional who has spent this limited time evaluating the child with relatively unreliable measures, in a context usually far removed from the ecological validity of the classroom setting, in an attempt to determine a diagnosis that is often irrelevant to classroom functioning. It is, of course, the school psychologist.[40]

How far-reaching and how wrong the decisions of the school psychologist, based on his unreliable measures, can sometimes be, is clearly illustrated by the following story:

> When Gregory Ochoa was a high school student in California, he and his classmates were given an IQ test. Gregory and the other students were told that the results would enable the school to place them in classes commensurate with their skills. It seemed like a fair thing to do; after all, they were all being given the same chance, the same test.

64

But, after looking at the questions, Gregory discovered that he just didn't understand many of the words, and he couldn't understand exactly what he was supposed to do. Spanish was the language spoken in his home, and his English skills were not quite equal to those of most of his classmates. Gregory, and a few others who were having the same trouble, pointed out their difficulty to the person who administered the test. They were told, "Do the best you can."

A few weeks after taking the test, Gregory found himself in a "special" class. Most of the other students in the class also had Spanish surnames such as Martinez or Gonzales. Gregory didn't fully realize what had happened. He never understood the term "educable mentally retarded" which was written on the teacher's letterhead and on the bulletin board in the classroom. All Gregory knew was that the special class didn't do regular school work. Gregory's teacher was sort of a coach, and they played a lot of soccer. Any class member interested in intellectual pursuits, such as going to the school library, found that such activities were out of bounds.

Gregory soon dropped out of school. He drifted about and got into trouble. He was sent to a reform school where he received some remedial teaching. After school he joined the navy. He scored well on the navy tests. They never told him what his IQ was on retesting, but they seemed pleased that a retarded person could do so well. While in the navy, Gregory earned high school credits, which eventually enabled him to attend college as a student on probation. His first quarter in college he received all A's. His second quarter he again received all A's, but he was kept on probation. Gregory finally graduated from San Jose City College on the dean's list as an honor student—on probation! The college was apparently unable to think of him as no longer "mentally retarded." By the age of forty, Gregory Ochoa was an assistant professor at the University of Washington in Seattle, where he taught classes in social casework.[41]

The story underlines the veracity of Langeveld's statement that nobody may ever be denied the opportunity to disprove test scores.[42]

It has been demonstrated clearly by numerous studies how unreliable test scores can be, and therefore any decisions that school psychologists might make on the basis of such scores. In one study, ninety-nine school psychologists independently scored an IQ test from identical records, and came up with IQs ranging from 63 to 117 for the same person.[43]

In another study, Ysseldyke et al. examined the extent to which professionals were able to differentiate learning-disabled students from ordinary low achievers by examining patterns of scores on psychometric measures. Subjects were 65 school psychologists, 38 special-education teachers, and a "naive" group of 21 university students enrolled in programs unrelated to education or psychology. Provided with forms containing information on 41 test or subtest scores (including the WISC-R IQ test) of nine school-identified LD students and nine non-LD students, judges were instructed to indicate which students they believed were learning disabled and which were non-learning disabled.[44]

The school psychologists and special-education teachers were able to differentiate between LD students and low achievers with only 50 percent accuracy. The naive judges, who had never had more than an introductory course in education or psychology, evidenced a 75 percent hit rate.[45] When Ysseldyke and Algozzine cite Scriven, they clearly show their belief that the current system is in trouble:

> The pessimist says that a 12 ounce glass containing 6 ounces of drink is half empty—the optimist calls it half full. I can't say what I think the pessimist could say about research and practice in special education at this point, but I think the optimist could say that we have a wonderful opportunity to start all over![46]

Notes:

1. Scriven, M., "Comments on Gene Glass," Paper presented at the Wingspread National Invitational Conference on Public Policy and the Special Education Task of the 1980s, cited in D. P. Hallahan, J. Kauffman & J. Lloyd, *Introduction to Learning Disabilities* (Englewood Cliffs, NJ: Prentice Hall, 1985), 298.
2. Franklin, B. M., "Introduction: Learning disabilities and the need for dissenting essays," in B. M. Franklin (ed.), *Learning Disability: Dissenting Essays* (Philadelphia: The Falmer Press, 1987), 1.
3. Sleeter, C., "Literacy, definitions of learning disabilities and social control," in Franklin (ed.), *Learning Disability: Dissenting Essays*, 67.
4. Kronick, D., *New Approaches to Learning Disabilities. Cognitive, Metacognitive and Holistic* (Philadelphia: Grune & Stratton , 1988).
5. Siegel, L. S., "Issues in the definition and diagnosis of learning disabilities: A perspective on Guckenberger v. Boston University," *Journal of Learning Disabilities*, 1 July 1999, vol. 32.

6. Du Preez, J. J., & Steenkamp, W. L., *Spesifieke Leergestremdhede: 'n Neurologiese Perspektief* (2nd ed.), (Durban: Butterworth, 1986).
7. Miles, T. R., *Understanding Dyslexia* (London: Hodder and Stoughton, 1978), 42.
8. Kavale, K. A., "Status of the field: Trends and issues in learning disabilities," in K. A. Kavale (ed.), *Learning Disabilities: State of the Art and Practice* (Boston: College-Hill Press, 1988), 7.
9. Swiegers, D. J., & Louw, D. A., "Intelligensie," in D. A. Louw (ed.), *Inleiding tot die Psigologie* (2nd ed.), (Johannesburg: McGraw Hill, 1982), 145.
10. Gould, S. J., *The Mismeasure of Man* (New York: W. W. Norton, 1981), 151-152, cited in R. L. Osgood, "Intelligence testing and the field of learning disabilities: A historical and critical perspective," *Learning Disability Quarterly*, 1984, vol. 7, 343-348.
11. Gould, *The Mismeasure of Man*, 153-154, cited in Osgood, "Intelligence testing."
12. Gould, *The Mismeasure of Man*, 159, cited in Osgood, "Intelligence testing."
13. Goddard, H. H., *Human Efficiency and Levels of Intelligence* (Princeton: Princeton University Press, 1920), 1, cited in Osgood, "Intelligence testing."
14. Linden, K. W., & Linden, J. D., *Modern Mental Measurement: A Historical Perspective* (Boston: Houghton Mifflin, 1968), cited in Osgood, "Intelligence testing."
15. Osgood, "Intelligence testing."
16. Armstrong, T., *In Their Own Way: Discovering and Encouraging Your Child's Personal Learning Style* (Los Angeles: Jeremy P. Tarcher, Inc., 1987), 27.
17. Dworetzky, J. P., *Introduction to Child Development* (St. Paul: West Publishing Company, 1981), 82-83.
18. Goddard, *Human Efficiency and Levels of Intelligence*, v-vii, cited in Osgood, "Intelligence testing."
19. Gould, *The Mismeasure of Man*, 167, cited in Osgood, "Intelligence testing."
20. Gould, *The Mismeasure of Man*, cited in Armstrong, *In Their Own Way*, 28.
21. Osgood, "Intelligence testing."
22. Buros, O. K. (ed.), *Mental Measurements Yearbook* (Highland Park, NJ: Gryphon Press), cited in Osgood, "Intelligence testing."
23. Armstrong, *In Their Own Way*, 27.
24. Bjorklund, D. F., *Children's Thinking: Development Function and Individual Differences* (Pacific Grove, CA: Brookes/Cole, 1989), cited in P. Engelbrecht, S. Kriegler & M. Booysen (eds.), *Perspectives on Learning Difficulties* (Pretoria: J. L. van Schaik, 1996), 109.
25. Broadfoot, P., cited in Engelbrecht et al. (eds.), *Perspectives on Learning Difficulties*, 109.
26. Dworetzky, *Introduction to Child Development*, 348.
27. Lippman, cited in N. J. Block & G. Dworkin (eds.), *The IQ Controversy: Critical Readings* (New York: Pantheon Books, 1976).
28. Armstrong, *In Their Own Way*, 26.
29. *New York Times*, August 1979, cited in S. B. Sarason, *Psychology Misdirected* (New York: The Free Press, 1981).
30. *National Education Association Handbook, 1984-85* (Washington, DC: National Education Association of the United States, 1984, 240), cited in Armstrong, *In Their Own Way*, 27.
31. Armstrong, *In Their Own Way*, 27.
32. Siegel, "Issues in the definition and diagnosis of learning disabilities."

33. Siegel, L. S., "IQ is irrelevant to the definition of learning disabilities," *Journal of Learning Disabilities*, 1989, vol. 22(8), 469-478.
34. Siegel, "Issues in the definition and diagnosis of learning disabilities."
35. Ibid; Siegel, "IQ is irrelevant to the definition of learning disabilities."
36. Siegel, L. S., & Metsala, E., "An alternative to the food processor approach to subtypes of learning disabilities," in N. N. Singh & I. L. Beale (eds.), *Learning Disabilities: Nature, Theory, and Treatment* (New York: Springer-Verlag, 1992), 45.
37. Smith, C. R., *Learning Disabilities: The Interaction of Learner, Task, and Setting* (Boston: Allyn and Bacon, 1991), 63.
38. Tyler, cited in A. Anastasi, (ed.), *Testing Problems in Perspective* (Washington, DC: American Council on Education, 1966).
39. Gould, *The Mismeasure of Man*, 199-212, cited in Osgood, "Intelligence testing."
40. Kavale, "Status of the field," 6.
41. Dworetzky, *Introduction to Child Development*, 347-348.
42. Langeveld, M. J., *Voraussage und Erfolg: Über die Bedeutung von Tests als Voraussage Kindlicher Entwicklung* (Braunschweig: Georg Westermann Verlag, 1973).
43. Cited in J. Sattler, *Assessment of Children's Intelligences and Special Abilities* (Boston: Allyn & Bacon, 1982), 60.
44. Epps, S., Ysseldyke, J. E., & McGue, M., "'I know one when I see one'—Differentiating LD and non-LD students," *Learning Disability Quarterly*, 1984, vol. 7, 89-101.
45. Ysseldyke, J. E., & Algozzine, B., "LD or not LD: That's not the question!" *Journal of Learning Disabilities*, 1983, vol. 16(1), 26-27.
46. Scriven, M., "Comments on Gene Glass," cited in Ysseldyke & Algozzine, "LD or not LD."

5.

Intervention

The decisive question is not what methods or procedures are employed, or whether they are old-fashioned or modern, time-tested or experimental, conventional or progressive. . . . The ultimate criterion for success in teaching is—results![1] – Mursell

Soon after the "discovery" of learning disabilities in the 1960s, remedial programs of different types were under way, ranging from small one-enthusi-astic-teacher size programs to large, nationally funded ones. However, a disappointing shock came to many special educators in the U.S.A. when the President's Report to Congress, reported by Nixon in 1970 in *American Education*, stated its findings. After the expenditure of one billion dollars on compensatory education, mainly reading, only 19 percent of children improved their reading significantly, 15 percent fell behind more than expected, and more than two thirds of the children remained unaffected. That is, they continued to fall behind.[2]

In 1972, Koppitz reported her findings in a five year follow-up of 177 LD students placed in special-education programs. Minimal progress had been made. Students had made a three to four months gain per year in reading and appeared to have reached a plateau in terms of academic progress.[3] Similar results were observed by Gottesman in 1979, who reviewed learning-disabled students five to seven years after initial placement in remedial programs. They showed an average gain in reading of only four months per year of remedial instruction,[4] which means that they continued to fall further behind. In order to catch up, their reading must improve by *more* than one year in every year of instruction.

After reviewing a set of long-term studies, Spreen concluded in 1982, "most children who are referred for a learning or reading disability do not catch up. In

69

fact, their disability is likely to become worse in time. In addition, remedial instruction has not been shown to improve the prognosis of these children."[5] A decade later no progress had been made. In 1992 Reiff and Gerber echoed Spreen's findings, stating that the "available literature of longitudinal and follow-up studies suggests that a learning disability is a lifelong condition."[6]

Since the beginning of the 1980s, ever-increasing attention has been directed toward the use of technology with individuals with LD. In the hope of improving methods of instruction and remediation, computers and other electronic devices have been integrated into resource rooms and mainstreamed classrooms. Reflecting over this decade, Hresko and Parmar stated in 1991, "no area [in the field on LD] has grown as significantly as high technology."[7] It was hoped that computers and high technology would be able to achieve what teachers and therapists could not. However, in regard to the benefits of computers in special education, Hresko and Parmar stated the following: "Although much has been expected of computers in the education of the exceptional child, those expectations have not been realized. Research to date has failed to substantiate significant or even moderate gains in the academic areas. Furthermore, although some researchers have focused on the potential effects of computers on thinking and reasoning ability, research has failed to show significant gains. Thus the widespread hopes for educational uses of the computer remain to be realized."[8]

This was, of course, to be expected. All the intervention efforts that had so far been tried by teachers and therapists were ineffective. Having them applied by computers would not suddenly make them effective.

Because of the inability of LD specialists to "fix" a learning disability, attention has shifted in the 1990s from remediation to compensation. Consequently, students with learning disabilities are taught ways of coping and adapting.[9]

Creating More Problems than it Solves?

Current federal law states that every handicapped child in the United States has the right to an appropriate education. Many parents whose children aren't learning in the schools have chosen to have their children tested and declared "learning handicapped" to make them eligible for special LD programs.[10] While the statistics above demonstrate quite clearly that there is often nothing "special" about these programs, they frequently cause more problems than they solve.

Like prisons, LD classrooms often serve as a training-ground for misbehavior, where a small number of children referred for severe emotional problems pass on their instability to the rest of the students. Carl Milofsky, a California sociologist who spent several months in classes for the education-ally handicapped wrote of his experience, "It was clear that, if anything, the special class made students more rebellious and harder to handle."[11]

A more serious problem with many LD programs is that by removing children from the "mainstream" of regular classroom life, there is a greater likelihood that these youngsters will fall ever further behind their peers. Lee Ann Trusdell of the City University of New York, in a study of remedial programs in New York City, observed that many students were receiving instruction in special classes that was totally unrelated to what was being taught in regular classes. As these children become more disconnected from their homeroom classes, it becomes that much harder for them to return. In fact, many of these youngsters, initially referred to special education for minor remediation, soon make a career out of their disability and slip more deeply into the LD labyrinth.[12] The following letter, posted on an LD bulletin board on the Internet, is just one example:

If you care at all for your children you will read this and take it to heart. I want to tell of my own nightmare, and how my schoolteachers and parents destroyed my interest in school.

First let me start by letting you all know that I was not a great student. I was an average student who mostly made C's and B's with an occasional A and an occasional D. But the D's were rare. And I loved school. I worked hard and did the best I could. I can honestly say, that going into fifth grade there was no one on this planet I trusted more than my parents and my schoolteachers. Despite average grades, I felt I was getting a lot out of school and found it fascinating. My standardized scores on tests like the CAT and CTBS were always in the average range—between the 40-60% range. I was about as average as I could be, but I was happy and I was in love with school.

Then, for some reason that puzzles me to this day, a nosy do-gooder, perfec-tionist teacher decided to stick her nose where it didn't belong. She coerced my parents into agreeing to a special education evaluation. NOW WHY ON EARTH WOULD SHE DO THAT TO ME?

My parents signed the evaluation—no questions asked. So one day I get called out of my classroom. I was told that I was going to be given a test. Mind you I was a ten-year-old boy. No one else was required to take the test. I was lead down the hall—all by myself—out of the door and down a breezeway to a stand-alone shack, my nerves building all of the way. I was terrified. "Why were they doing this to me?"

My nerves got the best of me. I did well on most of the tests, but my nerves overtook me and I did poorly enough on other parts of the test that I was placed in special ed. I was in classrooms with kids who . . . were clearly intellectually challenged. I was humiliated, degraded and worst of all betrayed. I now hated my teachers and barely cared for my parents. I started to hate school, whereas before then I loved school.

I was also in the worst of catch 22 situations, as there was no way out. What if I make all A's? Well it proves you need to be in special ed! What if I make all F's? Well it proves that you need more special ed. And sure enough I made A's in those pathetic little special ed classes. But what idiot would not make an A in them. The coursework was pathetically easy. Most of all, what was really bad—despite reassurances to the contrary—I was well aware of the fact that the coursework was not the same as what was in regular classes. I knew for a fact that I was not receiving an equal education. I knew it was unjust. Eventually it took its toll. I lost all interest in school and never made it past the eight grade. . . .

If one considers that less than two percent of students placed in special education ever return to regular education,[13] it is evident that the LD system has failed more children than it could help. A widespread feeling of dejection has taken root amongst its educators:

I have found that both learning disability specialists and administrators are among the first to tell me of their discouragement with the present system for helping students with learning problems. They are less satisfied with the system than their staunchest critics: they want the most for the students in their care, yet they see the inadequacy of both the special and the regular education systems to meet these needs.[14]

However, as Coles remarks, persistent academic failure should be no surprise. The invalid assumptions behind the explanation of learning disabilities center almost exclusively on what is happening inside children's heads, thereby misdirecting the diagnoses and remedial programs. At the same time, they hinder the pursuit of other, scientific explanations, of preventative strategies, and of truly effective methods for addressing the problems when they do occur.[15] As stated in the first chapter, there is only one way in which any science can make progress and that is if its point of departure is based on fact. At present, within the field of learning disabilities, it is based on a myth.

Besides failing due to its mythical foundations, remedial instruction and other intervention efforts of an educational nature also fail because to a large extent one of the most important principles of teaching is overlooked, that of sequence. Herbart, who made important contributions to the development of modern pedagogics, insisted that one never apprehends anything in isolation, but always in terms of one's background of previous experience and learning.[16] When teaching, it is therefore of extreme importance always to start with what is known to the pupil and then move to the unknown. In remedial education, this rarely happens, if at all.

A further, very important objection that can be raised against remedial education is that it is mostly symptomatic treatment and seldom deals with the cause of the problem it is supposed to address. A child's poor reading ability is the symptom of a deeper lying problem. Usually, in remedial education, only the reading problem itself, i.e. the symptom, is dealt with.

Stimulants

After remedial instruction, the most common intervention method in dealing with LD children is the use of stimulants. These psychoactive stimulants include Ritalin (methylphenidate), Dexedrine (dextroamphetamine), Cylert (magnesium pemoline) and numerous others.

The production of Ritalin has increased sixfold in the U.S. from 1990 to 1996. According to a report issued by the U.N.'s Vienna-based International Narcotics in February 1996, as many as 5 percent of all American schoolchildren—and 12 percent of all boys between the ages of six and fourteen—are being treated with Ritalin.[17] And the production is still increasing. According to Dr. Lawrence H. Diller, author of *Running on Ritalin*, stimulant drug use in children rose 23 percent between 1995 and 1999.[18]

Although stimulants are very often administered for other types of learning disabilities, it is especially prescribed for children suffering from a vaguely

73

defined syndrome, "attention deficit hyperactivity disorder" (ADHD). These children have trouble sitting still in class and giving attention. Eighty percent of children with ADHD also have problems with reading, spelling and writing.[19] Almost 60 percent would be anticipated to have failed one grade in school;[20] about a third fail to graduate from high school.[21]

Up to about 1957 hyperactivity was a rare phenomenon, with an incidence of perhaps one out of two thousand individuals. These rare individuals seemed to be driven by an inner whirlwind, not just in school, but constantly. They were always moving, climbing and knocking things over and were in constant danger of injuring themselves or others.[22] Today, on the contrary, children are being diagnosed as ADHD even if the symptoms of the "disease" occur *only* in the classroom. The same child can watch TV or tinker with something for hours without distraction.

The manner in which "attention deficit hyperactivity disorder" is diagnosed and the drug prescribed lends credence, as the U.S. Drug Enforcement Agency puts it, "to claims that methylphenidate is overprescribed and used indiscriminately in place of disciplinary measures at home and at school."[23]

One of the concerns about the use of medication for LD children is that the induction of pharmaceutical intervention frequently has not been based on the criteria published by the pharmaceutical companies and medical reference texts. This information is straightforward in the description of the indications, contraindications, and precautions that need to be considered before medical intervention is implemented. The medication is usually prescribed by a physician based only on parent or parent/teacher reports indicating problems with learning/attention. In many instances, sufficient data for a responsible decision is simply not obtained.[24]

The pertinent data on Ritalin is quite clear. Anxiety, tension, agitation, depression are among the contraindications for the prescription of Ritalin. In spite of these blatant warnings, Ritalin continues to be prescribed without data assessing these conditions. Warnings indicating that Ritalin should not be used for children under the age of six are ignored. Users are increasingly as young as two years of age.[25]

Stimulants often have side effects, the most commonly reported being the loss of appetite, serious weight loss, insomnia, depression, headaches, stomachaches, bed-wetting, irritability and dizziness. Reports also indicate severe psychological effects. In one case, as told by Schrag and Divoky, a six-year-old girl on Ritalin started showing bizarre behavior. She hid herself in a closet and cowered in a corner, became apathetic and mute, "almost like a vegetable," then again started babbling incoherently, staring into space, contorting her body. In another case, a ten-year-old boy started screaming in his sleep on the second day of a Ritalin regimen, then became more irritable, more hyperactive and physically abusive to younger children, saying that he "felt like he wanted to tear everything apart." He saw animals marching around in a whirlpool, food assumed a strange taste and his mouth went dry. Later he became weak and depressed. A six-year-old boy who had been "well adjusted except for hyperactivity," began to exhibit visual and tactile hallucinations, that included seeing and feeling "worms all over him."[26]

The history of violence by teenagers who have been subjected to psychoactive drugs cannot be ignored. T. J. Solomon, a fifteen-year-old at the Heritage High School in Georgia was being treated with Ritalin. On 20 May 1999, he opened fire on and wounded six classmates.[27] On 19 April 1999, Shawn Cooper, a fifteen-year-old student from Notus, Idaho, fired two shotgun rounds, narrowly missing students and school staff. He was taking Ritalin.[28] On 21 May 1998, before going on a wild shooting spree at his Springfield, Oregon high school that left two dead and twenty-two injured, fourteen-year-old Kip Kinkel had been attending anger control classes and was reportedly taking Prozac and Ritalin. Kinkel also shot his parents, killing them.[29] While on vacation in Las Vegas on 25 May 1997, eighteen-year-old Jeremy Strohmeyer raped and murdered a seven-year-old girl in the ladies rest room in a casino. He had been prescribed Dexedrine and started taking it a week before the killing.[30]

Except for short-term side effects, there are warnings in the literature that stimulants may have fundamental long-term effects, particularly on psychological drug dependence. According to one study, children treated with Ritalin are three times more likely to develop a taste for cocaine.[31]

Perhaps if stimulant treatment achieved positive results, one could ignore its critics. After all, as Bee remarked, we live in a "drug-taking culture. We pop aspirin into our mouths at the first sign of pain, decongestants when we have a cold, tranquilizers when we are nervous, and sleeping pills when we cannot sleep."[32] That however, does not seem to be the case. Except for keeping parents and teachers happy, there is scant evidence of improved academic performance with stimulant treatment. In *The Learning Mystique*, Gerald Coles confirms the findings of a 1978 review of both short and long-term studies on the use of stimulants with hyperactive and learning-disabled children. Of a total of seventeen studies included in this review, whether they were short or long-term, whether they met basic scientific criteria or not, all the conclusions converged: "stimulant drugs have little, if any, impact on . . . long-term academic outcome."[33]

It seems that for most children drugs provide only maintenance, and not "treatment." According to Schrag and Divoky, studies in which drug-treated children were followed into adolescence "suggest that the outlook for children treated primarily with drugs is relatively poor. In their teens, these children were still having trouble in their families, often behaving antisocially and presenting academic and behavioral problems in school."[34]

When considering the child who has difficulties with learning, or concentration, or behavior, the purpose of any intervention effort should be to improve the child's quality of life. Any intervention that does not achieve this, does not achieve anything at all. Besides remedial education and pharmaceutical intervention, that both—considered from this perspective—achieve very little, there is a legion of other controversial techniques and aids that achieve just as little, and often less.

The time has come to put the children first. They, the children, are the ones who are suffering while the wrangling and the arguing are continuing. The fact is that whatever is done under the umbrella of learning disabilities is contributing very little, if anything, towards improving the quality of life of children. In many cases it seems to be downright harmful. As stated by Mursell at the beginning of this chapter, results are the ultimate criterion for success in education. The only observable result that has so far emerged from the field of learning disabilities is the diversity of opinions. This is in agreement with present-day research practices in the human sciences, which are unfortunately not based on achievements, but rather on opinion and speculation.[35] This is not good enough for the children who depend on us for receiving a good education.

The purpose of this book is to indicate that it is possible to stop being satisfied with opinions and speculation when the lives and futures of children are at stake and to work towards achievement.

Notes:

1. Mursell, J. L., *Successful Teaching* (2nd ed.), (New York: McGraw-Hill Book Company, Inc., 1954), 1.
2. Nixon, R., "Message on education reform," *American Education*, 1970, vol. 6(3).
3. Koppitz, E. M., "Special class pupils with learning disabilities: A 5 year follow-up study," *Academic Therapy*, 1972, vol. 8(2), 133-139.
4. Gottesman, R. T., "Follow-up of LD children," *Learning Disabilities Quarterly*, 1979, vol. 2, 60-69.
5. Spreen, O., "Adult outcomes of reading disorders," in R. N. Malatesha & P. G. Aaron (eds.), *Reading Disorders: Varieties and Treatments* (New York: Academic Press, 1982).
6. Reiff, H. B., & Gerber, P. J., "Adults with learning disabilities," in N. N. Singh & I. L. Beale (eds.), *Learning Disabilities: Nature, Theory, and Treatment* (New York: Springer-Verlag, 1992).
7. Hresko, W. P., & Parmar, R. S., "Educational trends in learning disabilities," in D. K. Reid, W. P. Hresko & L. Swanson (eds.), *A Cognitive Approach to Learning Disabilities* (Austin, TX: PRO-ED, 1991), 45.
8. Hresko, W. P., & Parmar, R. S., "The educational perspective," in *A Cognitive Approach to Learning Disabilities*, 3-44.
9. "New perspectives on teaching from successful adults with learning disabilities," *Remedial and Special Education*, 1 January 1995.
10. Armstrong, T., *In Their Own Way: Discovering and Encouraging Your Child's Personal Learning Style* (Los Angeles: Jeremy P. Tarcher, Inc., 1987), 54.
11. Milofsky, C., *Special Education: A Sociological Study of California Programs* (New York: Praeger, 1976), 106, cited in Armstrong, *In Their Own Way*, 45.
12. Trusdell, L. A., "How pull-out programs can hurt," *Learning*, March 1980, 17, cited in Armstrong, *In Their Own Way*, 46.
13. Lytle, J., "Is special education serving minority students?" *Harvard Educational Review*, 1988, vol. 58, 116-120.
14. Bartoli, J. S., "An ecological response to Coles's interactivity alternative," *Journal of Learning Disabilities*, 1989, vol. 22(5), 292-297.
15. Coles, G. S., *The Learning Mystique* (New York: Pantheon Books, 1987), xiv.
16. Mursell, *Successful Teaching*, 210-211.
17. Barber, S., "High on discipline," *Sunday Times*, 3 March 1996.
18. "Into the mouths of babes. The drugging of preschoolers is on the rise, study shows," *The Education Reporter*, April 2000, no. 171.
19. Wolfish, M. G., "Attention Deficit disorder (the hyperactive child)," *Modern Medicine of South Africa,* November 1988.
20. Wodrich, D. L., *Attention Deficit Hyperactivity Disorder: What Every Parent Wants to Know* (Baltimore: Paul H. Brookes Publishing Co., 1994), 23.
21. Wallis, C., "Behavior: Life in overdrive," *Time*, 18 July 1994, 42.
22. Schrag, P., & Divoky, D., *The Myth of the Hyperactive Child and Other Means of Child Control* (Middlesex: Penguin Books, 1975).
23. Barber, "High on discipline."

24. Rooney, K. J., "Controversial therapies: A review and critique," *Intervention in School and Clinic*, 1991, vol. 26(3), 134-142.
25. "Into the mouths of babes," *The Education Reporter.*
26. Schrag & Divoky, *The Myth of the Hyperactive Child.*
27. O'Meara, K., "Guns and doses," *Insight*, 28 June 1999, cited in "Psychiatry creates senseless violence at society's cost," *Psychiatry: Cases of Fraud* (Los Angeles: CCHR, 1999), 32-33.
28. Ibid.
29. "Ruthless kids—Psychiatric drugs cause violence," *Psychiatry: Betraying and Drugging Children* (Los Angeles: CCHR, 1998), 16-17.
30. O'Meara, K., "Has psychiatry gone psycho?" *Insight*, 26 April 1999, cited in "Psychiatry creates senseless violence at society's cost."
31. Motluk, A. "Health institute conference will study Ritalin's kinship to cocaine," *Minneapolis Star Tribune*, 30 April 1998.
32. Bee, H., *The Developing Child* (3rd ed.), (New York: Harper & Row, 1981).
33. Barkley, R. A., & Cunningham, C. E., "Do stimulants drugs improve the academic performance of hyperkinetic children?" *Clinical Pediatrics,* 1978, vol. 17, 85-92, cited Coles, *The Learning Mystique*, 94.
34. Schrag & Divoky, *The Myth of the Hyperactive Child.*
35. Cf. J. Mouton & H. C. Marais, *Metodologie van die Geesteswetenskappe: Basiese Begrippe* (Pretoria: Raad vir Geesteswetenskaplike Navorsing, 1989), 146.

6.

At the Crossroads

The history of science is replete with theories that have been thoroughly believed by the wisest men and were then thoroughly discredited.[1] — Popkin & Stroll

It has always been typical of the human being that he wants an explanation for most phenomena he encounters. Having an explanation greatly contributes to his sense of security. This desire is so great that, if he comes across a phenomenon for which he cannot *find* a reasonable and a rational explanation, he will *fabricate* one himself. The ancient Greeks, for example, could not find a rational explanation for the changing seasons and then made up the story of Hades and Persephone.

Hades, they said, was the brother of Zeus and god of the underworld. He fell in love with Persephone, daughter of Demeter, the goddess of farming and the harvest. Hades abducted Persephone while she was gathering poppies in Sicily. Grieving over her daughter, Demeter wandered all over the world and in her sadness she forbid the earth to bring forth fruit. Zeus became afraid that all men would die and finally agreed that Persephone could leave Hades and return to her mother Demeter, provided she had not eaten in the underworld. Hades agreed to let her go but tempted her into eating a pomegranate. As a result, she had to spend half of every year with Hades in the underworld and the other half with Demeter. During the half of the year that she is with Hades, Demeter mourns and neglects her duties as goddess of farming and harvest. All the plants fade away and the earth is cold and bare. When she returns to her mother after six months, Demeter is happy and the earth grows warm and all the plants and flowers blossom.

Despite the scientific attitude of modern man, the desire to have an explanation for a puzzling phenomenon is still so overpowering that his opposing desire for logical and scientific thought will often fail to keep him from inventing "explanations" that are no less fictitious than the story of Hades and Persephone.

Since its inception, the learning disabilities field has been immersed in controversy and conflict. This is not surprising at all, if one considers that the popular explanation for learning disabilities—that of a neurological dysfunction—is nothing but a fabricated, mythical notion. The popularity of the idea does not give it any scientific validity. Before it was proved that the earth is round, everybody believed it to be flat. The popularity of the idea did not make it true. Science, therefore, does not always "advance by consensus," as is maintained by Galaburda.[2] In fact, as Heshusius rightly states, science does not advance by addition, but primarily by replacement and transformation.[3] When real progress happens, nothing stays the same, as Copernicus, Galileo and Einstein knew.

For as long as children with learning disabilities become adults with learning disabilities, it will certainly not be appropriate to attach the term "advancement" to this field. In fact, the statistics and subjective observations of scholars in the field indicate an explosion in the number of students with learning disabilities. This clearly indicates that there is no progress at all, but that the movement that is taking place is going downhill at an alarming rate.

From a medical frame of reference, this increase in the prevalence of learning disabilities is very difficult to explain. How can a noncontagious "ailment" spread at such a rate?

In evaluating the numbers across handicapping conditions, Edgar and Hayden noted that the number of individuals in all handicapping conditions in the U.S.A. had increased by 16 percent from 1976 to 1982. However, the number classified as learning disabled had increased by 119 percent. In 1976, the four major categories of handicapping conditions, in rank numbers served, were:

speech impaired   (1,302,600)
mentally retarded   (969,547)
learning disabled   (757,213)
emotionally disturbed (283,072).

In 1982, by contrast, rank order and numbers were:

learning disabled (1,745,871)
speech impaired (1,134,197)
mentally retarded (780,831)
emotionally disturbed (353,431).[4]

Within the next three years another nine percent increase in the LD category was noted. According to figures released by the U.S. Department of Education in 1991, the growth of the number of children in the LD category since 1985 amounted to another 32 percent.[5] The latest figures released by the U.S. Department of Education, those of the 1997-1998 school year, are as follows:

learning disabled (2,748,497)
speech impaired (1,065,074)
mentally retarded (602,111)
emotionally disturbed (454,363).[6]

The above figures represent the children formally classified in the special-education categories, not the total number of children whom scholars estimate could and should fall under the LD label at present.[7] Most estimates of this kind support a percentage of between 10 and 15 percent, although percentages as high as 40 percent are also suggested.[8] According to the Orton Dyslexia Society in America, at least one in every ten of otherwise able people has serious dyslexia problems.[9] The Foundation of Children with Learning Disabilities states that LD children represent more than ten million of the total population in the U.S.A.[10]

Many would argue that the increase in learning disabilities merely demonstrate the magnitude of a problem that was underreported or ignored before the 1960s. Others bring charges of overidentification and misidentification.[11] However, if one considers the increase in illiteracy and reading difficulties in general, both arguments go for a loop.

In 1910 the literacy rate was so high it was predicted that "the public schools will in a short time practically eliminate illiteracy."[12]

In 1930, illiteracy rates in the U.S.A. were as follows:

1. 1.5 percent among native-born whites.
2. 9.9 percent among foreign-born whites.

3. 9.2 percent among urban blacks.
4. 16.3 percent among blacks in general.

In 1935, a survey of the 375,000 men working in the Civilian Conservation Corps—a government-sponsored work project to provide employment—found an illiteracy rate of 1.9 percent. And this was among men primarily of low socio-economic status.[13]

Apparently—contrary to today's illiteracy rates—the illiteracy rates of the first half of the twentieth century reflected, for the most part, people who never had the advantage of schooling.[14]

Since the 1930s, something must have happened. . . . As Lionni and Klass point out, "Somewhere along the line our schools had lost the ability to routinely educate children and produce uniformly good results."[15] The erosion of America's educational performance, which seems to have started in the 1960s, and by now has assumed crisis proportions at all levels, is summarized in a 1976 *Los Angeles* article:

> After edging upward for apparently more than a century, the reading, writing, and mathematical skills of American students from elementary school through college are now in a prolonged and broad scale decline unequaled in history. The downward spiral, which affects many other subject areas as well, began abruptly in the mid-1960s and shows no signs of bottoming out.[16]

In its *Reading Report Card* (1985), the U.S. Department of Education found that 40 percent of the nation's thirteen-year olds and 16 percent of the seventeen-year-olds did not have intermediate reading skills (i.e., they could not find key information, link and compare ideas, or generalize, using materials in science, literature, or social studies). Only 5 percent of the seventeen-year-olds tested had advanced reading skills—the kind needed to understand complex ideas found in professional or technical journals and textbooks.[17]

The $14 million National Adult Literacy Survey of 1993 found that even though most adults in the survey had finished high school, 96 percent of them could not read, write, and figure well enough to go to college.[18] Even more to the point, 25 percent "were plainly unable to read," period.[19]

While learning disabilities and illiteracy have been, and are still growing, on the one hand, the standards of education have been declining—tragically and steadily—on the other:

For years, college professors have been complaining that students entering from high school lack such basic communication skills as the ability to read and listen with comprehension, to write and speak with clarity, precision, and correct grammar, and to spell even the simplest and most common words. . . . For the first hundred years of its existence, a college like Harvard would not graduate a student without a knowledge of Hebrew. Now the point is approaching when one can be graduated without a knowledge of English.[20]

Reading levels of young Americans fell so low in the 1970s that the Army was forced to rewrite its operating manuals in comic fashion.[21] Much reading material previously used for years in American schools became incomprehensible to present-day students and had to be simplified. For example, when a well-known history book was revised with an eye toward the high school market, words like "spectacle" and "admired" were removed. Apparently they were too difficult.[22]

On 26 April 1983, pointing to the literacy crisis and to the collapse in standards at the secondary and the college levels, the National Commission on Excellence warned: "Our nation is at risk." The report warned that America would soon be engulfed by a "rising tide of mediocrity in elementary and secondary school."[23]

Since the *Nation at Risk* report, education reforms have taken place in every state. New teaching methods and programs have been tried and evaluated.[24] But the overall goal set for the year 2000—to educate *every* child to a high standard—has remained a mere dream. "The nation is at even greater risk now," voiced Senator Edward M. Kennedy a decade after the famous report was published.[25] A newspaper reported in 1997 that the standards of education are so low in the U.S. that black Americans are returning to Africa, specifically Kenya, to get better schooling.[26] And if the article, published in *The Atlanta Journal and Constitution* in October 1999, part of which appears below, is only partially representative of conditions in the United States, it should cause great alarm:

In the aftermath of the Atlanta Public School's announcement that more than half the city's third-graders may flunk come spring, administrators, teachers and parents are grappling with questions about why the scores were so low and what can be done to improve them. Superintendent Beverly Hall last week revealed the stunning results of the Scholastic Reading Inventory, a criterion-referenced test that gauges a child's reading skills against what is expected for a child in that grade. Seventy-three percent of second-graders, 55 percent of third-graders, 57 percent of fourth graders and 49 percent of fifth-graders are not reading on grade level, according to the test.[27]

Australian children fare no better. The percentage of children that could read and write increased from 59.1 percent in 1871, to 79.8 percent in 1901, and 90.2 percent in 1911.[28] But something must have happened there too, as shown by numerous surveys conducted in the early 1970s. In Queensland, a survey given to eighth-grade students at the Mt. Gravatt High School showed 130 students out of 285 had reading problems varying from reluctance to retardation. A report on reading retardation at Liverpool Boys' High School, New South Wales, indicated that upwards of 500 pupils out of a total of 1,060 were in need of some form of remediation. The Bonorian High School advisory center in Victoria, surveyed more than 2,600 students in first and second forms (seventh and eight grades) in twelve eastern suburbs high schools. The results showed that 45.7 percent of those tested needed remedial specialist training if they were to profit from high school work, and 25 percent were found to read so badly that they could be classified as illiterate. All these surveys excluded children with acknowledged lower intelligence and migrant background.[29] But worse was yet to come. A survey of Australian adult literacy, reported in *The Australian* in 1990, found that 70 percent of a representative group of adults could not deal with concepts or arguments at the level of a standard newspaper editorial.[30]

According to the British Dyslexia Association 15 percent of children leave school with inadequate literacy.[31] According to a UNESCO report, more than two million Britons are completely illiterate. More than a third of the eleven-year-old children arriving at many secondary schools in Britain's inner cities are such poor readers that they cannot properly understand their textbooks.[32]

In Canada the estimates of learning-disabled children vary between 10 and 16 percent.[33]

While these figures vary because of differing definitions and research methods, taken together they suggest that millions of children worldwide are suffering from a disability that has been diagnosed in an increasing number of children and which should properly be recognized in even more.[34]

The situation raises the fear that we may be approaching another Dark

Age, with masses of illiterate people and only a handful of literate ones, like it was during the Middle Ages. In fact, Lewis Mumford concluded, "I have a book on my shelves by a man who says that the Dark Age is coming. I think the Dark Age is already here, only we don't know it."[35]

Not all countries face this "Dark Age." While the American nation was "at risk" in the 1980s, the Koreans and Chinese reported a very low rate of reading disabilities, and remedial reading facilities were not needed in Japan due to the rarity of reading problems.[36] That is another unexplainable phenomenon if one clings to the medical model. Why is this "ailment" more prominent in specific areas or countries? These differences surely cannot be attributed to neurological differences. Therefore some scholars attribute this phenomenon to the differences in writing systems. As the reader will see later, it is much easier to explain this phenomenon in terms of cultural differences.

During 1970, Professor Michael Rutter and his colleagues undertook a research study in the Isle of Wight, a relatively thriving rural district. They found that one out of every ten children had some kind of learning problem. In a follow-up study in London, this figure increased to one out of every six.[37]

Balow questioned how a reading disability can have a medical etiology if 60 percent of slum children and only two percent of suburban children had reading disorders.[38]

Adherents to the medical model also find it very difficult to explain why learning disabilities are more prominent among boys than girls. The statistics in the literature vary between 3:1 to 10:1. Knox, for example, states in his book *Learning Disabilities*, "One consistent fact is that 80 percent of dyslexics are male."[39]

The adherence to the LD explanation despite these discrepancies in statistics between different cultures, income groups and the two sexes reminds one of the pellagra incidences in the early twentieth century. The popular medical theory at the time was that the disease was caused by germs. However, Dr. Joseph Goldberger, who was asked to head an investigation into the situation in 1914, found that orphans and inmates contracted the disease, but staff never did. Goldberger knew from years of experience working on infectious diseases that germs did not distinguish between inmates and employees. Instead, he believed that the disease was caused by the insufficient corn-based diet of the poor.

Shipments of food, which Goldberger had requested from Washington, were provided to children in two Mississippi orphanages and to inmates at the Georgia State Asylum. Results were dramatic; those who were fed a diet of fresh meat, milk and vegetable instead of a corn-based diet recovered from pellagra. Those without the disease, who ate the new diet, did not contract it.

Amazingly, many of those convinced of the germ theory refused to abandon their view, even after Dr. Goldberger experimented on eleven healthy volunteer prisoners at the Rankin State Prison Farm in 1915. Offered pardons in return for their participation, the volunteers ate a corn-based diet. Six of the eleven showed pellagra rashes after five months. Angry because his experiment was dubbed "half-baked" and a fraud, Dr. Goldberger and his assistant injected each other with pellagrin blood, swabbed out the secretions of a pellagrin's nose and throat and rubbed them into their own noses and throats, and also swallowed capsules containing scabs of pellagrins' rashes. Volunteers joined them, yet none got pellagra. Despite these efforts, a few physicians remained opponents of his dietary theory. And Goldberger's warnings—which turned out to be true—to authorities of a dramatic increase in pellagra when the prices of cotton wool dropped dramatically in 1920, fell on deaf ears. They believed that any negative characterization of their region would discourage economic investment and tourism in the South. The Southern pride and prosperity were on the line.

The interesting end of this drama is that the land reform Goldberger believed necessary to eliminate pellagra was accomplished not by scientific reasoning but by the invasion of boll weevils. The insect destroyed cotton fields and forced Southerners to diversify their crops. By growing more food crops, they improved their diets and suffered less from pellagra.[40]

Unfortunately boll weevils will not invade the field of learning disabilities and lessen the suffering of children. It can only be done by educators—parents, teachers and specialists—who are serious about their educational task, who are willing to part with the illogical theory that learning disabilities have a biological cause and who are prepared to address the *true* cause. In the same way that the "pellagra germ" could not distinguish between inmates and employees, a "neurological deficit" also cannot distinguish between different cultures, income groups and the sexes.

The previous chapters—as well as this one—show that the field of learning disabilities is in a scientific crisis. Because one's pride is on the line, one can choose to ignore this crisis. One can side-step this crisis with something like Einstein's famous remark, "if the facts do not fit the theory, then the facts are wrong." One can also rationalize the crisis with the common suggestion that "LD is still new and experiencing growing pains."[41] Or one can help to change the system and thereby create new hope for a better quality of life for millions of children.

More and more experts, dissatisfied with the current status, are indeed declaring their willingness as well as their eagerness to consider alternative approaches. The field of learning disabilities is "in obvious turmoil, if not in disarray. We move to an uncertain future, but when was that not true? . . . We are ready for something better," remarked Gallagher.[42] Others call for "radical transformation."[43]

LD professionals, who acknowledge that a neurological explanation is unfounded, have been debating what changes the field should make. "If they consider the mythology on which the field has been built, the harmful effect it has had on children's academic development, and the ways in which it has helped cloak the causes of academic failure, perhaps the proper question is," states Coles, "whether the field should continue at all."[44] Maybe Blatt's wishes, already expressed in 1979, will come true: "My hope that this foolishness will stop is nurtured in the possibility that enough people will realize that the creators of this 'disease' have gone too far, and thus they expose themselves."[45]

It appears that the theory of learning disabilities has arrived at crossroads,[46] in a situation similar to Alice in Wonderland when she asked, "Would you tell me please, which way I ought to go from here?" And the Cheshire Cat responded, "That depends a good deal on where you want to get to."[47]

Notes:

1. Popkin, R. H., & Stroll, A., *Philosophy Made Simple* (London: WH Allen, 1969), 176.
2. Galaburda, A. M., "Learning Disability: Biological, societal, or both? A response to Gerald Coles," *Journal of Learning Disabilities,* 1989, vol. 22(5), 278-282.
3. Heshusius, L., "Why would they and I want to do it? A phenomenological-theoretical view of special education," *Learning Disabilities Quarterly,* 1984, vol. 7, 363-368.
4. Edgar, E., & Hayden, A. H., "Who are the children special education should serve and how many children are there?" *Journal of Special Education,* 1984-1985, vol. 18(4), 523-539.
5. U.S. Department of Education, *Thirteenth Annual Report to Congress on the Implementation of the Individuals with Disabilities Education Act* (Washington, DC, 1991).

6. U.S. Department of Education, *Twenty-first Annual Report to Congress on the Implementation of the Individuals with Disabilities Education Act*, website of the U.S. Department of Education, Office of Special Education Programs.

7. Coles, G. S., *The Learning Mystique* (New York: Pantheon Books, 1987), 11.

8. Knox, J. M., *Learning Disabilities* (New York: Chelsea House Publishers, 1989), 15.

9. *The Orton Dyslexia Society and the Problem of Dyslexia*, pamphlet by the Orton Dyslexia Society, cited in Coles, *The Learning Mystique*, 10.

10. *Understanding Learning Disabilities*, pamphlet by the Foundation for Children with Learning Disabilities, cited in Coles, *The Learning Mystique*, 10.

11. "The special/general education integration initiative for students with specific learning disabilities," *Journal of Learning Disabilities*, 1 September 1994, vol. 27, 435.

12. Blumenfeld, S. L., *NEA: Trojan Horse in American Education* (Boise, Idaho: The Paradigm Company, 1984), 102.

13. Blumenfeld, S. L., "Who killed excellence," *Imprimis*, September 1985, vol. 14(9), 5, cited in B. Wiseman, *Psychiatry: The Ultimate Betrayal* (Los Angeles: Freedom Publishing, 1995), 276.

14. Nash, R. H., "The three kinds of illiteracy," website address: www.christiananswers.net, 1999.

15. Lionni, P., & Klass, L. J., *The Leipzig Connection: The Systematic Destruction of American Education* (Portland, Oregon: Heron Books, 1980).

16. McCurdy, J., & Speich, D., "Student skills decline unequalled in history," *Los Angeles Times*, 15 August 1976, cited in "Education and social ruin," *Education: Psychiatry's Ruin* (Los Angeles: CCHR, 1995), 2-3.

17. Sherrow, V., *Challenges in Education* (Englewood Cliffs: Julian Messner, 1991), 21.

18. "A closer look—Special education," *Right to Read Report*, January 1994, vol. 1(8), 1-3, cited in Wiseman, *Psychiatry: The Ultimate Betrayal*, 275.

19. Baughman, F. A., Jr., "Johnny can't read because phonics is all but ignored," *The Daily Californian*, 16 February 1994, cited in Wiseman, *Psychiatry: The Ultimate Betrayal*, 275.

20. Lean, A. E., & Eaton, W. E., *Education or Catastrophe?* (Wolfeboro: Longwood Academic, 1990), 27-28.

21. Honig, B., *Last Chance for Our Children. How You Can Help Save Our Schools* (New York: Addison-Wesley Publishing Company, Inc., 1987), ix.

22. O'Brien, S., "The reshaping of history: Marketers vs. authors," *Curriculum Review*, 11 September 1988, cited in T. Sowell, *Inside American Education* (New York: The Free Press, 1993), 7.

23. Kantrowitz, B., et al., "A nation still at risk," *Newsweek*, 19 April 1993, 46-49.

24. Sherrow, *Challenges in Education*, 7.

25. Kennedy, E. M., "The nation is at even greater risk now," in J. F. Jennings (ed.), *National Issues in Education: The Past is Prologue* (Bloomington: Phi Delta Kappa, 1993).

26. "Illiterates swop slums for sums," *Sunday Times*, 27 July 1997.

27. Carter, R., "Schools struggle to find solutions. Dismal showing by lower grades on reading tests prompts some to ask why system has failed," *The Atlanta Journal and Constitution*, 14 October 1999, J1.

28. *Commonwealth Year Book 1924*, 477-478, cited in Cleverly & Lawry (eds.), *Australian Education in the 20th Century* (Longman, 1972), 1-2.

29. Wallis, J. M., *The Disaster Road* (Bullsbrook: Veritas Publishing Company, 1986), 92-93.
30. *The Australian*, 1990, cited in J. D. Frodsham, "Introduction," in J. D. Frodsham (ed.), *Education For What?* (Canberra: Academy Press, 1990), 1.
31. Coles, *The Learning Mystique*, 11.
32. "Illiteracy and crime: An international problem," *Education: Psychiatry's Ruin* (Los Angeles: CCHR, 1995), 20-21.
33. Coles, *The Learning Mystique*, 11.
34. Ibid.
35. Lean & Eaton, *Education or Catastrophe?* 31.
36. Sheridan, E. M., "Reading disabilities: Can we blame the written language?" *Journal of Learning Disabilities*, 1983, vol. 16(2), 81-86.
37. Hornsby, B., *Overcoming Dyslexia* (Johannesburg: Juta and Company Ltd., 1984), 14.
38. Balow, B., "Perceptual motor activities in the treatment of severe reading disability," *Reading Teacher*, 1971, vol. 24, 513-525.
39. Knox, *Learning Disabilities*, 27.
40. Kraut, A., "Dr. Joseph Goldberger and the war on pellagra," website address: www.nih.gov/od/museum/exhibits/goldberger/full-text.html, 1996.
41. Kavale, K. A., "Status of the field: Trends and issues in learning disabilities," in K. A. Kavale (ed.), *Learning Disabilities: State of the Art and Practice* (Boston: College-Hill Press, 1988), 17.
42. Gallagher, J. J., "Learning disabilities and special education: A critique," *Journal of Learning Disabilities*, 1986, vol. 19(10), 595-601.
43. Brantlinger, E., "Using ideology: Cases of nonrecognition of the politics of research and practice in special education," *Review of Educational Research*, 1997, vol. 67, 425-459; Lipsky, D. K., & Gartner, A., "Equity requires inclusion: The future for all students with disabilities," in C. Christensen & F. Rizvi (eds.), *Disability and the Dilemmas of Education and Justice* (Philadelphia: Open University Press, 1996), 144-155; both sources cited in J. M. Kauffman, "Commentary: Today's special education and its messages for tomorrow," *Journal of Special Education*, 15 January 1999, vol. 32.
44. Coles, *The Learning Mystique*, 307.
45. Blatt, B., "Bandwagons also go to funerals," *Journal of Learning Disabilities*, 1979, vol. 12(4), 222-224.
46. Lerner, J., *Learning Disabilities: Theories, Diagnosis, and Teaching Strategies* (4th ed.), (Boston: Houghton Mifflin Company, 1988), 497.
47. Kavale, "Status of the field," 18

7.

Creating an Alternative Possibility

The proper study of mankind is man[1] —
Alexander Pope

One of the most neglected questions in science is why it sometimes happens that a scientific field runs off the rails.[2] Of course, an answer to this question would hold the possibility of getting it back on track again. It is our considered opinion that there is only one reason why the LD study field has run off the rails. There is one very important key factor, which is being overlooked. This key factor is what has made it impossible for LD experts to correctly interpret the phenomenon of the child with a learning problem.

Before one starts talking about learning and behavior, according to W. H. O. Schmidt, author of *Child Development: The Human, Cultural, and Educational Context*, one should first try to define the important, *species-specific characteristics* of the species that one is studying.[3] In other words, what is so distinctive about a certain species that it allows us to distinguish it from any other species? If, for example, we were studying chickens, ducks or geese, we should take note of what is called their imprinted "following response."

In 1873, D. A. Spalding discovered that baby chicks tend to follow the first moving object that they see. This tendency seemed to exist either at birth already, or very shortly after hatching. Spalding speculated that the tendency to follow was probably innate, since it helped the chicks to survive. Because the mother hen was almost always the first moving object encountered, the instinctive "following response" had the survival value of keeping the baby chicks in the immediate vicinity of the hen.

To test his hypothesis, Spalding covered the chicks' heads with hoods immediately after they were hatched, before they had a chance to open their eyes. When the hoods were removed a few hours later, the chicks followed the first object that crossed their field of vision, regardless of what the object was. This demonstrated that the response was not learned, since experience could not have played a role.[4]

In 1937 Konrad Lorenz published a paper, describing the same "following response" in ducklings and goslings. On one occasion Lorenz made certain that he would be the first moving object that a number of ducklings saw. As a result, these ducklings proceeded to follow "Mama" Lorenz everywhere he went, even swimming. It seemed that the first object to move past these ducklings was "stamped into" the animals' brains as the object to be followed. Lorenz called this stamping-in phenomenon *imprinting*.[5]

This unique species-specific characteristic was the source of great childhood pleasure to 't Hart, who describes a trick his father used to play on the farm poultry. Whenever the opportunity arose, he would switch the eggs of a brooding duck with those of a brooding hen, later to enjoy the anxious antics of the hen when her brood takes to the water, and on the other hand the futile efforts of the duck to coax her hatchlings into the duck pond.[6]

Knowledge of this species-specific characteristic, however, has greater value than merely that it can raise a laugh. In fact, it may perhaps be the only factor between the lesser white-fronted goose and extinction. These very rare geese once hatched all over Lapland. Unfortunately, each year their migratory route would bring them to the Black and Caspian Seas where hunters awaited them, ruthlessly hunting them to a threatened extermination. In an effort to save the species, Christian Moullec and his wife Paolo bought some thirty eggs and got the geese imprinted on themselves and on their ultralight aircraft. Because the geese followed the aircraft, the Moullecs could lead the geese to a nature reserve in Germany. The couple plans to continue their mercy flights in the future.[7]

In the Moullecs' efforts to save the lesser white-fronted goose, knowledge of a particular species-specific characteristic of the goose proved to be of great importance. Just like these birds were hunted to near-extinction by hunters, literacy in children is at present, so to speak, also "hunted" to near-extinction. As in the study of ducks and geese, a viable point of departure would be to first determine whether there may not be some fundamental, species-specific characteristics of the species in question—the human child—that are being overlooked by learning-disabilities experts.

What is distinctive about being human? What characteristics of the human being are so distinctive that knowledge of them would make it impossible for us to confuse ourselves with the animals? Perhaps learning-disabilities experts have so far been groping in the dark because they have never realized the potentialities embodied in an investigation of such characteristics in the study of the learning and reading-disabled child. In the same way that knowledge of the important species-specific characteristics of the lesser white-fronted goose may perhaps save this species, knowledge of such characteristics of the human species may perhaps hold the key towards the correct interpretation of the phenomenon of the child with a learning problem.

The sciences that traditionally occupy themselves with the study of learning disabilities are mainly education, psychology, neuropsychology, speech and language pathology, neurology, psychiatry, ophthalmology, optometry, and occupational therapy. None of these has as its aim the discovery of the fundamental, species-specific characteristics of the human being. This is the task of philosophy, specifically of philosophical anthropology. From whatever scientific perspective one wishes to study the learning-disabled child, one would therefore have to check with the philosopher first, to find out what fundamental characteristics of the human being might play a role in the situation.

Philosophers have over the ages noted many species-specific characteristics of the human being. Schmidt, for example, states that the characteristic that stands out most clearly to him is man's ability to *symbolize*, with language and speech representing one form of symbolization.[8] Adolf Portmann, on the other hand, documented the view already expressed earlier by Johann Gottfried Herder in the eighteenth century, that the human infant is more helpless and, in proportion to its total life-span, is helpless over a longer period of time than the young of any other species. Simultaneously, however, the human being shows greater plasticity.[9]

The human being is such a complex and many-faceted creature, that it will probably never happen that any two philosophers will ever agree on which characteristics of the human being are the most important ones. However, after many years of intense study of the problems of the child with a learning disability, we have come to the conclusion that the most notable species-

92

specific characteristic of the human being, and the one that sheds the most light on the plight of the LD child, is to be found in the stories of feral children and children raised or kept in extreme isolation.

Feral Children

In the late eighteenth century a child of eleven or twelve was captured, who some years before had been seen completely naked in the Caune Woods in France, seeking acorns and roots to eat. The boy was given the name Victor and is often referred to as the Wild Boy of Aveyron.

When hearing of the capture, a minister of state with scientific interests, believing that this event would throw some light on the science of the mind, ordered that the child be brought to Paris. In Paris the boy became a nine days' wonder. People of all classes thronged to see him, especially since it was an opportunity to see the romantic theories of the famous Jean Jacques Rousseau in practice.[10] Rousseau, a passionate critic of society of his time, saw the possibility of reforming society through the education of children. In his *Émile* he posits a *natural* development of the child, which must be protected from the influences of society so that the child can grow up as Nature intended him to be. In essence, Rousseau believed that there is a natural development on which we can rely and which will inevitably take place, provided we can keep in check the "unnatural" influences of society.[11] So, with Victor, the people of Paris had the opportunity to see a child who had grown up according to Rousseau's ideals. . . .

What they did see was a degraded human being, human only in shape; a dirty, scarred, inarticulate creature who trotted and grunted like the beasts of the fields, ate with apparent pleasure the most filthy refuse, was apparently incapable of attention of even elementary perceptions such as heat or cold and spent his time apathetically rocking himself backwards and forwards like the animals at the zoo. A "man-animal," whose only concern was to eat, sleep, and escape the unwelcome attentions of sightseers.[12]

Expert opinion was as usual somewhat derisive of popular attitude and expectations. The great French educator and psychologist, Philippe Pinel, examined the boy, declaring that his wildness was a fake and that he was an incurable idiot.[13] He failed to explain how a mentally defective person could have been able to fend for himself in the wilds for any length of time.

Victor was assigned to Dr. Itard, who describes the behavior of the boy and his own efforts to teach him to do the things ordinary human beings do, including speaking and reading. Victor's tutor tells us that his senses were extraordinarily apathetic. His nostrils were filled with snuff without making him sneeze. He picked up potatoes from boiling water. A pistol fired near him provoked hardly any response, though the sounds of cracking a walnut caused him to turn around.[14]

Itard tried to teach Victor to speak and read. At the end of five years, Victor could identify some written words and phrases referring to objects and actions, and even some words referring to simple relationships such as big and small, and he could use word cards to indicate some of his desires. However, he did not learn to speak.[15]

Another story of feral children, and probably the best known, is that of two girls, Amala and Kamala, who were raised by a she-wolf. In 1920, as the story goes, Reverend J. A. L. Singh saw a mother wolf and cubs, two of whom had long, matted hair and looked human. After considerable preparations and difficulties, the two human creatures were captured. They turned out to be two girls whose ages were assessed by Singh at about eight years and one and a half years.

The creatures were taken to an orphanage in Mindapore, India, where the Reverend and his wife were stationed. Singh described them as "wolfish" in appearance and behavior. They walked on all fours and had calluses on their knees and palms from doing so. They were fond of raw meat and stole it when the occasion offered. They licked all liquids with their tongues and ate their food in a crouched position. Their tongues permanently hung out of their thick, red lips, and they panted just like wolves. They never slept after midnight and prowled and howled at night. They could move very fast, just like squirrels, and it was difficult to overtake them. They shunned human society altogether. If approached, they made faces and sometimes bared their teeth. With regard to the development of their senses, it was noted that their hearing was very acute and that they could smell meat at a great distance. Furthermore, while they could not see well during the day, they could orient themselves very well at night. In September 1921 both girls became ill, and Amala, the younger, died.[16]

By means of intimate and devoted contact with Kamala, by softening her skin with oil and massaging her, by feeding and caressing her, Mrs. Singh was able to win her confidence and to create the conditions in which Kamala would be willing to learn from her.

After five years at the orphanage, Kamala demonstrated some intellectual functions. She knew some of the names of the babies housed there; she understood the concept of color; she accepted food only from her plate and knew her glass from among the others. As far as language development is concerned, a visitor, Bishop H. Pakenham-Walsh, provides an outsider's description of this aspect of her progress: "When I saw Kamala she could speak, quite clearly and distinctly, about thirty words; when told to say what a certain object was, she would name it, but she never used her words in a spontaneous way. . . . I saw her again two years later . . . and she had learned a good many more words."[17]

By now Kamala's (and the Singhs') fame had spread. An invitation arrived from the Psychological Society of New York in 1928 offering to take Kamala to the United States where she could be presented to the public, but the invitation could not be considered, as Kamala grew weak. Her health grew less secure throughout the year, and somewhat unexpectedly, she died on the fourteenth morning of November 1929.[18]

There are many other stories of feral children in the literature, amongst others the story of a boy who lived in Syria, who ate grass and could leap like an antelope, as well as of a girl, who lived in the forests in Indonesia for six years after she had fallen into the river. She walked like an ape and her teeth were as sharp as a razor.[19]

Children Raised or Kept in Extreme Isolation

Besides children being raised in the "natural state" provided by the wild, there are also many cases of children who were raised or kept in extreme isolation. A popular story is that of Kaspar Hauser, told in *Wolf-children and Feral Man* by Singh and Zingg.[20]

Kaspar was first discovered on 26 May 1828, standing unsteadily in a square in Nuremberg, dressed in clumsy clothing. In his hand he held letters directed to the Captain of the 4th Esgataron of the Shwolishay regiment, which inter alia instructed the captain that ". . . if he isn't good for anything [the captain] must either kill him or hang him in the chimney."

95

The boy was about sixteen years of age, appeared unable to communicate, his eyes were red and unused to sunlight, he did not know how to use his fingers, and the soles of his feet, blistered from walking, were as smooth as the hands of a baby. He walked by placing both the ball and heel of the foot down at the same time. Like a child newly emerged from the womb, this adolescent boy seemed a complete stranger to almost everything in the world.

At first regarded as a vagabond and halfwit, he was taken to a prison cell where he was kept while the authorities tried to figure out what to make of him. He could utter only a few phrases, clearly meaningless to him, such as, "I want to be a rider like my father," and "Don't know," which he used to express everything from thirst to anxiety. When handed paper and pen, he wrote *"Kaspar Hauser."* He was unable to eat anything but bread and water, and reacted violently to most sensory impressions. The very smell of meat or alcohol would put him into terrible convulsions. When presented coffee, he would sweat and vomit. At night, he lay on his straw bed; during the day, he sat on the floor with his feet before him. When a mirror was shown to him, he looked behind him, as if to find the person seen in the mirror.

Hauser's keeper, Herr Hiltel, took Kaspar in his home, where Hiltel's son, Julius, was permitted to play with Kaspar. It was also Julius, writes Hiltel, who taught Kaspar to speak. Kaspar was also of interest to the mayor, Bürgermeister Binder, who most days had Kaspar brought to his house for conversation, and to a certain Professor Daumer, a teacher, who was to devote his time to the education of the boy.

The visits with the mayor led to the development of a more or less coherent study of Kaspar's whereabouts since birth. During their conversations, Herr Binder, who believed that he had communicated well enough with Kaspar, made the attempt to reconstruct Kaspar's former life. Some people doubted Herr Binder's recollection. They did not think Kaspar's speech at that time was enough advanced for him to provide a coherent story. Nevertheless, what Kaspar said, according to Herr Binder, was that he had lived upon bread and water in a small, dark cell. He had known only one person, alluded to by him as "the man," who periodically drugged him to clean him, change his clothes, cut his fingernails and hair and once hit him for being noisy. He was kept alive in this near vegetative state until his keeper appeared toward the end of his confinement, taught him to write Kaspar Hauser (he did not know the meaning), walk, and to speak a few rudimentary sentences. Equipped with only these and a rough collection of clothes, Kaspar had been led to Nuremberg market and abandoned there.

Two months after being discovered Kaspar went to live with Daumer, where he was provided round-the-clock education. He flowered under Daumer's gentle and compassionate tutelage and learned to read, write and even play chess.

The end of the story is not happy, though. Kaspar died on 17 December 1833, three days after a second attempt had been made on his life. Numerous conflicting explanations have been offered for Kaspar's murder. The most prevalent theory is that Kaspar Hauser was originally locked away because he stood in the way of possible succession to the state of Baden. When the result was obtained, Kaspar was released, so goes the story, with the letters he carried with him being written to mask the true reason. Fear that he would eventually expose his perpetrators, however, required his permanent removal.

Another, more recent story of a child raised in isolation is that of Isabelle, who was born in 1932. She was an illegitimate child and was kept in seclusion for this reason. Her mother had developed normally up to the age of two years and then, as a result of an accident, had become deaf-mute and had not been educated. From the day Isabelle was born until she was a little over six years of age, mother and child spent their time together in a dark room with the blinds drawn, separated from the rest of the family. The parents of the mother did not permit her to leave the house alone. She eventually escaped, however, carrying her child with her, and in this way Isabelle's case was brought to the notice of the authorities.

As a result of lack of sunlight, fresh air, and proper nutrition, Isabelle had developed a rachitic condition that made locomotion virtually impossible. This condition yielded to proper treatment, including surgery, and Isabelle learned to walk and move normally.

When her intelligence was first tested at the age of six and a half, her mental age appeared to be about nineteen months. In place of normal speech, she made a croaking sound.

By means of intensive training and a stimulating environment, Isabelle improved so much that she was considered a child of normal intelligence by the age of eight. Her language development had been rapid: by that time she already had a vocabulary of 1,500 to 2,000 words, she enjoyed and could recite nursery rhymes, she could tell a story and make one up. She could now create and share with others a world of imagination and was not confined in her use of language to the immediate and the concrete.[21]

Consider also the case of Genie, found in California in 1970. Genie was thirteen when she came to the attention of authorities. From the age of twenty months she had been kept in a small room in her parents' house. She had never been out of the room; she was kept naked and restrained to a kind of potty-chair by a harness her father had designed. She could move only her hands and feet. The psychotic father, who apparently hated children, forbade her almost blind mother to speak to the child. (He had put another child, born earlier, in the garage to avoid hearing her cry, and she died there of pneumonia at two months of age.) Genie was fed only milk and baby food during her thirteen years.

When the girl was found, she weighed only 59 pounds. She could not straighten her arms or legs. She did not know how to chew. She could not control her bladder or bowels. She could not recognize words or speak at all. According to the mother's report—the father killed himself soon after Genie was discovered—Genie appeared to have been a normal baby.

Over the next six years, Genie had plenty of interactions with the world, as well as training and testing by psychologists. She gained some language comprehension and learned to speak at about the level of a two or three-year-old: "want milk," "two hand." She learned to use tools, to draw, and to connect cause-and-effect in some situations. And she could get from one place to another—to the candy counter in the supermarket, for example—proving that she could construct mental maps of space. Her IQ score on nonverbal tests was a low-normal 74 in 1977. But her language did not develop further, and, in fact, she made types of language errors that even normal two-year-olds never make.[22] In keeping with the biologistic ideas of our times, the cause of Genie's language delay was sought in her brain only. Nobody ever thought to question whether the methods that were used to teach her had perhaps been inadequate.

A Species-Specific Characteristic of Homo Sapiens

If one reads these stories, one simply has to agree with Ashley Montagu, who stated in his book *On Being Human* that being human is not a status *with* which, but *to* which, one is born. While every creature that is classified physically as man is thereby called *Homo sapiens*, no such creature is really *human* until it exhibits the behavior characteristics of a human being. He, however, adds that one cannot deny the status of being human to a newborn baby because it cannot talk, cannot walk erect or reveal any of the other behavior characteristics of human beings. The way in which he reconciles this apparent contradiction with his previous statement is by pointing to the *promise* the baby shows of being able to develop the behavior characteristics of human beings. The wonderful thing about a baby is its promise, not its performance —a promise that can only come true with the required help and assistance. The development of *Homo sapiens*, however great the promise might be, into a human being with behavior characteristics of human beings, requires more than just being kept alive physically. A child only becomes a human being thanks to *education*.[23]

The essence of Montagu's message is that being human must be *learned*. Viewed differently, it can be stated that there is *nothing that any human being knows, or can do, that he has not learned*. This of course excludes natural body functions, such as breathing, as well as the reflexes, for example the involuntary closing of the eye when an object approaches it. This is a characteristic, which very clearly distinguishes man from the animals.

A bear does not have to learn to be a bear, he simply is one. A duck needs no lessons in duckmanship. And an ant leads a perfectly satisfactory life without any instruction from other ants.[24] Even when isolated from birth, animals usually retain clearly recognizable instincts. Jan (coauthor) tells the story of their dog, which had been taken from its mother at only two weeks. They had to bottle-feed it the first few weeks. They lived in a completely enclosed yard, and it was nearly a year old before it ever saw another dog, when they took it with on a picnic. In spite of its isolation from other dogs, and its constant human companionship, this dog did not eat with knife and fork, did not walk upright, and did not speak. It behaved just like any other dog, lifting its leg at every telephone pole and tree, and doing its very best to sink its teeth into the postman's leg. There are only a few exceptions, such as the lion cub, which would not be able to hunt the wildebeest when raised in isolation, and the nightingale that would not be able to sing. A human being, raised in isolation, however, as we have seen in the stories of Victor, Amala and Kamala, Kaspar, Isabelle and Genie, will not be able to exhibit any of the behavior characteristics of a human being.

This species-specific characteristic, that there is nothing that any human being knows, or can do, that he has not learned, has so far been ignored in the human sciences, for the simple reason that the human sciences have modeled themselves on the findings of psychology.

Psychology has, for the past more than a century, thought that its salvation was to be found in the physical sciences, specifically in biology. Consequently, psychology has been shaped in accordance with the physical sciences, often employing concepts borrowed from biology and using them sometimes as analogies or metaphors and sometimes as statements implying a fundamental identity between the functions of psychological processes from amoeba to mollusc to man.[25]

When Edward Lee Thorndike was appointed to the chair of educational psychology at Teachers College, Columbia University in New York, around 1900, his first innovation was to study the learning processes of animals—mainly cats in puzzle boxes—in order to throw light on the learning processes of children and of human beings in general. Rats, as is well known, had to run through mazes in order to satisfy the curiosity of psychologists as to how learning occurs, and projections to human learning have been made on that basis. Köhler, for some strange reason referred to as a *child* psychologist, studied the intelligence of *chimpanzees*, and for many years after that time (1917) Köhler's experiments were included in many discussions on learning and problem-solving processes in children. Harlow carried out work with monkeys on mother-child relationships, social development, conditions in which curiosity manifests itself, "learning to learn," and the acquisition of "concepts." All this was intended to throw light on human behavior. A considerable amount of work by a number of investigators has also been devoted to the study of the effects of sensory deprivation in young animals in order to better understand the effects of deprivation on cognitive development in children.[26]

More recent experiments include a thirty-year study of "the vocal learning" of birds, which researchers had hoped would offer insight into the learning and/or speech process of infants, children and adults.[27] A five-year study of budgerigars was conducted because researchers believed that "budgerigars may provide a unique system for examining how acoustic and visual information is coordinated in vocal learning."[28] In a five-year project that started in 1994, researchers studied "crickets and flies because these insects can serve as model systems for understanding sensory processing and communication in higher animals. . . ."[29] One could go on for a long time listing examples of the pervasive influence of the study of animal behavior on child psychology and educational psychology—and naturally also on the LD field.

When we compare man and animal from a biological perspective only, there are no fundamental differences. Man does not possess a single organ, no bone, no muscle, which is not also to be found in the vertebrate animals.[30] The only difference, seemingly, is the size of the brain.[31] But because there are similarities, it does not imply that there are not also dissimilarities. Every morning millions of people throughout the world get up, dress themselves, eat breakfast and then go to work or to school. In the afternoons they all come back home, do homework, eat their supper, sit in front of the television, or go to visit friends, or read a book. Has any person ever seen any animal doing any of these? As Schmidt said, if the child psychologist and the educational psychologist turn to the study of animal behavior and development, they will not only have to look for identities and continuities but also for contrast, and they will have to pay attention not only to differences in complexity but also to differences in kind.[32]

A century ago, Edmund Husserl argued that the human sciences were in a crisis.[33] In 1981 Sarason complained that the social sciences were in disarray,[34] while Schrag repeated exactly the same warning as Husserl, and gave exactly the same reason for the crisis: "The human sciences are suffering from a loss of center, from an occlusion of that point of origin at which man first asks the question about himself."[35] We must heed the wise counsel of Alexander Pope that the "proper study of mankind is man." It is impossible to understand the plight of the supposedly learning-disabled child unless one recognizes that he is a *human being*. A human being knows nothing, or cannot do anything, that he has not learned. If one accepts this as fundamental to humans, it opens up new avenues of interpreting the problem of the child with a learning disability. It implies that there is not necessarily anything wrong with a person who cannot do something. He may simply not have learned it yet—and any person can learn almost anything, provided that he is taught according to *viable* learning principles.

Notes:

1. Pope, A., Epistle II from "An Essay of Man," *English Verse, Volume III* (London: Oxford University Press, 1930), 164.
2. Blatt, B., "Bandwagons also go to funerals," *Journal of Learning Disabilities*, 1979, vol. 12(4), 222-224.
3. Schmidt, W. H. O., *Child Development: The Human, Cultural, and Educational Context* (New York: Harper & Row, 1973), xiii.
4. Dworetzky, J. P., *Introduction to Child Development* (St. Paul: West Publishing Company, 1981), 91.
5. Ibid.
6. 't Hart, M., *De Kritische Afstand. Agressieve Aantekeningen over Mens en Dier* (Amsterdam: Uitgeverij De Arbeiderspers, 1979).
7. Galloway, H., "Gans en al 'n leier...," *Huisgenoot*, 17 August 2000, 36-56.
8. Schmidt, *Child Development*, xiv.
9. Ibid.
10. Candland, D. K., *Feral Children and Clever Animals. Reflections on Human Nature* (Oxford University Press, 1993), 18.
11. Schmidt, *Child Development*, 5-6.
12. Itard, J. M. G., *The Wild Boy of Aveyron (Rapports et memoires sur le sauvage de l'Aveyron)*, translated by George & Muriel Humphrey, (New York: Century, 1932), cited in Candland, *Feral Children and Clever Animals*, 18.
13. Ibid.
14. Itard, cited in K. Davies, "Extreme isolation of a child," *American Journal of Sociology*, 1945, vol. 45, 563.
15. Schmidt, *Child Development*, 27.
16. Singh, J. A. L., & Zingg, R. M., *Wolf-children and Feral Man* (New York: Harper, 1939), cited in Schmidt, *Child Development*, 28, and in Candland, *Feral Children and Clever Animals*, 53-60.
17. Singh & Zingg, *Wolf-children and Feral Man*, xxvi-xxvii, cited in Candland, *Feral Children and Clever Animals*, 67.
18. Singh & Zingg, 113, cited in *Feral Children and Clever Animals*, 68.
19. Olivier, J., "Deur wolwe grootgemaak," *Huisgenoot*, 7 March 1985, 126-127.
20. Singh & Zingg, cited in *Feral Children and Clever Animals*, 38-51.
21. Schmidt, *Child Development*, 32-33.
22. Curtiss, S., *Genie: A Psycholinguistic Study of a Modern-Day "Wild Child"* (New York: Academic Press, 1977), cited in F. E. Bloom & A. Lazerson, *Brain, Mind, and Behavior* (2nd ed.), (New York: W. H. Freeman and Company, 1985), 266-267.
23. Montagu, M. F. A., *On Being Human* (New York: Abelard-Schuman, 1950), cited in Schmidt, *Child Development*, 22.
24. McKern, S. S., *The Many Faces of Man* (New York: Lothrop, Lee & Shepard Co., 1972), 128.
25. Schmidt, *Child Development*, 4.

26. Ibid.
27. Project number MH14651: "Comparative study of vocal learning," cited in "Sex, animals and financial waste," *Psychiatry: Cases of Fraud* (Los Angeles: CCHR, 1999), 24-27.
28. Project number MH00982: "Biological foundations of vocal learning," cited in "Sex, animals and financial waste."
29. Project number MH01148: "Neuroethological models for acoustic communication," cited in "Sex, animals and financial waste."
30. Vloemans, A., *De Mens als Waagstuk* (Den Haag: H. P. Leopolds Uitgevers-mij N.V., 1949).
31. Lieberman, P., *On the Origins of Language* (New York: MacMillan Publishing Co., 1975).
32. Schmidt, *Child Development*, 11.
33. Kearney, R., *Modern Movements in European Philosophy* (Manchester: Manchester University Press, 1986).
34. Sarason, S. B., *Psychology Misdirected* (New York: The Free Press, 1981).
35. Schrag, C. O., *Radical Reflection on the Origin of the Human Sciences* (West Lafayette: Purdue University Press, 1980).

8.

Learning and the "Learning Disabled"

> Learning was relegated to the psychologists much too hastily. Their efforts to study the phenomenon . . . have been badly hampered by the fact that no one had bothered to figure out what learning really is.[1] — McClellan

Whenever one is confronted by any problem, and one wishes to discover a *scientific* solution to the problem, one should make sure that proper scientific methods are followed. Unless the recognized precepts of scientific method are strictly adhered to, one cannot lay any claim to having found a scientific solution.

Williams has already pointed out in 1928 that any scientific theory or hypothesis must be proven first possible, then probable, then certain. This suggests that, when embarking upon an effort to discover a scientific solution to a certain problem, one should first try to discover *all* the *possible* solutions. To achieve this, one must determine the *exact nature* of the phenomenon one is dealing with. For example, if one desires to rescue an animal that became trapped in a poacher's snare, the possible methods of effecting such a rescue would very strongly depend on the kind of animal. Similarly, before possible solutions to the plight of the child, who has difficulties in the teaching/learning situation, become ascertainable, one should first try to determine the exact nature of the situation.

What is it that really happens in any situation where a child is being taught? Careful consideration of this situation will reveal that essentially it is a *communication situation.* There is a *communicator*—the parent or teacher, there is a *message*—the knowledge that is being passed on to the child, and there is a *recipient* of the message—the child. This is exactly in accordance with the so-called *communication triptych* that characterizes any communication situation. Like any other message, the message that is being passed on to the child has a very specific purpose, viz. that the child must learn. If the child does not learn, then it means that the message somehow failed.

This suggests that we should start by looking at the *possible* reasons why *any message* can fail. In any communication situation, there must be at least two reasons why the message can fail:

1. There may be something wrong with the receiver of the message. For example, if one tried to talk to a deaf person, then there would certainly be the possibility that the message would not be received.
2. There may be something wrong with the way in which the message is passed on.

If a person, who is blind, or unable to read, tried to read the message contained in this book, then the message, that we are trying to convey, would probably fail. On the other hand, however, it is certainly *our* responsibility to make sure that our message is passed on in accordance with certain principles that will ensure successful reception, or else it will certainly fail. *Misalnya, kalau kami menulis dalam bahasa asing. . . .* This message is directed at readers of the *English* language, and if we therefore wrote in a language *other than English*, the message will probably fail. We must also be careful that we write in accordance with English grammar, syntax and orthography, otherwise the message will probably also fail. If we rote in mjutilayted vurzhion of langwidge, or we if not put do words the logical order in a, then we can certainly not blame our readers if our message does not succeed. *However, as the reader will presently see, that is exactly what we are doing when we blame children of "learning disabilities."*

Most people have so far jumped to the—*very* hasty—conclusion that the first possibility mentioned above is the one that applies. However, from the above arguments it should be clear that there must be *two* possible reasons why some children fail to learn. There may be something wrong with the child, as is the assumption in LD, but there is also the possibility that the message fails because of the *way* in which it is passed on.

The purpose of the message in any teaching situation is that the child must *learn*. This means that the message must be passed on to the child in such a way that it will be *possible* for him to learn, which means that the message must be passed on according to *learning principles*—and this is where we have a big problem. *What* are the principles of learning that should be observed in such a situation?

As was indicated in the previous chapter already, most of what is "known" about learning today, has been gleaned from experiments with animals on "learning"—Thorndike with cats and rats, Skinner, Tolman and Miller with rats, Pavlov with dogs, Guthrie with cats, Harlow with monkeys and apes, Hebb with rats and chimpanzees, et cetera. The problem about such experiments is that they are based on the *assumption* that what we observe in humans and interpret as *learning* is the *same* as that which we observe in animals and that *appears* to us to be the same phenomenon. Because "no one had bothered to figure out what learning really is,"[3] we do not know whether in fact animals learn or not. The behavior that we see in them and that is interpreted as learning may, for all we know, be something quite different. Until such time as it has been verified that human learning and animal "learning" are indeed identical, we have to be very suspicious of animal experiments. Therefore, for the time being at least, learning theories that were based on, or that were perhaps influenced by such animal experiments, should be viewed with reserve.

Even stronger reason to be cautious about existing learning theories, is their very multifariousness. Many have attempted to define learning. Sutaria quotes quite a number of different definitions of learning, and then states, "It is obvious from the above samples that there are probably as many definitions of learning as there are of learning disabilities."[4] Because there is a large number of, generally conflicting, definitions on learning, there are also a large number of, equally conflicting, theories on learning. Hergenhahn (1982) describes eleven major ones with countless variations.[5]

If one drives from Los Angeles to San Francisco and one's car suddenly stalls and stops, there cannot be eleven different explanations of why this happened. There also cannot be eleven different explanations—with countless variations—of how human beings learn. Although it is true that all theories on learning are certainly not wrong in their entirety, it is equally true that there is as yet not *one* theory that adequately explains learning. The net result of this is that we must accept that we still know very little about learning. This means that jumping to the conclusion that the cause of a learning problem is intrinsic to the child, must at least be regarded as scientifically highly questionable. The shoe may well be on the other foot. We contend that we should all confess our ignorance and acknowledge that the second possibility should be considered very seriously indeed.

The symptoms and phenomena, that are noticed in the so-called "learning-disabled" child, have so far been misinterpreted as a "disorder" inherent to the child, for the simple reason that the learning disabilities theory is based on sensory observations, and its conclusions are in the form of correlations of observations.[6] The tendency prevails to focus on the *appearance* of these phenomena, instead of on their *reality*.

Whenever observations are made, it is always necessary to *interpret* such observations, and to draw conclusions about them.[7] The reason for this is that one must be able to distinguish between *veridical* impressions, i.e. those that are reflecting the true state of affairs, and those that are *illusionary*, i.e. those that are not in accord with the actual state of affairs.[8] We have all experienced that "the moon appears to be moving when it is visible through a cloud passing in front of it. However, we know that this is an illusion; the moon is *not* really moving through the clouds and so its apparent movement must be disregarded by the astronomer."[9]

There is only one way in which one can know that it is not the moon that is moving, but the clouds, and that is by *interpreting* the sensory impression in terms of foreknowledge and past experience. In the same way one has to interpret the phenomenon of the child who has difficulties in the learning situation. Because too little has so far been known about learning, it has been misinterpreted as a "disorder" inherent to the child.

In his research, Jan (coauthor) has discovered three learning principles that play a vital role in learning, and holds the key to unlocking a learning *IN*ability:

Human Learning is a Stratified Process

This is a self-evident fact, yet its significance in the situation of the "learning-disabled" child has apparently never been fully comprehended. Throughout the world in all educational systems it is commonly accepted that

107

a child must start at the lower levels of education and then gradually progress to the higher levels. If human learning had not been a stratified process, if it had taken place on a single level, this would have been unnecessary. It would then not have been important to start a child in first grade. It would have been possible for the child to enter school at any level and to complete the school years in any order.

Even more astounding is that this very important principle of learning is hardly noted in any of the present-day theories on learning. In fact, when this principle of learning is mentioned, it often happens by way of an *en passant* reference to discarded notions from the past:

> Baldwin (1896) introduced the concept of a hierarchy of senses and proposed that sense perception ability varied from person to person. As we ascend Baldwin's pyramidal scale we find that each capability rests on, and is chronologically and psychologically dependent on, all the capabilities below it (for example imagination, which could not act but for its predecessors perception and memory). This notion of training competencies hierarchically was the premise on which perceptual training and perceptual motor training were based.[10]

When this principle *is* noticed, then its significance is often distorted by reductionist thinking such as, "Cognitive abilities develop in a sequential fashion that cannot be altered,"[11] or, "Another prerequisite for reading includes a certain level of physiological development of the brain."[12]

The stratified nature of learning is an age-old—but ageless—principle. This principle was already pointed out by Herbart (1776-1841), and it is based on the further principle that

> One never . . . apprehends anything in isolation, but always in terms of one's background of previous experience and learning. So *the first consideration in properly organized learning would be to make sure that the learner had the right background* (our italics).[13]

By way of a simple and practical example we have to remind the reader of the fact that one has to learn to count before it becomes possible to learn to add and subtract. Suppose one tried to teach a child, who had not yet learned to count, to add and subtract. This would be quite impossible and no amount of effort would ever succeed in teaching the child these skills. Conceivably people who abide by the "learning disabilities" idea would also then conclude that the child "suffered" from a "minimal brain dysfunction," or from "dyscalculia," overlooking that the ability to count must have been acquired *first, before* it becomes possible to learn to add and subtract.

In the same way, there are also certain skills and knowledge that a child must have acquired *first, before* it becomes possible for him to benefit from a course in reading. Bartoli, who says that it is "the actual practice with the real task of reading that leads to more skilful reading," is only partially correct. "Of course," she adds, "any soccer, tennis, or basketball coach will tell you the same thing: If you want to get better, you have to play the game—not just practice skill drills."[14] Now, we know very little about tennis and basketball, but we do happen to know about soccer. The game of soccer consists of many fragmented elements or skills—passing, control, shooting, dribbling, goal keeping and heading. Before any child is expected to play in a full-game situation, he should first be trained to pass, head, control, dribble and shoot the ball.[15] In fact, until these skills have been *automatized*, the child will have two left feet on the soccer field.

The reading "game," just like the game of soccer, rests upon certain skills and until these skills have become automatized, the child will have "two left eyes" in the reading situation. The important thing, of course, is to know *what* these skills are.

Glenn Doman, whose work was mentioned earlier, eventually recognized this fact that human learning is a stratified process. In fact, his breakthrough in treating seriously brain-injured children can be attributed to this insight.

Children, treated by Doman and his team, were so severely disabled that they couldn't even walk. Initially, a multiplicity of techniques were used in their treatment, such as heat and massage of the affected limbs, exercise, orthopedic surgery to transplant muscles or to change bone structure and electrical stimulation to help maintain paralyzed muscles.

During 1950 the team decided to evaluate the results of their work. By that time they had been treating a group of a hundred brain-injured children for a number of years. The children themselves ranged in age from one to nineteen years. The results of this evaluation proved how tragically inadequate their methods were. Many of the children had not improved at all. What was even more discouraging was that many of the children were actually worse. The progress of those who had improved was so minimal and slow, that they were most probably going to be old aged before they could walk.

To justify their work in any way, they started to compare these hundred children in treatment with children whom they had evaluated but who did not return for treatment. Mostly they were children who were in some way underprivileged and whose parents could not afford the charges. The parents of others simply did not care enough to undertake treatment. After reevaluating these children, they came to an absolutely astonishing conclusion. The children who had been without treatment were almost overwhelmingly better than the children they had treated! Their conclusion: through all these years they had applied symptom-therapy, and never addressed the cause of the problem.

Their research now entered a new phase. They now focused their research on the *normal child.* They asked themselves the question, how do normal children develop until the walking phase, and the answer to this question explained why previous results were without avail. Along the road to walking, there are four important stages: The first stage begins at birth, when the baby is able to move his limbs and body but is not able to use these motions to move his body from place to place. This first stage Doman called "Movement without Mobility".

The second stage occurs later when the baby learns that by moving his arms and legs in a certain manner with his stomach pressed to the floor, he can move from Point A to Point B. This stage Doman called "Crawling."

Sometime later, stage three occurs, when the baby learns to defy gravity for the first time and to get up on his hands and his knees and move across the floor in this easier, but more skilled manner. This stage was called "Creeping."

The last significant stage occurs when the baby learns to get up on his hind legs and walk, which was, of course, called "Walking."

Parents sometimes report that their children did not creep. Doman answers: "Do you mean that this child simply lay in his crib or pushed himself on the floor until one day he jumped to his feet and then walked? . . . There [is] no way [for any child] to travel this road without passing each and every milepost, [but there can indeed be] a difference in time factors."[16]

If these basic stages were slighted, Doman discovered, as for example in the case of a child who had begun to walk before he had crept *enough*, there would be adverse consequences such as poor coordination.

The observations that followed left the team completely aghast: The children undergoing intensive training were almost everywhere except where they belonged. They were in braces, in casts, in wheel chairs, in standing tables, on crutches or canes, or in their mothers' arms. In short, they were every place except on the floor. This explained the results of the underprivileged children—the mother had placed the child on the floor and had allowed him to travel down this road in the normal manner.

Having made an error it was necessary to correct it—to put the brain-injured child on the floor, to stop all other treatment and to see what would happen. The results of this experiment, Doman says, were

> dramatic in the extreme and were destined to teach us many lessons we would never forget. While many additional techniques and methods had yet to be developed, many of them complex and highly scientific in their conception and execution, none to this day has achieved nearly the significance of just putting the child on the floor. When the children were placed on the floor, face down, we saw a reproduction of the exact stages we had seen in the normal child. The brain-injured children traveled down this road in exactly the normal order that has been described, without further treatment of any kind.[17]

Another point of interest is that Doman and his team only advanced in their field after focusing their attention on *normal* children. In the LD field, researchers should perhaps take note of Adelman and Taylor who (with our italics) say that we need "to base LD theories . . . on *normal* human development and functioning."[18] Until now they have been based on abnormal functioning, as a result of the work of Strauss and Werner.

The Ageless Principle of Repetition

A second learning principle of great importance is that learning cannot occur without repetition. As far as one can go back in history, repetition—also called rote learning or drilling—has been the backbone of successful teaching. But this is no longer the case:

> The jewel in the crown of American pedagogy has long been Columbia University's Teachers College. Its patron saint, and of American education more generally, is John Dewey, whose idea of school as engines of social change led his disciples in the 1920s and 1930s to define their task as replacing the rigid, the authoritarian, and the traditional with a school centered on the child's social, rather than his intellectual, functioning. The child would be

freed from the highly structured school day, from testing, rote memorization, and drill. Books were to take second place to projects, reading to "life experience." Cooperation would replace competition; the emphasis would be on the group rather than the individual. The elementary school pupil would learn about here and now, his neighborhood rather than places in the far-off past. The school was to be a socializing institute where children learned through active experience.[19]

One consequence of Dewey's influence was that repetition, rote learning and drilling became swear words in education. Today this form of learning is considered to be "out of style,"[20] "ghastly boring"[21] and even "mindless."[22] "Having to spend long periods of time on repetitive tasks is a sign that learning is not taking place—that this is not a productive learning situation," says LD expert Bartoli.[23]

We would like to ask the critics of repetition and drilling if they have a driver's license. If they have, we would like to know how they got it? Did they just jump in the car one day and off they went? No, the fact is that they repeated over and over—drilled and drilled and drilled—the same actions up to a point where they became *automatized.* Only then were they able to drive a car successfully. Why then, do they expect from *children* to learn successfully without repetition and drilling? Repetition creates confidence and builds a basis, a kind of springboard for them to conquer higher cognitive skills. One has to build that *first* and then branch out into "creative" and "critical" thinking and other approaches. They need a base for the higher functions. Today, however, children are required to think "critically" (a sacred cow in education) while they haven't learned anything to think critically about. As Professor Roger Shattuck so rightly states, public schools in the United States—and elsewhere—have put the cart before the horse.[24] Maybe what they really did was that they drowned the horse and burned the cart.

In recent years, neuroscientists have discovered that repetition is important in the "wiring" of a person's brain, i.e. the forming of connections or *synapses* between the brain cells. Without these connections, the brain cells are as useless as batteries standing in a row next to a torch. Only when the batteries and torch are connected, can they make a shining light.

The thing that wires a child's brain, say neuroscientists—or rewires it after physical trauma—is "repeated experience."[25] Without such repeated experience, key synapses don't form. And if such connections, once formed, are used too seldom to be strengthened and reinforced, the brain, figuring they're dead weight, eventually "prunes" them away.[26]

But mere repetition is not the end of the story. There must be *enough repetition for a beginner learner.* A beginner learner must start by repeating a limited amount of material many times over and over. Gradually, less and less repetition will be necessary to master new skills and new knowledge. This principle is especially noticeable when teaching mentally handicapped children. Since 1993 we have been actively involved in research in this area.

When teaching the mentally handicapped we follow a very intensive program, with counting being one of the first things to teach them. Especially in the initial stages, a great part of the daily program is used for this activity. This activity is also a good example to illustrate the above-mentioned principle.

When Chrizan B., an eight-year-old who had an IQ of 65 at the onset of intervention, was taught to count, it took three full days to teach her to count from one to three and back. On the fourth day, "four" was added. Chrizan immediately became completely confused and could no longer count from one to three. It again took three full days to teach her to count from one to four and back. When "five" was added, the same thing happened. She became completely confused and could no longer count from one to four. Again it required three days to teach her to count from one to five and back. Gradually, however, less time was required to add new numbers and she no longer became confused when new numbers were added. From eleven onwards, it took two days to add a new number and from twenty onwards, more or less one day was needed for every new number. From thirty onwards it was possible to add more and more new numbers on a daily basis.

The point is that much repetition was needed before Chrizan could count from one to three, one to four, and one to five. Gradually, however, it became easier and easier, until very little repetition was needed to add new numbers. No doubt it is the same with normal children, as the following story, taken from *Nurtured by Love: A New Approach to Education* by Suzuki illustrates:

> Since 1949, our Mrs. Yano has been working with new educational methods for developing ability, and every day she trains the infants of the school to memorize and recite Issa's well-known haiku. [A haiku is a short Japanese poem, consisting only of three lines.] Children who at first could not memorize one haiku after hearing it ten times were able to do so in the second term after three to four hearings, and in the third term only one hearing.[27]

This means that, if one systematically and regularly does repetition with a learner, it will gradually become possible for the learner to learn more and more with fewer and fewer repetitions. It is almost as if a "pyramid of repetition" has to be constructed first.

The importance of this "pyramid of repetition" is also seen in the learning of a first language. According to Dr. Beve Hornsby, it has been found that a child who is just beginning to talk must hear a word about 500 times before it will become part of his active vocabulary, i.e. before he will be able to say the word.[28] Two years later, the same child will probably need only one to a few repetitions to learn to say a new word.

Without building this "pyramid of repetition" first, later learning will always be time consuming and prone to failure. Unfortunately educators have ignored this learning principle and have removed most of the repetitive work that used to form part of education for so long. With few exceptions, this change is seen as a step forward. Doreen Kronick, in her book *New Approaches to Learning Disabilities*, stated that we "overlooked what our common sense told us, which was that the poems that we had learned in school were useless for helping us to remember what we needed to buy at the supermarket."[29]

It seems that people, like Kronick, who regard this as a step forward, are wrong. Maclean et al., for example, found that knowledge of nursery rhymes among three-year-olds was a significant predictor of later prereading skills even after the children's IQs and their mothers' educational levels were partialed out.[30] Even stronger evidence of Kronick's wrong assumption is the "explosion" of "learning disabilities" all over the Western world.[31] One of the reasons for this explosion is that repetition or drilling has been dropped out of the school system. As Kronick said—the memorizing of poems would not help you to remember what to buy at the supermarket. What she does not realize—and many others too—was that by reciting and repeating these poems over and over we were building this pyramid of repetition. Therefore it was not useless at all!

Educators should take into account that the learning material, that children are expected to master, continually becomes more, and more difficult, year after year. Unless the teaching methods take note of this—and due to the removal of repetition or drilling, modern-day teaching methods do not—it is inevitable that they will start battling, sooner or later. One can compare this to the story of Milo, the famous Greek wrestler from the sixth century B.C. He

114

is said to have carried a calf on his shoulders every day from its birth and eventually to have carried the grown cow around the Olympic stadium. Like the calf inexorably grew and therefore became heavier and heavier, the learning material, that children are confronted with year after year, also becomes more, and more difficult. The fact that Milo carried the calf *every day*, however, made it possible for him also to carry the grown cow. The repeated carrying of the calf had a permanent effect on Milo. In the same way repeated learning experiences also have a permanent effect on the learner.

In regards to building a "pyramid of repetition" there are two very important factors that should be kept in mind: The first is that there is great individuality among different people, and even within the same person, in the amount of repetition required to learn something. The amount of repetition that is enough for one person, may not necessarily be enough for another. The amount of repetition that a certain person requires in mastering a certain skill, may not necessarily be enough to master another skill. Mrs. Butler might need ten lessons to master the skill of driving, Mrs. Brown might need twenty, Mrs. Lane thirty and Mrs. Jones forty. Mrs. Jones, who struggled to learn to drive, may, on the other hand, need only ten lessons to become expert at sewing. One should note, however, that Mrs. Jones was not diagnosed as "driving disabled" because she needed forty lessons!

The second important factor is that one should not lose sight of the stratified nature of learning. If a child has not yet mastered the skill of counting, ten thousand repetitions in adding and subtracting will not teach him to add and subtract. The child needs to learn how to count *first*, although he may need more repetitions to master this skill than some other children.

Application

The third important learning principle is that there must be opportunities for *application*. Even while a child is learning to master the fragmented elements of soccer, he can and should already be given opportunities to *apply* these skills in an actual game. In the same way, while learning to master the skills that form the basis of reading, a child can and should already be given opportunities to apply these skills in the act of reading.

An important point is that these three fundamental learning principles should be looked upon as a whole and should not be viewed in isolation. Any botanist will tell you the same thing: it is the whole of the amount of water, sunlight and fertilizer that will cause a tree to bear large, juicy fruit. If you only water the tree six weeks after you have hoed the fertilizer into the ground, you are bound to return to a withered tree.

Notes:

1. McClellan, J. E., *Philosophy of Education* (Englewood-Cliffs: Prentice-Hall, 1976), 55.
2. Van Schoor, M., *Bestaanskommunikasie* (Bloemfontein: Uitgewery P. J. de Villiers, 1977).
3. McClellan, *Philosophy of Education*.
4. Sutaria, S. D., *Specific Learning Disabilities. Nature and Needs* (Springfield: Charles C. Thomas, 1985), 85.
5. Hergenhahn, B. R., *An Introduction to Theories of Learning* (2nd ed.), (Englewood Cliffs, NJ: Prentice-Hall, Inc., 1982).
6. Cf. T. Z. Lavine, *From Socrates to Sartre: The Philosophic Quest* (New York: Bantam Books, 1984).
7. Dane, F. C., *Research Methods* (Pacific Grove, California: Brooks/Cole Publishing Company, 1990).
8. Rock, I., *An Introduction to Perception* (New York: Macmillan Publishing Co., 1975).
9. Ibid., 2.
10. Kronick, D., *New Approaches to Learning Disabilities. Cognitive, Metacognitive and Holistic* (Philadelphia: Grune & Stratton, 1988), 6.
11. Lerner, J., *Learning Disabilities: Theories, Diagnosis, and Teaching Strategies* (4th ed.), (Boston: Houghton Mifflin Company, 1988), 173.
12. Lipa, S. E., "Reading disability: A new look at an old issue," *Journal of Learning Disabilities*, 1983, vol. 16(8), 453-457.
13. Mursell, J. L., *Successful Teaching* (2nd ed.), (New York: McGraw-Hill Book Company, Inc., 1954), 210-211.
14. Bartoli, J. S., "An ecological response to Coles's interactivity alternative," *Journal of Learning Disabilities*, 1989, vol. 22(5), 292-297.
15. Spindler, T., & Ward, A., *Knowabout Soccer* (Hampshire: The Automobile Association, 1990).
16. Doman, G., *What to Do About Your Brain-Injured Child* (New York: Doubleday & Company, Inc., 1982), 46.
17. Ibid., 50.
18. Adelman, H. S., & Taylor, L., "Summary of the survey of fundamental concerns confronting the LD field," *Journal of Learning Disabilities*, 1986, vol. 19(7), 391-393.
19. Kramer, R., "Inside the teachers' culture," *The Public Interest*, 15 January 1997.
20. Bremmer, J., "What business needs from the nation's schools," *St. Louis Post-Dispatch*, 19 April 1993.
21. Bassnett, S., "Comment," *Independent*, 14 October 1999.

22. Dixon, R-C. D., "Ideologies, practices, and their implications for special education," *Journal of Special Education*, 1994, vol. 28, 356.
23. Bartoli, "An ecological response to Coles's interactivity alternative."
24. Skube, M., "Professor out to put 'learning' back into education," *The Atlanta Journal and Constitution*, 12 March 2000.
25. Nash, J. M., "Special report: Fertile minds from birth, a baby's brain cells proliferate wildly, making connections that may shape a lifetime of experience. The first three years are crucial," *Time*, 3 February 1997.
26. Polaneczky, R., "How kids get smart: The surprising news," *Redbook*, 1 March 1998.
27. Suzuki, S., *Nurtured by Love: A New Approach to Education* (New York: Exposition Press, 1969).
28. Hornsby, B., *Overcoming Dyslexia* (Johannesburg: Juta and Company Ltd., 1984) 43.
29. Kronick, *New Approaches to Learning Disabilities*, 9.
30. Maclean, M., Bryant, P., & Bradley, L., "Rhymes, nursery rhymes, and reading in early childhood," *Merrill-Palmer Quarterly*, vol. 33, 255-281, cited in K. E. Stanovich, "Learning disabilities in broader context," *Journal of Learning Disabilities*, May 1989, vol. 22(5), 287-297.
31. Kramer, "Inside the teachers' culture."

9.

Things that Do not Fall from the Sky

The first consideration in properly organized learning would be to make sure that the learner had the right background.[1] — Herbart

Human learning, as we concluded, does not take place on a single level, but is a stratified process. There are certain preliminary skills that need to be mastered first, before any person can learn the skills of adding and subtracting, or the game of soccer. The same applies to reading. There are also skills and experiences that form the basis or *foundation* of reading and writing.

A "foundation," according to the dictionary, is the "natural or prepared ground or base on which some structure rests." This means that "foundational skills of reading" would refer to skills that form the prepared ground or base on which the structure of reading rests. This would further mean that, unless this base has been prepared adequately, no effective reading could take place.

The Foundational Skills of Reading

The reading act is a unitary occurrence, meaning that the actions taking place while one is reading occur simultaneously. However, for the purpose of this discussion, these actions will be divided into steps, and a schematic diagram representing these steps of the reading act is shown on the following page. It is suggested that the reader refer to this diagram throughout the rest of this discussion.

Reception

Reading must be regarded as an act of communication. There is a *communicator*—the author of the book that the reader is reading, there is a *message,* transferred to the reader via symbols on paper, and there is a *recipient* of the message—the reader.

ACT OF READING

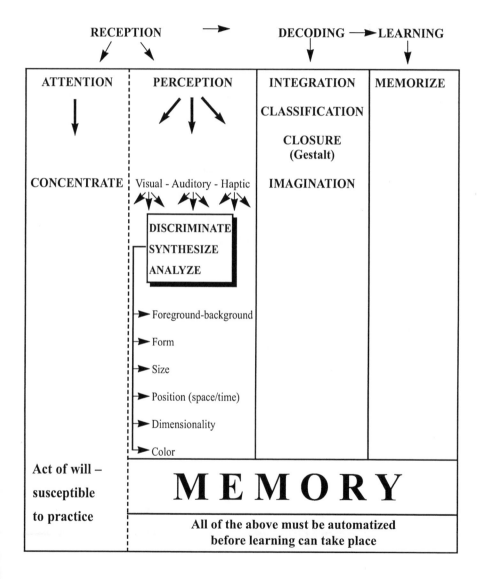

There are many factors involved in the reception of the message when a person is reading. The first of these is that the reader must *pay attention*. Paying attention is a body function, and therefore does not need to be taught. However, paying attention as such is a function that is quite useless for the act of learning, because it is only a fleeting occurrence. Attention usually shifts very quickly from one object or one thing to the next. The child must first be taught to *focus* his attention on something and to keep his attention focused on this something for some length of time. When a person focuses his attention for any length of time, we refer to it as *concentration.* Paying attention therefore, is the body function that makes the skill of concentration possible, just as the functions of seeing and hearing make the skills of looking and listening possible.

Concentration rests on two legs. First, it is an *act of will* and cannot take place automatically. The will to focus attention on the message must be sustained in order to carry out all the actions needed to fully comprehend the message. Second, it is also a skill, and therefore has to be *taught.*

Although LD specialists (with our italics) acknowledge that "the ability to concentrate and attend to a task for a prolonged period of time is *essential* for the student to receive necessary information and complete certain academic activities,"[2] it seems that the ability to concentrate is regarded as a "fafrotsky"— a word coined by Ivan T. Sanderson, and standing for "Things that . . . **FA**ll **FROm** The **SKY**."[3] Children who cannot concentrate—simply because they have not learned to do so—are therefore frequently diagnosed as suffering from ADD ("attention deficit disorder"). If one inquires what has been done to *teach* these children to concentrate, one invariably finds that nothing has been done at all. Concentration must be taught, after which one's proficiency can be constantly improved by regular and sustained practice. In the same way, one can also teach them all the other skills that are foundational to reading, and then one finds that the reading ability of a child, for whom reading previously was a seemingly endless nightmare, improves by leaps and bounds.

The next step in receiving a written message is that it must be perceived. In other words, *perception* must take place. Before one can read or learn anything, one has to become aware of it through one of the senses. Usually one has to hear or see it. Subsequently one has to *interpret* whatever one has seen or heard. In essence then, perception means interpretation. Of course, lack of experience may cause a person to misinterpret what he has seen or heard. In other words, perception represents our apprehension of a present situation in terms of our *past experiences*, or, as stated by the philosopher Immanuel Kant (1724-1804): "We see things not as they are but as we are."

The following situation will illustrate how perception correlates with previous experience:

Suppose a person parked his car and walks away from it while continuing to look back at it. As he goes further and further away from his car, it will appear to him as if his car is gradually getting smaller and smaller. In such a situation none of us, however, would gasp in horror and cry out, "My car is shrinking!" Although the sensory *perception* is that the car is shrinking rapidly, we do not *interpret* that the car is changing size. Through past experiences we have learned that objects do not grow or shrink as we walk toward or away from them. You have *learned* that their actual size remains constant, despite the illusion. Even when one is five blocks away from one's car and it seems no larger than one's fingernail, one would interpret it as that it is still one's car and that it hasn't actually changed size. This learned perception is known as size constancy.[4]

Pygmies, however, who live deep in the rain forests of tropical Africa, are not often exposed to wide vistas and distant horizons, and therefore do not have sufficient opportunities to learn size constancy. One Pygmy, removed from his usual environment, was convinced he was seeing a swarm of insects when he was actually looking at a herd of buffalo at a great distance. When driven toward the animals he was frightened to see the insects "grow" into buffalo and was sure that some form of witchcraft had been at work.[5]

A person needs to *interpret* sensory phenomena, and this can only be done on the basis of past experience of the same, similar or related phenomena. Perceptual ability, therefore, heavily depends upon the amount of perceptual practice and experience that the subject has already enjoyed. This implies that perception is a skill that can be improved tremendously through judicious practice and experience.

A further important point about perception is that the stratified nature of learning also applies here. Perception in itself consists of a large number of subskills, that can all be automatized. First, there are various ways of perceptualizing, namely visual, auditory and haptic. The latter includes touch perception and kinesthetic perception. Because we read with our eyes, visual perception plays the most important role in the reading act, and will therefore be discussed at some length.

When a person is reading, visual *discrimination* must take place. All printed letters are set against a certain background. The most important difference between the letters and the background is that they differ in color. Obviously, the first discrimination will therefore be in terms of *color*. The second discrimination is in terms of *foreground-background*. The particular letter, or word, or sentence, that the reader is focused on is elevated to the level of foreground, whereas everything else within the field of vision of the reader (the rest of the page and the book, the desk on which the book is resting, the section of the floor and/or wall that is visible, etc.) is relegated to the background. Our Latin alphabet consists of twenty-six letters, each with its corresponding capital letter with a difference in size and sometimes in shape compared to the lower case counterpart. The letters all differ in *form* or *shape* and must be discriminated accordingly. Capital letters, being used at the start of a sentence, sometimes look exactly the same as their lower case counterparts, and must therefore be discriminated mainly with regard to *size*. The letters in *dyslexia* and *DYSLEXIA* may all differ in terms of form and size, but must nevertheless be interpreted as constituting the same word. One also does not only read letters, but thoughts, all compiled from a conglomeration of words. A word is made up of a number of letters arranged in a particular sequence. The reader must therefore be able to discriminate the letters in terms of their *positions*. If a sketch or picture is included in the text, there must be discrimination of *dimensionality* as well.

One of the most obvious—and one of the most common—telltale signs of dyslexia is reversals. People with this kind of problem often confuse letters like *b* and *d*, either when reading or when writing, or they sometimes read (or write) words like *no* for *on*, or *pot* for *top*. One invariably *also* finds that these people find it difficult to distinguish between left and right, or that they find it difficult to cross the middle line. These difficulties are not signs of minimal neurological damage, as is often asserted, but simply signs that not enough had been done to teach these people to distinguish between left and right, or to cross the middle line.

The human body consists of two halves, a left side and a right side. The human brain also has two halves, which are connected by the corpus callosum. Mindful of the wise words of Immanuel Kant that man does not see things as they are but as *he* is, it is inevitable that a person will interpret everything in terms of his own sidedness. A child or adult, who has not learned to interpret correctly in terms of his sidedness yet, who has not learned to distinguish properly between left and right, will inevitably experience problems when he finds himself in a situation where he is expected to interpret sidedness. (See the *Act of Reading* diagram in this chapter—sidedness is a "position in space" interpretation.) One such a situation, where sidedness plays a particularly important role, is when a person is expected to distinguish between a *b* and a *d*. It is clear that the only difference between the two letters is the position of the straight line—it is either left or right.

It is important to note that people who are confused about left and right cannot use mnemonics or memory aids while reading, as is often advised by experts. Susan Hampshire, for example, advises that children should remember that "left" is the side on which they wear their watch. Girls, she says, sometimes enjoy having their right hand marked with a pretty ribbon.[6] Serfontein advises that one should put nail polish on the little finger of the student's left hand in order to teach him that reading and writing start on the left-hand side of the paper.[7] These tricks never work to improve reading ability. This is just like going to China with a Chinese dictionary and then hoping to be able to speak Chinese. One has to *learn* to speak Chinese. In the same way one has to *learn* to interpret sidedness. As all the other skills foundational to reading, the ability to distinguish between left and right must be drummed in so securely that the person can apply it during reading without having to think of it at all.

After having discriminated every letter in terms of color, foreground and background, form, size and position, letters must be combined into words. The reader must thus be able to perceive individual parts as a whole. In other words, he must be able to *synthesize*.

Although the ability to *analyze*, i.e. to perceive the whole in its individual parts, does play a role in reading, this ability is of the utmost importance in spelling. To be a good speller, one must be able to analyze.

The above events sound very complex, and indeed must be recognized as being just that. In reality they take place all the time—at lightning speed—while a person is reading, but a good reader is unaware of these events because they have been automatized. It can be compared to driving a car. Try to remember your first driving lesson. How hard you had to concentrate on *what* to do *when* to prevent the car from wrapping itself around the nearest tree! Now, after many years of experience and of doing it over and over, your driving has become an automatism and you need not even think while you drive. In fact, your mind is probably on something else most of the time, like talking to the other people in the car, or listening to the radio, or looking at the beautiful scenery outside.

Speaking is another example of the importance of drilling some activities to such an extent that they become automatic. Any person, who speaks a language that he knows well, does not concentrate on vocabulary, or on sentence structure, or on grammar. His mind is focused on what he wants to say.

Decoding

However, when a person attempts to speak a language in which he has not become automatic yet, he will necessarily have to divide his attention between the content of his message and the language itself. He will therefore speak haltingly and with great difficulty. As explained in the *Journal of Learning Disabilities*, "if the skill on the primary task is automatized, it will not be disrupted by concurrent processing on the secondary task because automatic processing does not take up attentional resources. If, on the contrary, the skill is not automatized, it will be disrupted by concurrent processing of a second skill because two skills are then competing for limited attentional resources."[8] This also applies to the act of reading. The child, in whom the above-mentioned foundational skills of reading have not yet become automatic, will read haltingly and with great difficulty. The poor reader is forced to apply all his concentration to the reception of the message, and therefore has "no concentration left" to decode the message.

The decoding of the message is a very important aspect of the reading act. Without being able to decode the message, the receiver cannot understand it. This explains why some children can "read" without understanding what they are reading.

Decoding implies that the reader is able to decipher the message, in other words, he is able to ascribe meaning to the written word. This becomes possible first by *integrating* the message that he is reading with his foreknowledge. Foreknowledge can be defined as the range of one's existing knowledge and past experiences. If one reads something that cannot directly be connected to or tied in with knowledge that one already possesses, one cannot decode or decipher the contents of the message. As Harris et al. state, "What a child gets from a book will often be determined by what the child brings to the book."[9]

It has been found that LD students often fail to integrate what they are reading with their foreknowledge.[10] The main reason for this has already been explained, i.e. that the poor reader is forced to apply all his concentration to the reception of the message, and therefore has "no concentration left" to decode the message.

A decoding skill that is closely related to that of integration is *classification*. When a person sees a chair, although he may never have seen a chair exactly like this one, he will nevertheless immediately recognize it as a chair, because he is familiar with the *class* of objects we call "chair." This implies that, whenever a name is ascribed to an object, it is thereby put into a specific class of objects, i.e. it is *classified*.

The Gestalt principle of *closure* means that the mind is able to derive meaning from objects or pictures that are not perceived in full. W- -re s-re th-t y-- w-ll b- -ble to und-rsta-d th-s s-ntenc-, although more than 25 percent of the letters have been omitted. The mind is quite able to bridge the gaps that were left in the sentence. The idea of closure is, however, more than just seeing parts of a word and amplifying them. It also entails the amplification of the author's message. No author can put all his thoughts into words. This stresses the importance of foreknowledge. If it were possible for an author to put everything related to the subject he is dealing with on paper, the possession of foreknowledge would not have been necessary. That, however, is impossible, as an author can at most present a very limited cross-section of reality and the reader must be able to expand on this before comprehension becomes possible. Poetry is a good example of the importance of foreknowledge. Any person, who is unfamiliar with the Arthurian legend, will probably derive little meaning from a reading of *Morte d'Arthur* by Alfred Lord Tennyson.

Lastly, *imagination* plays a role in decoding. It is doubtful whether a person really understands something unless he is able to think about it in terms of pictures. When we read or hear a message, the words and thoughts comprising the message call up images in our mind's eye. If this does not occur, the message will not make any sense. If you read or hear a sentence in an unfamiliar language, it will not make any sense to you, simply because none of the words will call up any pictures in your mind's eye. This ability plays a very important role in the decoding of the message. Furthermore, by using one's imagination while reading, one's emotions can be addressed during the reading act.

Learning

Only after a person has decoded a message can learning take place. To learn, a person must be able to store something that he has perceived and decoded, so that he will be able to recall this information at a later stage. It is the ability to *recall to memory* or to remember that makes learning possible.

Memory is one of the foundational skills of learning that is of special importance in the so-called learning subjects at school or university, where information is presented to the learner, and it is expected that he be able to reproduce it as accurately as possible. However, memory is a skill that is also of great importance to the reading act. For example, recognizing the shapes of the different letters comprising a particular word is an act of memory. Every word also consists of letters in a particular sequence, and one has to remember what word is represented by the sequence of letters in question. Simply by changing the sequence of the letters in *name*, it can become *mean* or *amen*.

It is widely accepted that LD students have poor memories. Scruggs and Mastropieri state, "One of the most commonly described characteristics of learning-disabled students is their failure to remember important information."[11] The problem with LD experts, however, is that they view memory as a "fafrotsky." For a long time it was firmly believed that IQ was biologically determined. In the same way, it is widely believed that biology decides whether a person has a good memory or a bad, and those who believe that memory can be improved are ridiculed:

> For many centuries it was felt that mind-brain with its memory component was like a muscle—if you exercised it enough, it became bigger, healthier, and more efficient [cf. chapter three]. When I was young, most college-bound high school students were forced to study Latin. They were told that this study was good exercise for their brains and memories. With enough study of Latin, they would be able to learn practical disciplines more efficiently. Today, the analogy of memory and muscle causes chuckles of amusement at the innocence and simplicity of former educational and psychological theory. Today, most students of cognitive psychology believe that memory is physically determined. Individual differences allow for some small improvement, but generally a good memory remains good and a poor memory remains poor. Not much hope for the learning disabled here.

> However, some modern researchers feel that memory can improve dramatically with training. (They studiously avoid the muscle analogy or the word *exercise*. Who wants to be laughed at?)[12]

Frankly, when we know that we are right, we do not mind at all being laughed at. The important question is, who laughs last?

In an article to the *Learning Disabilities Quarterly* Scruggs and Mastropieri evaluated the results of mnemonic instruction in learning disabilities intervention, and concluded, "mnemonic instruction delivers the greatest learning increases seen in the history of learning disabilities intervention research."[13]

Defined in broad terms, a *mnemonic* is a device, procedure, or operation that is used to improve memory. Defined in narrow terms—and what Scruggs and Mastropieri mean by the word—a mnemonic is a specific reconstruction of target content intended to tie new information more closely to the learner's existing knowledge base and, therefore, facilitate retrieval. Mnemonics have been used for thousands of years. Having limited access to writing materials, the Ancient Greeks developed complex mnemonic systems for remembering stories, poems, plays and lectures. Many of the Ancient Greek techniques were revived in the Middle Ages, where they were sometimes associated with mysticism and the occult.[14] However, with the invention of the printing press these ancient arts became lost as more and more people relied—sometimes exclusively—on note-taking and on the printed page.

There are a variety of mnemonic techniques, including keywords, pegwords, acronyms, loci methods, spelling mnemonics, phonetic mnemonics, number-sound mnemonics, and Japanese "Yodai" methods. An example of an *acronym* is to remember the word HOMES to make recall of the names of the Great Lakes possible: *H*uron, *O*ntario, *M*ichigan, *E*rie, and *S*uperior. The purpose of *number-sound mnemonics* is to recall strings of numbers, such as telephone numbers, addresses, locker combinations or historical dates. To use them, learners must first learn the number-sound relationships: 0=s; 1=t; 2=n; 3=m; 4=r; 5=l; 6=sh, ch, or soft g; 7=k, hard c, or hard g; 8=f or v; and 9=p. To remember the date 1439, for example, the learner uses the associated consonant sounds, t, r, m and p, and will insert vowels to create a meaningful word or words. In this case, the word "tramp" can be used. *Spelling mnemonics* is intended to help us remember the spelling of words. In order to remember that the word "cemetery" is spelled with three e's, for example, one can picture a lady screaming 'E-E-E' as she walks past the cemetery.

In their research Scruggs and Mastropieri synthesized the results of twenty-four experimental investigations of mnemonic instruction in special education settings. They found that the overall effect size of these combined investigations was 1.62 standard deviation units. According to them this was the highest measure of treatment effectiveness reported at the time.[15] For comparison, Kavale and Forness reviewed previous quantitative syntheses of special education interventions, reporting overall effect sizes ranging from -0.12 to +0.58, for such interventions as reduced class size, special class placement, psycholinguistic training, perceptual-motor training, stimulant and psychotropic drugs, and diet interventions.[16]

Scruggs and Mastropieri demonstrate, first of all, that memory *can* be trained, and second, the importance of memory training in helping LD children. There are, however, at least two problems in improving memory by means of mnemonic instruction. *One* is that it overlooks the sequential fashion of learning. Mnemonics instruction is, to a large extent, instruction in memory *techniques*, which should be taught only *after* the *skill* of memory has been learned. It can be compared to a child being taught soccer tactics, such as the "wall pass," while he has not yet adequately mastered the skill of passing the ball. As stated in *Knowabout Soccer*, "No matter how good your passing technique, if the quality of your passing is poor, your technique will not be effective."[17] *Two* is that by teaching the child to use memory crutches, the result is, as Scruggs and Mastropieri acknowledge, "On more complex applications, generalization attempts have been less successful."[18] If the *skill* of memory is taught, however, the child can apply it in any situation.

The Role of Language

Di dunia kini kita, tiap orang harus dapat membaca…

If one accepts the theory of a so-called "attention deficit disorder" or ADD, lately a very popular idea in the LD field, then those who are unable to read the above sentence all suffer from IRDD, or an "Indonesian reading deficit disorder." Of course this is a ridiculous idea, but then, as already implied earlier, the idea of ADD, and a learning disability too, must be equally ridiculous. Unless one has *first* learned to speak Bahasa Indonesia, there is no way that one will be able to read the above Indonesian sentence.

Language plays a vital role in reading. Its role in reading can be compared to the role of running in the game of soccer or ice-skating in the game of ice hockey. One cannot play soccer if one cannot run, and one cannot play ice hockey if one cannot skate. One cannot read a book in a language unless one knows that particular language. If a child's knowledge of English is poor, then his reading will also be poor. This means that the cause of a reading problem can go even deeper than merely that the foundational skills of reading have not been adequately mastered.

If a child's grasp of the English language is inadequate, the only way through which his reading could be improved, would be by not only teaching the skills foundational to reading, but by also improving his command of English. Without effectively working at improving his English, the reading ability of the child will *not* improve. Let us refer to this kind of problem as a "language problem." Comprehensive reviews of the evidence that links reading problems and language problems have been extensively presented in the literature. The following are just a few examples:

- A study in 1970 of Doctor Renate Valtin of Germany, based on hundred pairs of dyslexic and normal children, found indications of backwardness in speech development and a greater frequency of speech disturbances among dyslexics than among normal children.[19]
- According to Doctor Beve Hornsby it has been stated that about 60 percent of dyslexics were late talkers.[20]
- According to Janet Lerner, "language problems of one form or another are the underlying basis for many learning disabilities. Oral language disorders include poor phonological awareness, delayed speech, disorders of grammar or syntax, deficiencies in vocabulary acquisition, and poor understanding of oral language."[21]

Preschool children suffering temporary deafness over a period of time due to infections of the ear, or children, who have been diagnosed as hard of hearing at a late stage, will often have a language problem. However, the most common indication of a language problem is that the child started talking late, or is *language delayed*,[22] as this problem is referred to in the literature.

In most cases, a baby should be able to understand simple words and commands from the age of nine months. From around a year, he should start saying his first words. From about two years, he should be able to use simple phrases, and by three he should be able to use full sentences. By four, he should be fully able to talk, although he may still make grammatical errors.

By five, he should have acquired basic language.

If a child talks immaturely, or still makes unexpected grammatical errors in his speech when he is five years old, this should alert the parents to probable later reading problems. The parents should immediately take steps to improve the child's language. Even when a child is older already, but has a history of late talking, the parents should also follow the advice given in part two of this book to improve the child's language. The method that will be explained has proved to be extremely effective, but it will also be explained to the reader how and why it works.

Let us consider how a child learns language. Remember that it was explained that there is nothing that any human being can do which he has not learned to do. This is especially true of language. One very often encounters the expression "language development" when referring to the child's acquisition of language. By this expression it is often intended to imply that the child's acquisition of language is an automatic process.

This is a completely misguided idea. Language development should not imply that it is an innate and "natural process" or that the child's knowledge of language grows by itself as the child's physical body grows. In fact, his body will also not grow if the child is not fed regularly. Even physical growth then, does not happen by itself.

Parents should start talking to their little baby from the day he is born. Some mothers are by nature quiet and reserved. Others have the unfortunate idea that it is foolish to talk to their babies, knowing that they do not understand. The mother, who does not talk continually while feeding, bathing and dressing her baby, is laying the foundation for a late talker.

The baby learns language in one way only, and that is by hearing language as the parents talk and talk to it. The more a parent can talk to a child, often repeating the same words, the same phrases, the same structures over and over, the sooner the child will learn language.

An important thing to note here is that by the time a baby is about nine months old, as was mentioned above, he should be able to understand simple words and commands. He may perhaps also be able to say a few simple words already. Invariably, however, one finds that the baby understands much more than he is able to say. In fact, this remains so of any person throughout his life. One is always able to understand more of any language, even one's mother tongue, than one is able to use in active speech. This is even more so of any second or third languages that a person is able to speak.

This shows that we have two more or less separate masses of language knowledge, our *passive* knowledge (also called receptive language) on one hand, and our *active* (expressive language) on the other. When we listen or read, we make use of our passive vocabulary, and when we speak or write, of our active vocabulary. An important thing to note here is that the child's passive vocabulary came into being through constant repetition of words, phrases or structures. Once a word, phrase or structure has been repeated often enough, it also becomes part of the baby's active vocabulary. As stated by Dr. Beve Hornsby, a child who is just beginning to talk must hear a word about 500 times before it will become part of his active vocabulary.[23] Long before that it will already form part of his passive vocabulary.

This shows that the active vocabulary can only be improved *via* the passive. The stratified nature of learning therefore also applies here.

Solving Dyslexia

It was already stated in the first chapter that the key to the solution of most problems is that one must know what *causes* the problem. Consider again the people who died of pellagra during the early part of the twentieth century. Dr. Goldberger discovered that the disease was caused by a diet deficiency. However, by the time of his death in 1929, he still hadn't discovered precisely what was missing from the diets of pellagrins. During the next decade, Conrad A. Elevjhem learned that a deficiency of nicotinic acid, better known as B vitamin niacin or vitamin B3, resulted in canine black tongue disease. In studies conducted in Alabama and Cincinnati, Dr. Tom Spies found that nicotinic acid cured human pellagrins as well. Tulane University scientists discovered that the amino acid tryptophan was a precursor to niacin. When tryptophan was added to commercial foods such as bread to "fortify" them, it prevented the scourge of the South. Thanks to all these efforts that resulted in knowledge of the *cause* of pellagra, one doesn't hear about it any more, except for infrequent occurrences during times of famine and displacement.[24]

Problems with reading, or dyslexia, are at present a very common problem in most parts of the world. The reason for this is simply that the cause of dyslexia has so far remained a mystery. The only way in which the seemingly inexorable downward spiral in reading ability could be reversed, would be if the cause of dyslexia could be discovered.

From the explanation in this chapter and in the previous one, the reader should not find it too hard to come to the logical conclusion that the *cause* of dyslexia is none other than that the foundational skills of reading and spelling—and often language as well—have not been automatized. These foundational skills of reading, as all other human abilities or skills, are not dormant. They need to be taught, and only by building a "pyramid of repetition," can they be taught successfully. This implies not only that dyslexia can be "fixed" and "cured," but also that it can be *prevented*. If all educators—parents and teachers—take this message to heart, we have no doubt that dyslexia, like pellagra, will soon be eradicated.

Notes:

1. Mursell, J. L., *Successful Teaching* (2nd ed.), (New York: McGraw-Hill Book Company, Inc., 1954), 210-211.
2. Lerner, J., *Learning Disabilities. Theories, Diagnosis, and Teaching Strategies* (4th ed.), (Boston: Houghton Mifflin Company, 1988), 211.
3. Sanderson, I. T., *Investigating the Unexplained: A Compendium of Disquieting Mysteries of the Natural World* (Englewood Cliffs: Prentice Hall, Inc., 1972).
4. Dworetzky, J. P., *Introduction to Child Development* (St. Paul: West Publishing Company, 1981), 183.
5. Turnbull, C. M., "Some observations regarding the experiences and behavior of the Bambuti Pygmies," *American Journal of Psychology,* 1961, vol. 74, 304-308.
6. Hampshire, S., *Every Letter Counts. Winning in Life Despite Dyslexia* (London: Corgi Books, 1991), 309.
7. Serfontein, G., *The Hidden Handicap* (Sydney: Simon & Schuster, 1990), 179.
8. Yap, R L., & Van der Leij, A., "Testing the automatization deficit hypothesis of dyslexia via a dual-task paradigm," *Journal of Learning Disabilities*, 1 December 1994, vol. 27, 660.
9. Harris, K. R., Graham, S., & Pressley, M., "Cognitive-behavioral approaches in reading and written language: Developing self-regulated learners," in N. N. Singh & I. L. Beale (eds.), *Learning Disabilities: Nature, Theory, and Treatment* (New York: Springer-Verlag, 1992), 423.
10. Ibid., 424.
11. Scruggs, T. E., & Mastropieri, M. A., "Mnemonic instruction for students with learning disabilities: What it is and what is does," *Learning Disability Quarterly*, 1990, vol. 13, 271-280.
12. Lyman, D. E., *Making the Words Stand Still* (Boston: Houghton Mifflin Company, 1986), 124.

13. Scruggs & Mastropieri, "Mnemonic instruction for students with learning disabilities."
14. Yates, F., *The Art of Memory* (Chicago: University of Chicago Press, 1966), cited in Scruggs & Mastropieri, "Mnemonic instruction for students with learning disabilities."
15. Scruggs & Mastropieri, "Mnemonic instruction for students with learning disabilities."
16. Kavale, K. A., & Forness, S. R., *The Science of Learning Disabilities* (San Diego: College Hill Press, 1985).
17. Spindler, T., & Ward, A., *Knowabout Soccer* (Hampshire: The Automobile Association, 1990), 48.
18. Scruggs & Mastropieri, "Mnemonic instruction for students with learning disabilities."
19. Vatlin, R., *Legasthenie—Theorien und Untersuchungen* (3rd ed.), (Weinheim: Beltz, 1974), cited in R. Valtin, "Dyslexia: Deficit in reading or deficit in research?" *Reading Research Quarterly*, 1978-1979, no. 2.
20. Hornsby, B., *Overcoming Dyslexia* (Johannesburg: Juta and Company Ltd., 1984), 32.
21. Lerner, *Learning Disabilities*, 320.
22. Ibid., 322.
23. Hornsby, *Overcoming Dyslexia*, 43.
24. Kraut, A., "Dr. Joseph Goldberger and the war on pellagra," website address: www.nih.gov/od/museum/exhibits/goldberger/full-text.html, 1996.

10.

"Learning Disabilities" in Perspective

> To be a possible theory, it must be reconcilable with many facts; to be a probable theory, it must be reconcilable with many more; to be a certain and proven theory, it must be reconcilable with ALL the facts.[1] — Williams

In the sixth chapter it was stated that there are certain aspects regarding "learning disabilities" that are difficult to explain if one adheres to a medical frame of reference. The first of these is that the incidence of learning disabilities is on the increase. How is it to be explained that more and more children are born with mysterious brain problems? If, on the other hand, one accepts the ideas expressed on the foundational skills of reading, a completely logical explanation becomes available—that is, if one simultaneously keeps in mind the effect of certain changes in our society.

Children usually learn to read and write during the first year in school. This implies that the skills that are basic to the reading act must have been mastered *before* school. If a child is unable to learn to read, then it means that not enough was done while he was preschool to enable him to master the required skills, or to acquire sufficient mastery of them.

It is important to bear in mind that there are two modes of learning, viz. *incidental* and *intentional* learning. Incidental learning implies that learning occurs without any prior intention to learn. For example, if a person bumps his head against an object, he would learn to be more careful the next time he walks past that object. Intentional learning, on the other hand, means that purposeful learning is taking place.

A few decades ago, everyday life circumstances were such that more opportunities were provided by the daily environment so that preschool children could, to a great extent, master the foundational skills of reading in an incidental manner. Since then, drastic changes have occurred in our life circumstances. As a result of these changes, the opportunities for mastering these skills incidentally have gradually decreased.

Today, children and their families are bombarded by a great many more demands on their time and attention. In the 1950s there were but a handful of activities available for children. Today, a profusion of options compete for the child's attention, for example television, video games, computer games, et cetera. This has certainly had a great influence—not necessarily a good one—on the intellectual development of children.

Although television was available in the 1950s, it was a far cry from the multi-channel cable and satellite dish offerings of today, which has definitely changed family life. There has been a drastic decline in interpersonal communication between family members. A child can easily isolate himself by sitting in front of the television, while the rest of the family "forgets" about him. In 1951 Maccoby found that television drastically shortened children's play time, and that children were less willing to assist in household chores.[2] Four decades later, the average American child's weekly diet of TV amounted to twenty-seven hours, consisting of prime time, soap operas, sports, cartoons, et cetera. And this figure is minimal; one out of every four children view at least forty hours of television per week.[3] The problem is that TV cannot replace education. Even the so-called educational programs, researchers have found, only have an impact if a parent participates and draws the child's attention to interesting aspects of the program. If the child sits on his own, he becomes a mere passive spectator.[4]

The present-day toys attest to the great technological advances that have been made. The more technologically advanced the toy, the less is left to the imagination of the child, with the result that there are fewer opportunities for the development of the child's cognitive abilities. Contrary to the opinion of most people, children who had to make their own toys were better off than children who are addicted to video and computer games.

Other important changes include urbanization, forcing many children to grow up in restricted, less stimulating environments—think of the Pygmies—and the decline in time parents have available to spend with their children. Today, a larger number of mothers are working than was the case a few decades ago. This has led to fewer opportunities for communication between mother and child. Many fathers have also, in our modern world, become so involved in the rat race, that they have withdrawn from the education of their children, leaving whatever involvement is still left between parents and children to their spouses. Leete-Guy and Schor have found that the annual hours of work of employed Americans have increased markedly—by approximately 140 hours, or more than an additional three weeks—since 1969. This includes both hours on the job and time spent working at home. As a result, leisure, or free time—and of course time parents spend with their children—has declined.[5]

Then how can this problem be solved? Should we return to the old system? Should all mothers quit their jobs, all television sets be banished from our homes and should we all move back to rural areas? That would be a rather absurd idea. What needs to be done, however, is that parents must *compensate* for things that were previously provided by the everyday environment. Because opportunities for *incidental* learning have decreased, parents must create more opportunities for *intentional* learning. Parents must especially make sure that their children receive the necessary training they need to develop the skills that form the basis of the reading act.

The second unaccountable phenomenon, from a medical point of view, is the fact that the percentage of children with "learning disabilities" varies among countries and areas. As previously stated, the incidence of reading disabilities in the 1980s was particularly low in the East Asian countries—Japan, China and Korea. It is hardly possible to attribute this fact to the idea that the brain structures of these people are better equipped than those of the Westerner, and adherents of the medical model therefore maintain that this phenomenon should be attributed to the difference in writing systems between the East Asians and Westerners. Let us investigate the Japanese written language to see if that may be true.

Between 25 and 35 percent of the words in Japanese texts are written in Chinese characters and are referred to as *Kanji*. However, all pronunciation and the meaning of some Kanji characters are different from that of the Chinese. Approximately 70 percent of the words in Japanese texts are written in one of two Japanese *syllabaries*. Syllabaries are writing systems where each sign represents a separate syllable. The two Japanese syllabaries together are called *Kana*, consisting of both *Hiragana* and *Katakana*. Each of the Kana syllabaries has 46 basic letters, which represents 46 different syllables. With the possible addition of other marks adding additional phonetic values, related or secondary letters can be created bringing the total to 71 syllables that can be written in either Hiragana or Katakana. The Hiragana script is used to represent words that are Japanese in origin, about 65 percent of the text. Those words written in Katakana script, about four percent of the text, are loan words from European languages. The two Kana syllabaries along with a core of 1,850 Kanji ideographs borrowed from Chinese make up the daily reading demand in Japan. The remaining one percent of textual material in Japanese is written in Arabic numerals and Roman letters or *Romanji*.[6]

When reading is introduced to children in Japan, the Kana syllabaries are generally introduced before Kanji characters.[7] At the end of nine years of compulsory schooling, children have learned the 1,850 Kanji characters used in Japanese.[8]

One can perhaps argue that the Kanji ideographs, where each symbol represents a thing or an idea rather than a sound, are easier than our Latin alphabet. However, the Kana syllabaries, like our alphabet, use symbols to represent sounds,[9] and it would therefore be difficult to argue that reading problems were virtually nonexistent in Japan because their written language is easier than the Latin alphabet. The difference in incidence must simply be sought in *cultural differences*. The Japanese communities were more traditional. Children grew up in an environment that put a higher premium on *parental involvement,* especially in terms of the written word, than is the case in Western society. (Note that we are using the past tense in this discussion. Unfortunately, the problem of parental neglect has seemingly taken root in Japan in the 1990s, and is growing fast.[10] Unless this tide can be turned, one can expect an "explosion" of learning disabilities in the future, followed by a lowering of Japan's educational standards.)

By the time children entered first grade in Japan, only one percent of them could not recognize any Hiragana symbols. It was not unusual for four-year-olds to read books entirely in Hiragana. More than 93 percent of Japanese parents read to their children *regularly* by the time their children were four years old. This emphasis on parent reading began as a nationwide movement after World War II. There was a wide variety of books and magazines available for preschool children that were bought by parents on a regular basis. One preschool magazine sold more than a million copies per year, and 95 percent of two-year-olds owned a book. Reading readiness was attained by 4½ years of age.[11]

There was a high degree of parent involvement with children's education in Japan. Children were required to attend school six days a week. Homework assignments were given not only every day but also on weekends, holidays, and over summer vacations. Sakamoto reported that even though the children hated it, parents supported this practice and encouraged their children to complete their homework.[12]

Surprisingly—or maybe not surprisingly—in Japan "excessive reading," as opposed to lack of interest in reading, was a far more widely recognized problem.[13]

Parental involvement in Japan certainly paid off. While only 75 percent of U.S. high school students graduated in the 1980s, Japan succeeded in leading fully 91 percent of their students through a much more challenging school curriculum.[14] According to Thomas Rohlen, the Japanese high school diploma was arguably the equivalent of a U.S.A. bachelor's degree. "I found this conclusion hard to believe at first," he wrote. "But the more I looked at the fundamental facts, the more convinced I became that the majority of high school graduates in Japan would compare well with our university graduates in terms of basic knowledge in all fields and in mathematics and in science skills."[15] And the last sobering piece of news is that Japan averaged forty-one students per class, compared to twenty-six for the United States,[16] and the over-all per-pupil expenditure in Japan was 50 percent less than in the U.S.A.[17]

But to those who still insist that the difference in writing systems, and not the high degree of parental involvement, explains the low incidence of dyslexia in the East Asian countries, the research of Barbara Schneider and Yongsook Lee (1990) might be an eye-opener. They compared the academic performance of East Asian American school students to that of Anglo American students (whites whose ancestors immigrated from Western or Northern Europe). Excluded from both groups were students in special classes who had learning disabilities or physical handicaps. Both groups were compared as to their ability in the Latin alphabet.

Data collected indicated that East Asian academic performance on achievement tests and report card grades was higher than that of the Anglo students in all areas, with the exception of language skills. Differences in language performance could be attributed to the fact that many of the East Asian students were at a disadvantage because their parents did not speak English.

Schneider and Lee found only cultural differences—all related to *parental involvement*—to explain the East Asian Americans being "superior" to the Anglo Americans. For example, 22 out of 37 of the East Asian parents reported that they had spent time teaching their children reading, writing, and simple arithmetic skills before entering kindergarten. Only 4 out of 25 Anglo parents indicated that they had engaged in similar activities. East Asian parents closely monitored and controlled their children's use of time on academic and social pursuits and they placed high value on education. "There is nothing without education," one parent remarked. "Education is more important than money."[18]

Third, if one attempts to explain learning disabilities from a constitutional perspective, it is very difficult to understand why this "ailment" is encountered more often among boys than girls. (How lucky for the female sex to have better developed brain structures than their male counterparts!) But if one takes certain differences between the two sexes into account, this riddle can easily be solved.

As formerly indicated, the preschool phase is the most important time for the development of the skills foundational to reading. When left to themselves, preschool boys and girls involve themselves in different activities. Little girls usually keep themselves busy with activities that are more conducive to the acquisition of these foundational skills than the activities that boys prefer. When left on their own, little boys prefer activities that promote gross motor development. As a mother of two sons, Susan (coauthor) can testify to this. The solution is that the parents must intervene, and intentionally and on a regular basis involve the preschool boy in activities that exercise the foundational skills of reading.

If one accepts the theory expounded in this book, even the matter of heredity can be explained. The fact that learning disabilities seem to run in families does not necessarily imply that it is genetically determined. If the idea of the foundational skills of reading is accepted, an alternative possibility presents itself. Seeing that these skills must be *taught*, it is impossible for a dyslexic parent to teach his child the skills which underlie the reading act—simply because he has not mastered them himself. It is equally impossible for a non-French speaking parent to teach his child to speak French!

Lastly, it must be added that schools are all but blameless for the increase in learning disabilities. If the educational system had been effective, many of the "at risk" children could have been saved. Unfortunately, for the greater part, it is no longer effective. One of the reasons, as discussed in a previous chapter, is that repetition no longer forms the backbone of the educational system.

A further factor, that may have contributed to the worldwide downward trend in educational standards, may have been a general attitude of sloppiness and carelessness that has crept into education. Lean and Eaton, in their book *Education or Catastrophe?* state:

> To the elder educational statesman of today, brought up many years ago in a rigorous system emphasizing high standards and an uncompromising striving for excellence, the current scene in the United States gives little comfort and much cause for alarm. On all sides they see the gradual disappearance of the once common teacher-scholar at all levels of schooling, the debasement of quality, the "anything goes" and "do your own thing" philosophy. Carelessness and sloppiness seem to pervade the academic world from bottom to top, reflecting an undeniable trend in society as a whole.[19]

These are harsh words, and tragically they may be true in many cases. We, however, are convinced that there are many caring teachers, who would make a difference in the lives of children, if only they knew how.

By turning the page, they will learn how. . . .

Notes:

1. Williams, W. A., *The Evolution of Man Scientifically Disproved* (Camden, New Jersey: Author's publication, 1928).
2. Maccoby, E. E., "Television: Its impact on school children," *Public Opinion Quarterly,* 1951, vol. 15, 421-444.
3. Lean, A. E., & Eaton, W. E., *Education or Catastrophe?* (Wolfeboro: Longwood Academic, 1990), 78.
4. Friedrich, L. K., & Stein, A. H., "Aggressive and prosocial television programs and the natural behavior of pre-school children," *Monographs of the Society for Research in Child Development,* 1973, vol. 38(4), serial no. 151.
5. Leete-Guy, L., & Schor, J. B., *The Great American Time Squeeze: Trends in Work and Leisure, 1969-1989,* 1992, cited in D. P. Hallahan, "Some thoughts on why the prevalence of learning disabilities has increased," *Journal of Learning Disabilities,* 1992, vol. 25(8), 523-528.
6. Sakamoto, T., "Preschool reading in Japan," *The Reading Teacher,* 1975, vol. 29(3), 240-

244; Sakamoto, T., "Writing systems in Japan," in J. E. Merritt (ed.), *New Horizons in Reading* (Newark, Del.: International Reading Association, 1976), 244-249; Taylor, I., "Writing systems and reading: Papers in language use and language function (no. 3)," Scarborough College, University of Toronto, Ontario, April 1978; all sources cited in E. M. Sheridan, "Reading disabilities: Can we blame the written language?" *Journal of Learning Disabilities*, 1983, vol. 16(2), 81-86.

7. Taylor, "Writing systems and reading," cited in Sheridan, "Reading disabilities: Can we blame the written language?"

8. Sakamoto, "Preschool reading in Japan," cited in Sheridan, "Reading disabilities: Can we blame the written language?"

9. Bloom, F. E., & Lazerson, A., *Brain, Mind, and Behavior* (2nd ed.), (New York: W. H. Freeman and Company, 1985), 287.

10. Larimer, T., et al., "Young Japan: From we to me with its in-your-face style and endless thirst for thrills, Japan's new generation wants to transform the nation," *Time*, 3 May 1999.

11. Namekawa, M., "Children's literature and reading," in J. E. Merritt (ed.), *New Horizons in Reading* (Newark, Del.: International Reading Association, 1976); Sakamoto, "Preschool reading in Japan"; Sakamoto, T., "Beginning reading in Japan," in L. Ollila (ed.), *Beginning Reading Instruction in Different Countries* (Newark, Del.: International Reading Association, 1981), 16-25; Sakamoto, T., & Makita, K., "Japan," in J. Downing (ed.), *Comparative Reading* (New York: MacMillan Company, 1973), 440-465; all sources cited in Sheridan, "Reading disabilities: Can we blame the written language?"

12. Sakamoto, "Writing systems in Japan," cited in Sheridan, "Reading disabilities: Can we blame the written language?"

13. Sakamoto & Makita, "Japan," cited in Sheridan, "Reading disabilities: Can we blame the written language?"

14. Honig, B., *Last Chance for Our Children. How You Can Help Save Our Schools* (New York: Addison-Wesley Publishing Company, Inc., 1987), 30.

15. Rohlen, T. P., *Japan's High Schools* (Berkeley: University of California Press, 1983).

16. McKnight, C. C., et al., *The Underachieving Curriculum*, 56-57, cited in T. Sowell, *Inside American Education* (New York: The Free Press, 1993), 12.

17. Perlman, L. J., Hudson Institution Briefing Paper, May 1990, no. 120, cited in Sowell, *Inside American Education*, 12.

18. Schneider, B., & Lee, Y., "A model for academic success: The school and home environment of East Asian students," *Anthropology & Education Quarterly*, 1990, vol. 21, 358-377.

19. Lean & Eaton, *Education or Catastrophe?* 19.

Part Two

Practice

Preface to Part Two

Audiblox opens up new vistas for all those with learning and reading problems. It is based on *scientific* learning and reading principles that have been researched over a period of years by Dr. Jan Strydom. This explains why *Audiblox* is being employed so successfully in solving learning and reading problems.

It provides answers to many of the riddles that have been plaguing experts on the subject of learning and reading problems. Scientists from many fields of enquiry would do well to take note of Dr. Strydom's work and should put *Audiblox* to the test, so that they may also discover its effectiveness. Educationists, educational authorities and teachers especially should take the new prospects made available by *Audiblox* very seriously. It offers many possibilities of application in education, because it improves reading and spelling ability, sharpens concentration, develops perception and memory, and enhances logical thinking. It can put innumerable pupils, at present experiencing failure at school, on the road to successful learning.

For the first time there is real hope in the battle against learning and reading problems, not only inside the classroom, but also outside. Dr. Strydom must be congratulated on a revolutionary, brilliant, but at the same time simple and easily applicable program.

Prof. E. J. van Niekerk
University of South Africa

A large number of students are at present experiencing problems with learning. These are evidenced, for example, in a short attention span, in reading and spelling problems, in difficulties with math, in restlessness, etc.

On the causes of such problems there will probably never be complete agreement, but of far greater importance is the question: what can one do to help such students?

Over the past six years I have had the privilege of getting to know Dr. Jan Strydom's *Audiblox* program. I have referred many students so that they might follow the program, both in individual and group situations. Without exception

I was impressed by the positive results that were achieved. A factor that, in my opinion, enhances the value of the program, is the fact that such positive results could be noticed in all age groups—toddlers, children, young university students and adults.

The benefits of the program also extend beyond its use merely for the solution of specific learning problems. Also to persons who wish to improve their cognitive abilities—even when no specific learning problem is present—the program has shown its undeniable value.

Dr. B. H. du Toit
Senior Student Counselor
University of Pretoria

Dr. Jan Strydom is the lifeboat we all have been waiting for. *Audiblox* holds wonderful prospects for children with learning problems. The most important rule to remember is that it depends on you, the parents. It's like going to the doctor if you have a cold. He will give you the correct medicine to take but if you don't take it, you cannot blame the doctor if you do not get better. The same with *Audiblox*.

We started on the 12th of August with both our children. By the 7th of October we had been informed that Bronwen had passed. That in a nutshell, says it all. It had taken just forty days for Bronwen to be on *Audiblox*. No mention of special class. Just a straight pass into a normal third-grade class. Charnell also benefited from the program. In the June exam she got an E for English. In her finals she got a B.

I'd like to take this opportunity to say THANK YOU to you, Dr. Strydom. For sharing your knowledge with us, the parents. Of all the angels, you are the ombudsman. You've made teachers and everybody else involved with education sit up and listen to you. There is no point in teaching remedial. You have to go back and find out just where our children have missed out. *Audiblox* does this for our children. You have made parents aware that the problem really lies within them but now they have a chance to correct their mistakes. *Audiblox* holds wonderful prospects for children. You see, God really does answer prayers.

Mrs. B. J. Horne

11.

The Key to Success
by Susan du Plessis

His IQ was 148, yet eighteen-year-old Werner Louw could hardly read. When his reading efficiency was assessed by means of an *ophthalmograph* or *eye-camera* on 9 March 1990—one of the many assessments he had undergone in his life—it was found to be equal to that of a second-grade child. This meant that his reading ability was about ten years behind his chronological age. His eyes fixated 164 times and regressed 36 times with every one hundred words of reading. His reading speed was only 107 words per minute. It is therefore quite understandable that Werner had been battling since his first year in school. He attended third grade in a remedial class for two years, after which he was placed in a school for learning-disabled children, repeating third grade for the third time. His condition was diagnosed as "minimal brain dysfunction." Although his parents went from pillar to post to try and solve his reading problem, nothing seemed to help. As he grew older, a sense of inferiority took hold and he had to receive treatment for depression. "I didn't know what to do, which way to turn. Nothing we did seemed to help his problem," his mother told a reporter.[1] It was therefore with great skepticism that the Louw parents came to see Dr. Jan Strydom, a South African educationist and philosopher, and coauthor of this book, to try yet another avenue.

In March 1990 Werner became the first client of a newly founded Center for Dyslexia. Intervention commenced a few days after his reading efficiency was assessed. Five months later, after working faithfully according to Dr. Strydom's recommendations for two half-hour sessions per day, five days per week, Werner's reading efficiency was retested. It then equaled a ninth-grade level. The number of fixations dropped to 37 and regressions to three. His reading speed was now 163 words per minute.

Six months after this second reading test, Werner's reading efficiency was tested once again and found to be equal to a second-year college level. His eyes now fixated only 37 times in one hundred words. The number of regressions, already low, remained the same. He could now read 230 words per minute. This means that, in less than one year, Werner's reading efficiency level improved by twelve years.

Needless to say, this newly found reading ability changed Werner's life. His story illustrates that ten years ago the problem of dyslexia could already be solved very adequately through a method that addresses the *cause*. Since that time, thousands of others, children and adults, have also been helped successfully to a better reading ability.

The Eye-Camera and its Application

At the time when the above-mentioned Center for Dyslexia was founded, the eye-camera was still a very popular instrument to assess reading ability. It measured the time it took a person to read a piece of text, and from this his *reading speed* per minute was calculated. The movements of the person's eyes were photographed and represented on a reading graph.

This reading graph could be analyzed to determine the number of eye *fixations* that occurred during reading. When a person reads, his eyes engage in a series of quick movements across the page with intermittent fixation pauses. The more often the eyes have to pause for fixations, the slower the reading speed will be. A dyslexic person will be inclined to pause more often, and the duration of each fixation will be longer than that of the typical reader. After this, it was possible to calculate the person's recognition span. This referred to the average number of words the person could recognize in one fixation, as well as to the average duration of such a fixation.

By analyzing the reading graph one could also determine whether any *regressions* occurred in the eye movements of the reader. A regression occurred when the eyes moved toward the left to look again at words that had been covered already. The dyslexic person is inclined to have more regressions than the normal reader.

After reading the piece of text, the person doing the test was required to answer a number of questions on the contents. This was to determine his *comprehension*, which was expressed in a percentage. Lastly, the *relative reading efficiency* could be calculated, which was expressed in year levels.

The test results of Werner are presented on the following page. The solid line represents the first reading test on 9 March 1990, the thin dashed line the retest on 5 August 1990, and the thick dashed line the second retest on 12 February 1991.

The test results of the second and third clients of the Center for Dyslexia, A. van Niekerk, a fifth-grade student, and F. Joyce, a sixth-grade student, are also presented on the following page. The solid lines represent their first reading tests on 9 March 1990, and the dashed lines their retests on 5 August 1990.

The Audiblox Story

The changes in these children's lives were brought about by a program named *Audiblox*. *Audi* is derived from "auditory," because the program—among others—enhances auditory skills, while *blox* refers to the main materials used in the program—little colored blocks.

Audiblox has a long history. Just like penicillin, X-rays, and a host of others, serendipity played a strong role in its invention. It started life as a school readiness program in the 1970s.

Dr. Jan Strydom, inventor of the *Audiblox* program, believes that the first formative years of a child's life are of the utmost importance. Therefore he spent a lot of time preparing his own children for formal school learning. However, only when the youngest one was preschool did he hit on the idea of devising a more or less formal school readiness program for her. He continues the story:

When this daughter entered school, it soon became evident that she was able to learn to read exceptionally quickly and also remarkably well. Soon after school entrance, her teacher remarked that she had never before encountered a child who was so perfectly ready for school as this little one was. From this, I concluded that the program was effective enough to justify making it available to other parents.

At first I recommended the program only to parents with preschool children. By that time I had already completed a master's degree in education, and was often consulted by parents about their children's learning problems—mostly reading problems—but I never thought of using *Audiblox* in such cases.

NAME: Werner Louw

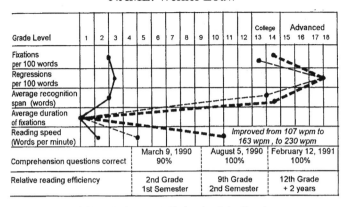

Grade Level	1	2	3	4	5	6	7	8	9	10	11	12	College 13 14	Advanced 15 16 17 18

Fixations per 100 words

Regressions per 100 words

Average recognition span (words)

Average duration of fixations

Reading speed (Words per minute) — *Improved from 107 wpm to 163 wpm, to 230 wpm*

Comprehension questions correct	March 9, 1990 90%	August 5, 1990 100%	February 12, 1991 100%
Relative reading efficiency	2nd Grade 1st Semester	9th Grade 2nd Semester	12th Grade + 2 years

NAME: A. van Niekerk, 5th Grade

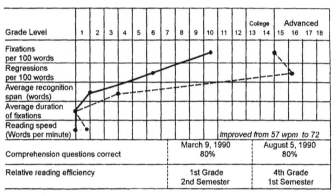

Grade Level	1	2	3	4	5	6	7	8	9	10	11	12	College 13 14	Advanced 15 16 17 18

Fixations per 100 words

Regressions per 100 words

Average recognition span (words)

Average duration of fixations

Reading speed (Words per minute) — *Improved from 57 wpm to 72*

Comprehension questions correct	March 9, 1990 80%	August 5, 1990 80%
Relative reading efficiency	1st Grade 2nd Semester	4th Grade 1st Semester

NAME: F. Joyce, 6th Grade

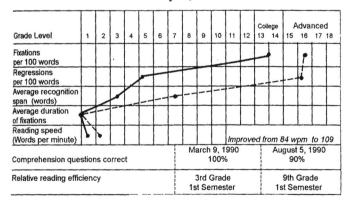

Grade Level	1	2	3	4	5	6	7	8	9	10	11	12	College 13 14	Advanced 15 16 17 18

Fixations per 100 words

Regressions per 100 words

Average recognition span (words)

Average duration of fixations

Reading speed (Words per minute) — *Improved from 84 wpm to 109*

Comprehension questions correct	March 9, 1990 100%	August 5, 1990 90%
Relative reading efficiency	3rd Grade 1st Semester	9th Grade 1st Semester

Late in September 1980 parents approached me about their son who had been diagnosed as "learning disabled." The boy was then in a third-grade remedial class, and had already been referred to a special school for the following year. While interviewing the parents, the idea occurred to me to try the *Audiblox* program with the boy. I told the parents that it would be purely an experiment, because I had never before tried it with children with learning difficulties.

I don't know who was the most surprised by the outcome of the experiment—the parents or me. Within a mere two months it became quite evident that it would be a grave error to allow this boy to go to a special school. This became apparent not only to his parents and to me, but also to the boy's teacher. She brought this to the attention of the principal of the school, who then called in the school psychologist. After reassessment, it was decided not to send the boy to a special school, but to promote him to the next class the following year.

Later, this boy became a top achiever with marks usually above eighty percent and often above ninety percent. I remember the year he was in seventh grade his father phoned me one evening early in December. They had just returned from the school where their son had been awarded the prize for the top achiever in the school.

This event convinced him that there were far greater possibilities in the *Audiblox* program than he had imagined. Thereafter he started using the program more and more for children with learning difficulties, mostly with resounding success. At first, he used it only for smaller children, but as his confidence grew, he later started to use it for elementary school children in the senior classes, still later for high school children, and still later for adults. In 1990 a Center for Dyslexia was founded to deal specifically with reading, spelling and writing difficulties.

Eventually, he adapted his program so that it could also be used in a classroom situation. In this way, not only one at a time, but a whole class full of children could simultaneously benefit from the program. One of the first schools to use the program on a large scale was a school in Johannesburg. Every class in the school had one *Audiblox* period per day. Mr. Jan Venter, who has in the meantime retired, was at the time the principal of the school. He reported that, before he introduced *Audiblox* in his school, he used to require help from the school psychological services for up to 15 percent of his approximately 400 pupils. After introducing this program, the teachers were able to deal with all but one or two who were in need of individual tutoring.[2] Many other mainstream schools have since also introduced this method with great success. Most report satisfactory results if it is implemented in their first-grade *or* first-grade and second-grade classes only. This seems sufficient to build a firm foundation for the ensuing school years.

Many years after its first inception, with more research and many adjustments to the program, it could also be implemented with great effect for the mentally handicapped and *truly* brain damaged.

For many years after its initial publication, one question had been plaguing Dr. Strydom. *Why* does a program that he devised for *school readiness* achieve such phenomenal results when used for children with *learning difficulties*? "I always believed that any practice should be supported by a sound theory," he said. "With *Audiblox* I had accidentally stumbled upon a practical method that could achieve wonderful results when used for learning-disabled children, but I had no theoretical explanation for the success of the program. Why was it possible with such a simple program to achieve what learning disabilities experts throughout the whole world had asserted to be impossible—to cure a learning disability? What in *Audiblox* made it possible to help learning-disabled children to become at least normal, often very good, and sometimes even top achievers at school?"

After an intensive study over many years of the literature on a variety of subjects, including learning and learning disabilities, studying them from as many angles as possible, the answer to this riddle gradually started dawning upon him. This answer is given in part one of this book.

The more he learned about theoretical considerations, the more it became possible to further improve the practical program. Part two consists of the eleventh revised edition of the *Audiblox* program for individual use, which has been dubbed *Audiblox 2000*. Note that it is not exclusively for dyslexia. It can also be used to improve the learning and reading abilities of schoolchildren who have no problems at all. A program for preschool children, intended to *prevent* learning and reading difficulties, is provided in the last chapter.

Please note that I take no credit for the practical side of *Audiblox*. My contribution is only theoretical in nature, and my coauthorship thus ends with this chapter.

I have no doubt that parents and teachers will derive great pleasure from the program. Over the years, there have been thousands who have done just that. A few of these cases are presented below.

It Certainly Brings Results

Terry-André E. had had remedial lessons for three years for his reading problem. "I have taught him to cope with the work but I have not been able to teach him to read. His reading has always been a serious problem and he has been diagnosed as dyslexic," wrote Jennie van Zyl, Terry-André's remedial teacher.

In the mid-year of fourth grade Terry-André's reading ability was, according to Mrs. van Zyl, like that of a first-grade/second-grade child. His spelling was poor, he confused b's and d's, and found creative writing a problem. According to his class teacher, Mrs. Leslie, he was very untidy, always in a hurry, happy with second best and just generally not coping at all. Because the children laughed at his efforts, reading in front of the class caused him great embarrassment.

Terry-André started on *Audiblox* in the third term of fourth grade, a few weeks before the examination. He and Mrs. van Zyl spent half-hour, five days per week, on the program. He nevertheless failed third term with an aggregate of 54 percent.

Rapid improvement was noted during the fourth term. By the end of the school year Terry-André was no longer reversing letters. "The other day," Mrs. van Zyl reported, "he picked up a book and I was amazed to hear him actually reading without any stammering, hesitation or repetitions. It was the first time he had ever managed without being taught the words first. Now, whenever there is any spare time, he asks if we can read." His class teacher reported, "He has settled down, completes all his tasks to the best of his ability and takes pride in his work. He is also able to read aloud in from of the class without any of the problems which had caused him such embarrassment before."

Terry-André passed fourth grade with an aggregate of 66 percent.

Three months later Mrs. van Zyl sent in a report once more: "It gives me great joy to listen to him and see his incredible progress. Thank you for your program. It certainly brings results."

An example of Terry-Andre's schoolwork just before he started on *Audiblox,* and another example after six months, are presented on the following page.

my sisters went to the S.A. champenchip for croaty. My two sisters left erly this morning and they went with a croaty traner and my mother and my dad said good and we will hold they thums

champion ship	championship
karaii	karaii
carly	early
trainer	traner
thumbs	thumb

whinter is the time for hanting my dad and I and other hanters go hanting the best place to sheoot it is in the hed and in the sholder and when you have and you ma biltong it is the nisht time for hanting

hunting	hunting
nice	nice
shoulder	shoulder
head	head

An example of Terry-Andre's schoolwork just before he started on Audiblox.

Experiment 1

Aim: To prove that there is air in water.

Apparatus: syringe; water and beaker

Method: I drew water into the syringe until it was one third full. I closd the opening and drew the plunger further out. I then let the plunger go.

Result: Air bubbles appeared in the syringe when I drew out the plunger. When I let go of the plunger it moved back and the bubbles went away.

Conclusion: There is air in water.

The striking improvement in Terry-Andre's schoolwork after only six months.

It's Perseverance That Counts

Before embarking on the *Audiblox* program, parents often wonder how they will be able to motivate their child to do the daily exercises. One usually finds, however, that children enjoy the program. After about six weeks, after the novelty has worn off, some children become stubborn and resistant. In such a situation the parent must remember that the program was not devised to entertain the child, but to help him overcome his learning problem. It is the parent's duty to ensure that continuity is maintained. After a further six weeks to two months, most children regain their initial enthusiasm for the program.

Mark M. was one of the children who did not always enjoy doing *Audiblox*. Yet his mother was adamant that they should continue, and their perseverance was greatly rewarded.

During Mark's first school year, it became evident that he had serious scholastic difficulties. He experienced great problems with reading, spelling, phonics and creative writing. His concentration was poor, as well as his memory. His work tempo was slow and his handwriting untidy. He was very shy and reserved, with no confidence to express himself in front of others. He didn't enjoy school.

During Mark's first year in second grade he received remedial help. Two months before the end of the school year, his parents were not satisfied with his progress and started Mark on *Audiblox*. As is sometimes the case, progress in the initial stages was painfully slow and, according to his mother, often discouraging. Mark failed second grade.

With much perseverance, noticeable improvement started showing the following year. Mark's mother reported that his reading became more fluent and correct, and his spelling and creative writing improved remarkably. His handwriting and neatness improved to the extent that he received an award at year-end ceremonies. According to his teacher, "Mark has made the best progress of any of the pupils I had repeating second grade in my class."

The improvement in Mark's school report says it all:

	TERM 4: 2ND GRADE	TERM 4: 2ND GRADE (REPEAT)
ENGLISH		
Oral	B	A
Reading	D	B+

155

Phonics	D	B+
Creative writing	D	B+
SECOND LANGUAGE	C	B+
MATHEMATICS	C+	B+
HANDWRITING	C+	A

For Mark's mother, his most delightful improvement was his self-confidence. Once a boy without confidence, he has now played one of the leading roles in his school's second-grade concert. He came second in the Speech and Drama Contest and was asked to give his speech again at year-end ceremonies in front of a large audience.

An example of Mark's schoolwork just after he started on *Audiblox*, and another example after fifteen months, are presented on the following page.

A New Lease on Life

One factor that can influence the success of the *Audiblox* program, is an emotional problem. A child who is emotionally unstable, and especially one who has a behavior problem, will often not benefit from *Audiblox* until such problems have been addressed. In many cases, however, emotional problems are brought about by the fact that the child has already experienced so many intellectual failures that he believes himself to be inferior to other children. By helping the child to improve his reading and learning skills, and thereby to start experiencing success, such emotional problems are frequently alleviated. This is what happened to Allan R.

Allan started his first school year, like most other children, with eagerness and enthusiasm. His enthusiasm, however, was short-lived, because he soon discovered that he could not learn to read and write like most of the other children.

At the beginning of second grade, his parents were informed that Allan would have to attend two remedial sessions per week at the school. A few months later the school arranged for an appointment for Allan at the Child Guidance Clinic. The psychologist, who tested him, came to the conclusion that Allan was behind in both reading and spelling and the remedial classes at

My News

On friday mt chirstian
came to sleap at my hows
that mt cras a stam ant
it wark us all upe
then we had sum coklet
ther I went to slep the
nesd day I got a dall later
we went to Monganc we
went for a long wall wen
we wer ver ey hot sow
we swam then we swang
on a monkey rowp yoy holl
arowp and you fall on a big
net. then we had sm mor
fun in the pool with big
trator toups. we had a dry
then we went home

A copy of Mark's schoolwork during his first year in second grade, just after he started on Audiblox.

My news
Mini-cricket was OK this
week. After cricket we
went to the library. Later
in the afternoon my dad
and I painted our garage
door. We also had a swim.
We had great fun playing
with our big tractor
tubes in the water.
I am working on my
picture for the Audi-Blox
competition. I can win
R100 if my picture gets
chosen.

Mark's work during his second year in second grade, 15 months after starting to do Audiblox.

the school continued as before. In spite of this help, Allan continued falling further and further behind.

Allan's third-grade teacher recommended that he should be taken to an occupational therapist. The therapist found nothing wrong with Allan and said that therapy would not help him. Allan became more and more uncertain of himself, was sometimes very emotional and started hating school.

In fourth grade, because there was still no progress, his teacher asked his parents to take Allan to a neurologist. After an EEG was done, the doctor prescribed medication. Two years later his parents stopped the medication, because they still did not notice any improvement in either Allan's schoolwork or his emotional condition. His work tempo was painfully slow, and he complained that he could not concentrate on his schoolwork.

In the fifth month of sixth grade Allan's mother started with *Audiblox*. The improvement in Allan's school report, within seven months, explains why she writes that he is a "different person." (Note that intervention commenced one month before the exam of the second term):

	TERM 1	TERM 2	TERM 3	TERM 4
First Language	38%	36%	53%	53%
Second Language	41%	44%	49%	57%
Mathematics	43%	45%	45%	55%
Geography	50%	26%	63%	65%
History	36%	43%	68%	83%
General Science	66%	66%	76%	82%
Health Education	55%	95%	65%	95%
Writing	60%	50%	40%	40%
Crafts	63%	70%	66%	70%
Average of pupil	45.5%	45.6%	56.1%	63.1%
Average of grade	57.6%	56.8%	58.7%	59.5%

Allan's brother, who did ninth grade in a technical high school, also did *Audiblox*. His school marks also improved substantially. His average for the first term was 47.1 percent. He scored 19 percent for math. His average for the last term was 57.2 percent, and he scored 64 percent for math.

From Underachiever to Top of the Class

No human being likes to be branded as a failure. The child with a learning problem very often experiences failure, and this can have a very adverse effect on his self-image and thereby on his quality of life.

A child's self-image is based mainly on his interpretation of what other people think of him. No matter how much a parent tells a child he is wonderful, if the child senses insincerity or feels himself to be clumsy or incompetent, he will see himself as less worthy.

One of the clearest indications of what other people think of him, is the child's school report. There he sees in black on white what his teacher thinks of him. No amount of reasoning will change the child's interpretation of this.

In our modern world academic achievement has become very important. The school report therefore plays a major role in determining the quality of life that the child enjoys.

Any form of help that is offered to the child must at least lead to an improvement in the child's quality of life by being reflected in the school report. If it does not, it is merely a waste of time, as young Ruaan V. could testify.

Ruaan, now one of *Audiblox's* many success stories, once struggled to read a sentence in even the simplest book.

After consulting countless speech therapists, occupational therapists and having his eyes tested, his parents could still not pinpoint the nature of young Ruaan's problem. And a problem it was—he was seemingly dyslexic, reversing words when he read, reading very slowly and not comprehending the material. When he had a spelling test every Friday, he would study all week and still score only about 30 percent. With Ruaan being in third grade in one of the top schools in the country, his parents were convinced that he would have to be taken to a specialist school.

As an interim measure, they decided to try the *Audiblox* program. After only four months there was a remarkable improvement in Ruaan's reading and comprehension. To his delight, he was scoring high marks even for unprepared spelling tests. Not only did his reading improve dramatically, but so did his mathematics. So much so that he was awarded the school's mathematics prize.

After eighteen months on *Audiblox*, Ruaan's problem was nonexistent and he could discontinue the program. He now had time to participate in sports—a thing that most children with learning problems have to forego because they have to spend so much time on extra study—in which he is showing great potential. Despite the many hours that he is spending on the sports field, he is now far from an underachiever, because his report cards display only A's and B's.

Notes:

1. Kelly, D., "Overcoming dyslexia," *The Citizen*, 24 April 1991, 21.
2. Bassett, H., "Dyslexia: New therapy, new hope," *Fair Lady*, 12 August 1992, 130-132.

12.

Welcome to Audiblox 2000

Before embarking on the *Audiblox 2000* program, it is important to have a sound knowledge of the theory underlying the program. A person, who does not know how the engine of a car works, will not be able to fix the car when it stops. Similarly, a person who knows nothing about learning will not be able to "fix" a "learning disability." The most important theoretical considerations are discussed in part one of this book. Please study them carefully.

Part two of this book contains a practical program, divided into four levels. Each level consists of a program of exercises that needs to be done, preferably on a daily basis (see chapter 20). These exercises are described in the subsequent chapters (chapters 13-19). Before embarking on the program, it is essential that you carefully study the relevant exercises.

In the explanations of the various exercises, for the sake of convenience, the parent or teacher is referred to as "the tutor" or "she," while the person with whom the exercises are done is referred to as "the learner," or "he."

How to Get Started

In order to follow the *Audiblox 2000* program, some teaching materials are required. You can collect and/or make these yourself. Information on how to do this is given below. Alternatively, you can order the required materials from the address given on page 169.

Blocks

You will need at least 72 blocks, equally divided in six different colors: white, black, red, yellow, green, and blue. Each block must be a *perfect cube*, about $^3/_4$ by $^3/_4$ by $^3/_4$ inch (20 X 20 X 20 mm).

Instead of collecting your own blocks, you can order an *Audiblox Learner set*. The *Learner set* is a box, containing the required blocks, the screen card (explained below), and a set of color cards. The color cards are preprinted patterns, which are required for *Pattern exercise 1: Variation 2*.

Screen

You will need a screen, which you can make from an oblong piece of cardboard of 17 by 3½ inches (430 X 90 mm). Fold the cardboard as shown in *figure 1 (at the top)*. The cardboard can stand upright and serve as a screen to shield blocks from the learner. In some of the exercises this is of great importance.

Box

You will need an oblong box to do the *Spatial exercise*, discussed in chapter 18. The box should close with a lid, as shown in *figure 1 (bottom left)*. When not in use, the blocks can be stored in the box.

Reading book

You will need a suitable reading book. Find a book in which the type set is not too small and in which the text is neither interrupted by illustrations nor pictures. It does not matter if there are full-page illustrations, but there must not be pages on which the text is interrupted by illustrations. You will need the first five chapters of this book for the reading exercises.

Alternatively, you can order the book *Rainbow Dreams* from the address on page 169. It contains a story made up of the 800 most commonly used English words. It is available in both American and British English. Word cards of chapters one to three of *Rainbow Dreams* are included.

Word cards

You will have to make a word card of *every* word that appears in chapter one of the reading book, including names and words starting with capital letters. If, for example, the word "learn" appears twice, once starting with a capital letter and once with a small letter, you will have to make a word card for both.

The words of chapter one should all be made on *yellow* cardboard. The size of the word cards should all be exactly the same, about 2^1/$_2$ by 1^1/$_4$ inches (65 X 30 mm). *See figure 1 (bottom right).*

Figure 1

Once you have completed level one of the program, as set out in chapter 20, you will have to make a word card of every *new* word that appears in chapter two of the reading book. The new words of chapter two should all be made on *white* cardboard.

Once you have completed level two of the program, as set out in chapter 20, you will have to make a word card of every *new* word that appears in chapter three of the reading book. The new words of chapter three should all be made on *blue* cardboard.

Once you have completed level three of the program, as set out in chapter 20, you will have to make a word list containing every *new* word that appears in chapter four of the reading book. Also make a word list of every *new* word that appears in chapter five of the reading book. Type the words in three columns.

Arrows chart

Take a piece of paper or cardboard of $8^1/_2$ by 11 inches (A4-size), and with a thick Koki or felt-tipped pen draw several arrows on it, as shown in *figure 2*. You can also make one on your PC. (Note that an arrows chart is not included in the *Audiblox Learner set.*)

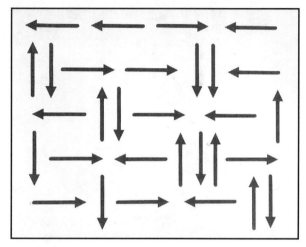

Figure 2

You will also need a clock with a second-hand, as well as two beanbags, a telephone directory, scrap paper and shoeboxes for the exercises described in chapter 17. Note that the beanbags and shoeboxes are *only* required for children in elementary school, and only from Level 2 of the program.

Video

A video, demonstrating the various *Audiblox 2000* exercises, is available from the address on page 169, and is highly recommended. It is available in both NTSC and PAL format.

Important Notes

When arranging rows of blocks in the *Audiblox 2000* exercises, it is important to note that the rows must always be arranged from *left to right*.

This is a very important point, because it is the reading direction in the English language.

The tutor must sit opposite the learner, which means that her directional orientations of left and right are reversed. When the learner puts a block to his right, from the tutor's point of view it will be to her left. It takes some time to get used to this reversed orientation. Later on, with more experience, the chances that one would make mistakes with left and right are slim, but at first, one needs to be extremely careful.

Another point is that, when doing an *Audiblox* lesson, it is important that the tutor offers as little help as possible. In some of the exercises it is extremely important to offer no help at all. This is especially important in the exercises performed with the blocks. The tutor may not through word or gesture indicate to the learner whether he is on a right or a wrong track while he is busy arranging the blocks by way of an answer to an exercise.

Imagine, for example, that during a lesson, the learner picks up a block in his hand—say a red one—and then looks at the tutor. The tutor shakes her head, and then the learner takes a blue one, again looking at the tutor, upon which the tutor nods. The tutor would probably do this almost imperceptibly, but nevertheless such a lesson would be of little value to the learner, who is merely making guesses and the tutor is green-lighting the correct guesses.

While the learner is busy with an exercise, the tutor must refrain from offering any form of help. For example, after she has shown him a pattern for *Pattern exercise 1*, she must keep absolutely quiet while the learner builds his pattern with the blocks. Don't, for example, say to a learner, "You must think carefully." That is as good as saying, "What you have in front of you is wrong."

In other exercises, such as the *Arrows exercise, Spatial exercise, Counting exercises* and *Reading exercises,* the tutor will preferably give him another chance so that he may correct his mistake before saying the correct answer. She will for example say, "Look again, what word is this?" before correcting his mistake.

For the purpose of foreground-background discrimination, the table upon which the exercises are done should be of a different color than the blocks.

Lastly, keep record of the learner's progress. You never know, he could perhaps win the *Audiblox Learner of the Year Competition*. Make a video recording of his reading before embarking on the program, keep copies of his handwriting, school reports, et cetera. Contact the address on page 169 for details and an entry form.

What to Do about a Language Problem

When a child has a language problem, that is, when it is suspected that his vocabulary is not up to expected standards, then there is only one way in which this can be remedied, and that is by providing the child with enough opportunities to hear language. There must also be enough repetition of the same words, phrases and grammatical structures.

A practical way of providing the child with enough opportunities to hear language, is by following the five steps below:

1. Make a recording of chapter one of the reading book. (If you are using *Rainbow Dreams*, make a copy of *Looking for a Dream*.) Read this chapter on tape, taking pains to read as clearly as possible. Copy this recording over and over on both sides of a blank cassette.

2. This recording must now be played to the child for at least three hours every day. What is needed is complete immersion. Playing the tape only two or three times a day will not achieve much. However, it is not necessary for the child to sit still and listen all the time. A background of language must be created for the child, so that he can continue with his other daily activities against this background. This can best be accomplished by using a portable auto-reverse cassette player (a "walkman") with earphones, instead of a regular cassette player. The walkman can be clipped on to the belt or garment of the child or be put into a belly bag.

3. As was mentioned above, repetition must form the backbone of this background. The *same* story must be played over and over until the words, phrases and grammatical structures in the story have become part of his active vocabulary. This will take about *three months,* and in some cases even longer.

4. After at least three months, the same procedure must be followed with chapter two of the reading book. (If you are using *Rainbow Dreams*, read the story *Following the Dream* on tape.) The child must listen to it continually, again for at least three months.

5. In this way one continues, playing the same story over and over for at least three months, using a new story every three months, until the child's active vocabulary is up to standard.

The correct teaching methods always deliver excellent results. Even a very severe language problem can, by using the correct method and creating a sufficiently stimulating environment, be overcome. The following letter was received from a mother whose child had a severe language problem. As she does not want her son's identity to be revealed, it has been changed to "Billy." Apart from the name, the rest of the letter is unchanged:

Billy was first tested when he entered a top private nursery school. I was told that he needed both occupational and speech therapy which I agreed to without undue concern. I first found out that he had serious "learning problems" at the end of the year when he was five years old and about to enter his final year at nursery school. His teacher, the principal and two school psychologists told me that Billy's abilities were significantly below the required level for his age group and that he would probably need remedial education. On one report, under the heading "child's strengths," the psychologist had written the word "none." I had to fight, beg and plead with the school to allow Billy to progress with his classmates to the higher nursery school class!

Although I was devastated, part of me refused to believe that there was anything wrong with my son. I instinctively knew that he was intelligent and set out to prove this. Immediately I visited bookstores and purchased a pile of workbooks and began teaching Billy formally at home. I also increased both his speech and occupational therapy sessions from once a week to twice a week.

Around the middle of the year Billy was retested by the school and, although an improvement was noted, the tests showed that he was still materially behind for his age group and remedial education was still everyone's recommendation. Again I was very distressed, particularly because I had been working very hard with Billy and I felt that he had made great progress. In fact, I was more convinced than ever that he was an intelligent child who was quick to learn.

I then decided that the school was biased against Billy and that I would prove them wrong by having him independently tested by the country's top therapists. Despite the high cost and trauma to Billy, I dragged him off to an occupational therapist, speech therapist, psychologist and remedial therapist for testing. Yet again the recommendation was for Billy to attend a remedial school. The therapists explained that a child, who had as many weaknesses as Billy did, would be unable to cope in an ordinary school. I felt totally disillusioned and confused.

The turning point came when my sister told me that she had heard wonderful reports about a program called *Audiblox*. I went along to the interview with mixed feelings. On the one hand I had a glimmer of hope and on the other I was dreading the prospect of hearing more negative reports about Billy. I needn't have worried because for the first time ever I was told that there was nothing at all wrong with Billy that could not be remedied.

I started the *Audiblox* preschool program in September and, at the same time, I began to play the tapes [as discussed above] repeatedly to solve Billy's language problem. In the early days a difficult step for me was to stop doing formal work with Billy (there just wasn't time). I had to reread the *Audiblox* literature to reassure myself that the program made sense and would work. I soon became confident because I was learning too. Many times I thought that Billy would not get to a higher level and many times I was pleasantly surprised. Over time, and with much evidence, I have learned not to place limits to the ability of the mind.

By the end of the year the most remarkable improvement that I had noticed was in Billy's language skills and, as a result, I lost my motivation to play the story tapes repeatedly. Although I knew Billy was benefiting from *Audiblox*, my first indication that some improvement was being noticed at school came when I met the principal and his teacher. They said that he was doing a bit better and they seemed less opposed to the idea of Billy attending an ordinary school. At this stage, I decided to discontinue Billy's speech and occupational therapy.

Billy started first grade the following year and I began to do the *Audiblox* program for schoolchildren with him. At the end of the first term, I finally got the confirmation I was waiting for that *Audiblox* was really working. Billy's report was full of praise about how good he was at EVERYTHING and his teacher's comment to me was "academically Billy is doing very well and you certainly have nothing to worry about." I truly feel grateful to *Audiblox*.

A year later, Billy's mother was still doing *Audiblox* with her son. Even the death of Billy's father had no effect on his schoolwork. In fact, his teacher was complaining that he was "too advanced" for the other children in his class.

Audiblox Contact Details

P. O. Box 31186, 0134 Totiusdal, South Africa
Tel: (+2712) 332-3734   Fax: (+2712) 332-4259
Website: www.audiblox2000.com (goods can be ordered online).

13.

Pattern Exercises

Foundational reading skills mainly exercised by these variations are:

- concentration;
- visual discrimination of foreground-background;
- visual discrimination of form;
- visual discrimination of position in space;
- visual discrimination of color;
- visual memory, especially of shapes.

There are two pattern exercises, *Pattern exercise 1* and *Pattern exercise 2*. There are two variations of *Pattern exercise 1*. The first variation is for users of the program who do not have an *Audiblox Learner set*, while the second variation is for users who have an *Audiblox Learner set*. *Pattern exercise 1: Variation 2* also exercises long-term memory, which *Pattern exercise 1: Variation 1* does not do.

Pattern exercise 1 should be replaced by *Pattern exercise 2* as soon as the learner has managed to arrange successfully a pattern with ten blocks.

Pattern Exercise 1: Variation 1

Summary of the exercise

1. The tutor shows a pattern of blocks to the learner for as many seconds as there are blocks.
2. The tutor hides the pattern behind the screen.
3. From memory, the learner uses the blocks to build a replica of the pattern.
4. Again show the pattern to the learner, so that he may check whether his version is correct.

Full description

For this exercise, the tutor will need a clock with a second-hand. It is easier to work with a fairly large clock, rather than with a watch.

The tutor must let the learner sit opposite herself at a table. The box with blocks is in front of the learner on the table, a small distance away from him so that there is a clear space right in front of him on the table.

The tutor must now build a pattern with two blocks behind a screen. One must be careful when taking the blocks, so that the learner will not see which colors one selects and takes from the box for the exercise. All the blocks that make up the pattern should touch and only vertical or horizontal connections should be used, not diagonal connections. *See figure 3.*

Examples of correct connections:

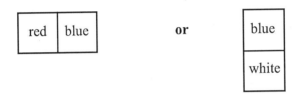

An incorrect connection:

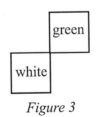

Figure 3

The tutor must make sure that the learner is ready to concentrate on the pattern. She must now lift the screen to reveal the two blocks to the learner for two seconds. *See figure 4.*

After exactly two seconds—she should look at the second-hand of the clock to measure the two seconds—she puts the screen back on the table, so that it again hides the pattern. The learner must now build the pattern from memory.

171

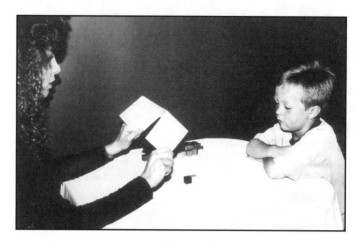

Figure 4

Note that the learner may not touch the blocks in the box until the pattern has been hidden by the screen.

After the learner has constructed the pattern from memory, again remove the screen, so that he may check whether his version is correct.

If the learner did not remember the pattern correctly, i.e. if his version differs in any way from the tutor's pattern, she must allow him to discover and correct the mistake himself. Afterwards, she builds a different pattern of two blocks and shows this to him for two seconds. If, however, the learner succeeds in remembering the pattern correctly, the tutor subsequently builds a pattern with three blocks. This is then shown to the learner for three seconds.

The exercise is continued in this way. If the learner makes a mistake, the same pattern is redisplayed to allow him to discover and correct the mistake. Then another pattern with the same number of blocks is shown. If the learner remembers a pattern correctly, a pattern consisting of one block more should be shown. One should bear in mind, however, that the learner must then also be allowed one second more in which to memorize the pattern. Suppose, for example, that you do this exercise with the learner, using a pattern with four blocks, and the learner successfully reproduces the pattern. Afterwards, let the learner do a pattern with five blocks. If he succeeds with this task also, give him a pattern with six blocks. If he fails with this, give him another one with six blocks. If he fails with this, and you decide to stop there for the day, make a note of the fact that he failed with six. The next time you do this exercise, continue doing patterns with six blocks, and continue doing so until the learner succeeds in remembering a pattern with six blocks correctly. Then move on to seven.

Pattern exercise 1 should be replaced by *Pattern exercise 2* as soon as the learner has managed to arrange successfully a pattern with ten blocks.

Pattern Exercise 1: Variation 2

Summary of the exercise

1. Show one of the color cards to the learner for as many seconds as there are blocks on the card.
2. Remove the card.
3. From memory, the learner uses the blocks to build a replica of the pattern.
4. Again show the color card to the learner, so that he may check whether his version is correct.

Full description

For this exercise, the tutor will need a clock with a second-hand. It is easier to work with a fairly large clock, rather than with a watch.

The color cards show patterns that can be built with the blocks. The tutor must sort the color cards in sequence of the number of blocks on the cards, i.e. she must put all the cards with two blocks together, and all those with three, four, five, six, seven, eight, nine and ten blocks together. By turning a card through 90 degrees, a different pattern is displayed.

The tutor must let the learner sit opposite herself at a table. The box with blocks is in front of the learner on the table, a small distance away from him so that there is a clear space right in front of him on the table.

The tutor should say to the learner, "I am going to show you a pattern consisting of two blocks for two seconds. Then I want you to arrange a duplicate of the pattern on the table in front of you."

The tutor must make sure that the learner is ready to concentrate. She now takes one of the color cards with two blocks and holds it horizontally in front of the learner. *See figure 5.*

Figure 5

After exactly two seconds—she should look at the second-hand of the clock to measure the two seconds—she removes the card again, so that the learner can build the pattern from memory. Note that the learner may not touch the blocks in the box until the color card has been removed.

After the learner has arranged his version of the pattern, again show the color card to the learner, so that he may check whether his version is correct.

If the learner did not remember the pattern correctly, i.e. if his version differs in any way from the pattern on the card, she must allow him to discover and correct the mistake himself. Afterwards, she selects a different card with a pattern of two blocks and shows this to him for two seconds. If, however, the learner succeeds in remembering the pattern correctly, the tutor subsequently selects a pattern with three blocks. This is then shown to the learner for three seconds.

The exercise is continued in this way. If the learner makes a mistake, the same pattern is redisplayed to allow him to discover and correct the mistake. Then another card with the same number of blocks is shown. If the learner remembers a pattern correctly, the next card must have a pattern with one block more. One should bear in mind, however, that the learner must then also be allowed one second more in which to memorize the pattern. Suppose, for example, that you do this exercise with the learner, using a pattern with four blocks, and the learner successfully reproduces the pattern. Afterwards, let the learner do a pattern with five blocks. If he succeeds with this task also, give him a pattern with six blocks. If he fails with this, give him another one with six blocks. If he fails with this, and you decide to stop there for the day, make a note of the fact that he failed with six. The next time you do this exercise, continue doing patterns with six blocks, and continue doing so until the learner succeeds in remembering a pattern with six blocks correctly. Then move on to seven.

Pattern exercise 1 should be replaced by *Pattern exercise 2* as soon as the learner has managed to arrange successfully a pattern with ten blocks.

Pattern Exercise 2

Summary of the exercise

1. Build a pattern with blocks behind a screen.
2. Lift the screen to display the pattern for as many seconds as there are blocks in the pattern.
3. Put the screen back, so that the pattern will again be hidden for the learner.
4. From memory, the learner uses blocks to build a replica of the pattern.
5. Lift the screen again to show the pattern to the learner, so that he may check whether his version is correct.
6. The learner must put all his blocks back into the box.
7. If the learner's version was incorrect, she will show him the same pattern again. However, if he succeeded in correctly reproducing the pattern, the tutor adds more blocks to the existing pattern without disturbing or changing it.
8. She lifts the screen and shows the larger pattern to the learner, again for as many seconds as there are blocks in the pattern.
9. She continues in this way, adding blocks to the pattern when the learner reproduces the pattern correctly, and showing the same pattern again if he makes a mistake.

Full description

For this exercise, the tutor will again need a clock with a second-hand. It is easier to work with a fairly large clock, rather than with a watch.

The tutor now builds her own pattern with the blocks behind a screen. One must be careful when taking the blocks, so that the learner will not see which colors one selects and takes from the box for the exercise. All the blocks that make up the pattern should touch and only vertical or horizontal connections should be used, not diagonal connections.

When starting the exercise, she should arrange a pattern with three blocks. *See figure 6 for an example.*

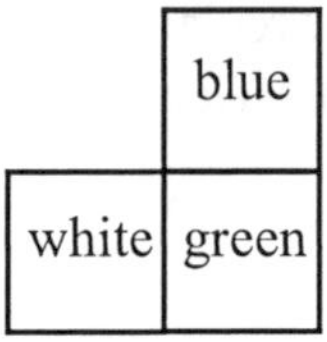

Figure 6

With her eyes on the second-hand of the clock, she then raises the screen to allow the learner three seconds to study the pattern. She must look at the second-hand of the clock to measure the seconds. Then she replaces the screen, so that the learner can build the pattern from memory. As soon as he is finished with his version of the pattern, the tutor raises the screen again, so that the learner may compare his effort with the original. If there is any difference, he must first correct the mistake and then put all his blocks back into the box. The tutor replaces the screen, makes sure that the learner is ready to study the pattern again, and then raises the screen to give the learner another opportunity to study the pattern.

However, if the learner succeeds the first time to reproduce the pattern correctly, the tutor again hides her pattern behind the screen and then, behind the screen and out of sight of the learner, adds two more blocks to the existing pattern, without in any way changing or disturbing the original pattern. The new blocks must just be added to the pattern so that the blocks now form a pattern consisting of five blocks. Only vertical or horizontal connections should be used, no diagonal connections. *See figure 7 for an example.*

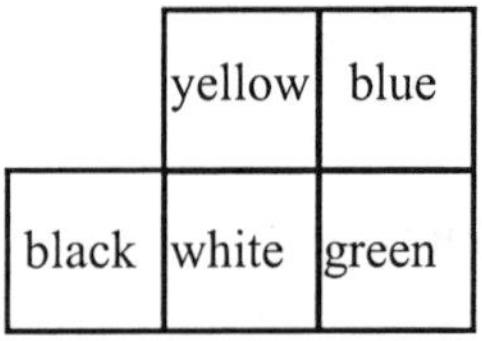

	yellow	blue
black	white	green

Figure 7

176

The tutor must first make sure that the learner is ready to study this new pattern. She then lifts the screen for five seconds, measuring the seconds by watching the second-hand on the clock. Again she hides the pattern behind her screen, allowing the learner time to build the new pattern from memory. As soon as he has completed his effort, the tutor again takes away the screen so that the learner may compare. If there are any mistakes, the leaner must first correct and then put all the blocks back into the box. The same pattern is then shown to him again for another try.

However, if the learner's effort was correct, the tutor will add two more blocks to the existing pattern and then show the new pattern to the learner, again for as many seconds as there are blocks in the pattern, i.e. seven seconds. *See figure 8 for an example.*

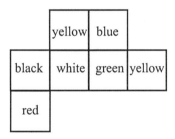

Figure 8

The exercise is continued in this way, making the pattern larger and larger, until the time that had been set aside for this exercise in the program is up. Every time the learner succeeds, the tutor adds two more blocks. When he makes a mistake, the tutor shows him the same pattern again.

Once the learner has made some progress, one can make the exercise more difficult by starting with more blocks and also by adding more blocks to the existing pattern. If the learner is able to correctly reproduce from memory a pattern of 21 blocks, and do so within the time set aside for this exercise in the program, then the tutor can start the exercise with five blocks, still adding two every time the pattern is correct. This can be summarized as follows: 21→⑤/2/0

If, with this more difficult target, the learner succeeds in getting to a pattern of 23 blocks in the time allotted for the exercise, the tutor can again make it more difficult, by still starting with five blocks, but now adding three every time the learner has the pattern right. This can be summarized as: 23→⑤/3/0

When the learner gets to twenty-six: 26→⑥/3/0.

When he gets to thirty: 30→⑥/4/0.

14.

Sequencing Exercise 3

Foundational reading skills mainly exercised in this variation are:

- concentration;
- visual discrimination of position in space;
- visual discrimination of color;
- imagination;
- visual memory, especially of sequence.

For this exercise the tutor will need a clock with a second-hand. It is easier to work with a fairly large clock, rather than with a watch.

The tutor must let the learner sit opposite herself at a table. The box with blocks is in front of the learner on the table, a small distance away from him so that there is a clear space right in front of him on the table. The tutor must put the screen upright in front of herself. She then takes three blocks, say a red, a green and a yellow, and puts them in a row behind the screen, building from her right to her left (from the learner's point of view, the blocks are arranged in the reading direction, i.e. from left to right). One must be careful when taking the blocks, so that the learner will not see which colors one selects and takes from the box for the exercise.

The tutor should instruct the learner, "I am going to show you a row consisting of three blocks for three seconds. Then I want you to arrange a duplicate of the row on the table in front of you."

The tutor must make sure that the learner is ready to concentrate on the three blocks, and then, while watching the second-hand of the clock, she must lift the screen to reveal the three blocks to the learner for three seconds. *See figure 9.*

Then she puts the screen back on the table, so that it again hides the row of

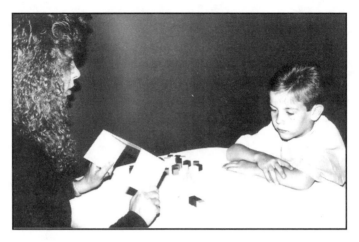

Figure 9

blocks. The learner may not touch the blocks in the box until the row has been hidden by the screen.

The learner must now take three other blocks from the box and from memory construct a duplicate of the row of three blocks. When finished, the tutor must remove the screen, so that the learner can compare whether his version is correct. If not, he must correct.

The learner must now return his three blocks to the box. The tutor must leave her three blocks undisturbed, and again hide them behind the screen.

If the learner's effort to reproduce the row of three blocks was correct, the tutor takes two more blocks, and adds them to the row of three already behind the screen. Naturally, she must add the two new blocks to her own left, so that, when the learner looks at the row of blocks from his side of the table, the two blocks will have been added to his right. While adding the blocks the tutor will ask the learner, "How many blocks did we have?" If the learner correctly answers, "Three," the tutor will say, "I am going to add two more blocks. How many shall we have then?" The learner should answer, "Five."

Again the tutor lifts the screen to reveal the row of blocks to the learner, this time allowing him five seconds. She again hides the blocks from the learner's sight, for him to try and reproduce the row of blocks from memory. If the learner again succeeds in arranging all five colors in the correct sequence, the tutor will proceed exactly as before. While the learner returns his five blocks to the box, she will add two new blocks to the row behind the screen. She will again ask the learner, "How many blocks did we have?" If the learner correctly answers, "Five," the tutor will say, "I am now going to add two more blocks. How many shall we have then?" The learner should answer, "Seven."

In this way the tutor will continue to add two blocks to the row every time the learner correctly reproduces the row. However, if the learner fails to correctly duplicate the row of blocks, she will not add any blocks, but will allow the learner another opportunity to study the same row of blocks. If, for example, the learner makes a mistake in his attempt to arrange a row consisting of seven blocks, the tutor will not add two more blocks, but will say, "I am going to show you the same seven blocks again," and will again remove the screen for seven seconds so that the learner can study the row.

An important point is that, when the row reaches eleven blocks, the eleventh block should not be placed next to the tenth block. One should start a second row with it. From the learner's point of view it should be placed in front of the first block. *See figure 10.*

Figure 10

The twenty-first block should also not be placed next to the twentieth block, but, from the learner's point of view, it should be placed in front of the eleventh block.

181

To sum up

1. Every time the learner has it right, add two more blocks.
2. After every mistake, show the same sequence of blocks again, without adding anything.

Continue in this way, making the row of blocks longer and longer, until the time that had been set aside in the program for the exercise is up.

Once the learner has made some progress, one can make the exercise more difficult by starting with more blocks, and by adding more blocks every time. If the learner is able to correctly reproduce from memory a row of twenty-one blocks, and do so within the time set aside for this exercise in the program, then the tutor can start the exercise with five blocks, still adding two every time the row is correct. This can be summarized as follows: 21→⑤/2/0.

If, with this more difficult target, the learner succeeds in getting to a row of 25 blocks in the time allotted for the exercise, the tutor can again make it more difficult by still starting with five blocks, but now adding three every time the learner has the row correct. This can be summarized as: 25→⑤/3/0.

When the learner gets to twenty-nine: 29→⑥/3/0.

When he again gets to thirty-six: 36→⑥/4/0.

On every new day, one should start with a new row of colors. However, whenever two or more lessons are done on the same day, and this exercise is therefore repeated during that day, one simply continues with the *same* row, making the same row longer and longer. This is a very good exercise for long-term memory. It is advised that the tutor then arranges the blocks on a cardboard, and not on the table. In this way, she can put the rows of blocks aside and continue with the other exercises until the time arrives to continue with this exercise. Please note that, for the purpose of foreground-background discrimination, the cardboard should be of a different color than the blocks.

15.

Auditory Exercises

Foundational reading/learning skills mainly exercised in these variations are:

- concentration;
- auditory and visual discrimination of foreground-background;
- auditory and visual discrimination of position in space;
- auditory and visual discrimination of color;
- auditory and visual analysis of position in space;
- auditory and visual synthesis of position in space;
- auditory and visual discrimination of dimensionality;
- integration;
- imagination;
- auditory memory.

Auditory Exercise 1

Summary of the exercise

1. Read a color combination twice.
2. The learner builds the combination from memory.
3. Read the color combination again, so that the learner may compare.

Full description

The tutor must let the learner sit opposite herself at a table. The box with blocks is in front of the learner on the table, a small distance away from him so that there is a clear space right in front of him on the table.

The color combinations that one needs for this exercise follow immediately after the description of the exercise. The tutor must select any of the color combinations, and read it aloud *twice*, slowly and clearly, while the learner listens with his *eyes closed.*

The combinations vary from *four* to *eighteen* blocks. When doing the exercise, the tutor should first explain to the learner what to do, and should also demonstrate if necessary. As soon as she is sure that the learner understands exactly what to do, she must tell him to wait until she has read the whole combination twice before he starts building. Then she reads the whole combination twice, slowly and clearly, while the learner listens with eyes closed. After this, he must build the combination as he remembers it.

It is important to let the learner build from left to right. The color that the tutor reads first must be placed on the left, and subsequent colors must be added towards the right. If the learner succeeds in reproducing the combination correctly, one would read another with one block more. The tutor must not forget also to read this new combination twice, *slowly* and *clearly*, while the learner listens with eyes closed. If, however, the learner makes a mistake in his reproduction of the combination, then the tutor rereads the same combination, while the learner corrects the mistake(s). Afterwards, the tutor reads another combination, which contains the *same number of blocks* as the one on which he failed.

The following instruction could be given to the learner: "I am going to read a combination consisting of four blocks. I shall do this twice, and then you must arrange the four blocks. All four blocks will be in a straight line. You must arrange them in front of you, from left to right. Close your eyes and listen: *yellow red blue green.* Listen again: *yellow red blue green.* Now arrange the blocks in front of you."

When the learner has finished his attempt, seen from his side, it should look like *figure 11*.

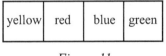

Figure 11

If the learner fails to arrange the combination with four blocks correctly, then the tutor should first read the same combination again, so that the learner can correct, and then she should read aloud twice another combination with four blocks. If, however, he was able to correctly reproduce the combination with four blocks, then the tutor must read one with five blocks.

The following instruction could be given to the learner: "Now I am going to read a combination of five blocks. Four blocks will be in a straight line, and the fifth block will be on top of one of the other blocks. I shall do this twice, and then you must arrange the blocks. Close your eyes and listen: *blue red yellow black, white on yellow*. Listen again: *blue red yellow black, white on yellow*. Now arrange the blocks in front of you."

When the learner has finished his attempt, a side view of the combination, seen from his side, should look like *figure 12*.

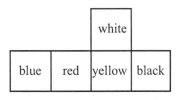

Figure 12

If the learner fails to arrange the combination with five blocks correctly, then the tutor should first read the same combination again, so that the learner can correct, and then she should read aloud another combination with five blocks twice. If, however, he was able to correctly reproduce the combination with five blocks, then the tutor must read one with six blocks.

The following instruction could be given to the learner: "Now I am going to read a combination of six blocks. Four blocks will be in a straight line, and the fifth and sixth blocks will either be in front of, behind, or on top of the other blocks. I shall do this twice, and then you must arrange the blocks. Close your eyes and listen: *red black green yellow, white on black, blue behind yellow*. I repeat: *red black green yellow, white on black, blue behind yellow*. Now arrange the blocks in front of you."

Seen from above, and from the learner's perspective, this combination will look like *figure 13*. Remember that, seen from above, the black block will be under the white one, and will therefore not be visible. Also remember that one always interprets space from inside one's own body. When the learner arranges this combination, in order to put the blue block *behind* the yellow,

185

the blue block will be *further away* from him than the yellow. The yellow block will be between the learner and the blue block.

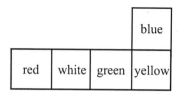

Figure 13

If there is any doubt in either the tutor's own or the learner's mind about this, they should do the *Spatial exercise*. It should then become quite clear what is meant by "behind" and "in front of." Many people, even adults, are uncertain of or inconsistent about these spatial terms. The important thing to remember, as already mentioned, is that one always interprets space from inside one's body.

When deciding how many blocks to use for this exercise, the tutor should keep in mind that the exercises in this program must always be done on a level that will present a challenge to the learner. Suppose, for example, that on any day, you do this exercise with the learner, using a combination with four blocks, and the learner successfully reproduces the combination. Afterwards, let the learner do a combination with five blocks. If he succeeds with this task also, give him a combination with six blocks. If he fails with this, give him another one with six blocks. If he fails with this, and you decide to stop there for the day, make a note of the fact that he succeeded with five and failed with six. The next time you do this exercise, start with a combination of six blocks.

Instead of only listening to the combination, the learner can be taught to also use his sense of touch to memorize the blocks. Each finger, starting with the little finger of the left hand, can represent a block in the row. *In front of* will be on the fingertip, *on* will be on the knuckle and *behind* will be on the nail of the finger. Some learners might find it hard to manage this right from he start. If so, first teach him the exercise, and then later to use his hands also.

Color combinations for Auditory exercise 1

4 blocks

1. yellow red blue green.
2. green black blue white.
3. black green white yellow.
4. white black yellow red.
5. yellow blue green black.
6. red green black white.
7. blue black white yellow.
8. green white yellow red.
9. black yellow red blue.
10. white red blue green.

5 blocks

1. blue red yellow black; white on yellow.
2. red black yellow blue; green on blue.
3. yellow white green red; blue on white.
4. black green white blue; yellow on black.
5. white blue yellow red; black on red.
6. green red blue yellow; black on blue.
7. blue green yellow white; red on green.
8. yellow red blue black; green on blue.
9. blue white black yellow; red on blue.
10. red yellow white blue; green on white.

6 blocks

1. red black green yellow; white on black, blue behind yellow.
2. blue red black white; green in front of blue, yellow on black.
3. black white blue red; yellow on black, green behind white.
4. green yellow red blue; black in front of yellow, white on red.
5. yellow green white black; red behind yellow, blue on black.
6. white black yellow green; blue in front of black, red on green.
7. red blue green yellow; white on blue, black behind yellow.
8. white red blue black; green on white, yellow in front of blue.
9. red blue white yellow; black in front of blue, green on yellow.
10. blue black yellow green; white behind blue, red on black.

7 blocks

1. yellow white green red; yellow on white, black in front of green, blue behind red.
2. blue yellow red green; black behind blue, red in front of yellow, white on green.
3. white black yellow blue; green in front of black, red on yellow, white behind blue.
4. green red blue yellow; white on green, green in front of red, black behind yellow.
5. red green white black; blue behind red, yellow on green, black in front of white.
6. yellow blue red green; black behind yellow, red on blue, white in front of green.
7. blue yellow black red; green on blue, white in front of black, blue behind red.
8. yellow black blue green; blue behind black, red in front of blue, white on green.
9. black red white blue; green in front of black, yellow behind red, white on blue.
10. green white yellow black; blue on green, red behind yellow, white behind black.

8 blocks

1. black yellow green black white; yellow on first black, blue in front of green, red behind white.
2. red green red white yellow; blue behind first red, black on second red, green in front of yellow.
3. green white black white blue; yellow on first white, red on second white, green in front of blue.
4. white yellow blue red white; black in front of first white, green behind red, blue in front of second white.
5. yellow blue yellow green red; white on first yellow, red in front of blue, black behind second yellow.
6. blue black white blue green; red on first blue, yellow on white, white on green.
7. black red green yellow black; white behind red, blue in front of yellow,

188

red on second black.

8. red white blue red black; green in front of white, yellow on second red, green behind black.

9. green yellow green blue red; black in front of yellow, white behind second green, black on red.

10. white black red white blue; green on first white, yellow behind black, green behind blue.

9 blocks

1. green white blue black yellow red; blue on white, yellow behind blue, green in front of red.

2. white green black white yellow blue; red behind first white, green on second white, yellow on blue.

3. blue red yellow green white red; black on blue, white behind green, yellow behind second red.

4. black yellow red white black green; blue in front of first black, yellow on white, red in front of green.

5. yellow black green yellow red white; blue on black, black in front of second yellow, green behind red.

6. red blue white blue black yellow; green on first blue, black in front of white, yellow behind black.

7. green white blue red yellow white; blue on first white, black on red, green behind second white.

8. white red yellow black blue white; black on red, red behind black, green on second white.

9. blue red black blue green white; green in front of red, yellow on second blue, red behind white.

10. black green green yellow red blue; white on second green, blue behind yellow, black in front of red.

10 blocks

1. yellow white blue yellow white black; blue on first yellow, green on first white, red on blue, black in front of second white.

2. white black red black blue red; green in front of first black, yellow behind first red, white in front of second black, green on second red.

3. blue green white green blue black; yellow on first green, white in front of

189

white, black in front of second green, red on second blue.

4. black red black red white green; green in front of first black, yellow behind first red, white in front of second black, blue on second red.
5. red yellow white blue yellow red; black in front of first red, blue on first yellow, green in front of white, white on second yellow.
6. green blue black blue red green; yellow in front of first green, white on first blue, yellow behind black, red behind second blue.
7. yellow yellow red black white white; green in front of first yellow, red behind second yellow, green on black, blue on first white.
8. black red red black white green; yellow in front of first red, green behind second red, blue on second black, white on green.
9. red green blue green yellow yellow; white in front of first green, black on blue, red behind first yellow, black in front of second yellow.
10. green white yellow white green red; black on first green, blue behind yellow, black behind second white, yellow in front of red.

12 blocks

1. red green yellow green black blue; blue on red, yellow in front of green, red on yellow, black behind green, yellow behind black, white on blue.
2. blue red green yellow black green; white on blue, black in front of red, blue behind green, white in front of yellow, blue on black, red on green.
3. yellow blue red black white green; green behind yellow, white on blue, yellow in front of red, red on black, blue behind white, yellow on green.
4. blue green black yellow white green; red on blue, yellow in front of green, white behind black, red behind yellow, blue in front of white, white on green.
5. blue green green yellow red red; white behind blue, black on green, blue in front of green, black on yellow, white in front of red, yellow on red.
6. white green black red yellow blue; red behind white, black on green, blue in front of black, yellow behind red, green on yellow, white behind blue.
7. green yellow red white black yellow; red in front of green, blue on yellow, black behind red, red behind white, white in front of black, black on yellow.
8. white green red blue yellow white; green in front of white, red on green, blue on red, white behind blue, black on yellow, red in front of white.

190

9. green white yellow green red blue; red on green, blue behind white, white in front of yellow, black behind green, white behind red, black on blue.
10. white black blue white black yellow; green on white, blue behind black, yellow on blue, red in front of white, green on black, blue behind yellow.

14 blocks

1. yellow yellow red black green black blue; red behind yellow, white in front of yellow, green on red, blue in front of black, yellow on green, green behind black, white on blue.
2. black yellow green white red green black blue; blue behind black, green on yellow, red in front of green, yellow behind white, blue on green, white behind blue.
3. yellow blue white yellow green black white blue yellow; black on yellow, red behind yellow, blue on white, green in front of blue, red on yellow.
4. yellow red blue yellow green white red; green on yellow, yellow behind red, black in front of blue, white on yellow, blue behind green, black behind white, yellow on red.
5. black green red blue green red black; red behind black, yellow in front of green, black on red, red behind blue, blue on green, blue behind red, white on black.
6. red black green blue black yellow blue white; white in front of red, blue on black, red behind green, green on black, yellow in front of blue, green behind white.
7. white green red black black white yellow; black on white, red behind green, yellow in front of red, green on black, blue behind black, blue in front of white, white on yellow.
8. yellow white blue green white black yellow; red behind yellow, yellow in front of white, black on blue, yellow behind green, red on white, blue behind black, green on yellow.
9. red white yellow blue red green white black; black behind red, green on white, white in front of blue, black behind red, red on white, green in front of black.
10. black red white green yellow red blue; green on black, yellow behind red, black on white, blue behind green, red in front of yellow, black on red, white behind blue.

191

16 blocks

1. green blue white red blue green yellow black; black behind green, black in front of blue, green behind white, white on red, yellow in front of blue, red behind green, green on yellow, yellow behind black.
2. blue black yellow green red white green red; black behind blue, yellow on black, white in front of yellow, blue on green, white in front of red, black on white, yellow behind green, blue in front of red.
3. blue red yellow green black blue white red; white on blue, green behind red, black on yellow, yellow in front of green, white behind black, yellow on blue, red in front of white, black behind red.
4. white yellow blue white red yellow green black; green behind white, black on yellow, red in front of blue, blue behind white, yellow in front of red, blue on yellow, red behind green, green on black.
5. yellow red green green black blue yellow white; black behind yellow, blue on red, red on green, blue behind green, white behind black, green on blue, red in front of yellow, blue on white.
6. red green yellow green white yellow blue black; white behind red, black on green, white in front of yellow, red behind green, blue on white, black behind yellow, green in front of blue, white on black.
7. yellow green blue black white green yellow red; red behind yellow, white in front of green, yellow on blue, blue on black, yellow behind white, red in front of green, white on yellow, black on red.
8. green red black blue white red blue black; yellow in front of green, white behind red, green on black, black in front of blue, green in front of white, yellow on red, red behind blue, white on black.
9. white green blue white black blue yellow red; blue behind white, red on green, white in front of blue, green on white, white behind black, red on blue, black in front of yellow, green behind red.
10. red white green black blue green red black; green on red, yellow behind white, blue on green, yellow in front of black, green behind blue, yellow behind green, blue in front of red, red on black.

18 blocks

1. red green green yellow white black blue green red; yellow on red, black behind green, red on green, black on yellow, blue in front of white, white on black, yellow behind blue, black in front of green, white on red.

2. red black yellow green white blue green black white; blue on red, green on black, red on yellow, black behind green, yellow in front of white, red on blue, yellow behind green, red in front of black, blue on white.

3. red yellow red green white green black blue white; blue on red, black in front of yellow, white on red, yellow behind green, blue on white, black behind green, yellow in front of black, red on blue, green in front of white.

4. red black white red yellow yellow blue red blue; white on red, yellow in front of black, green on white, blue behind red, black on yellow, white behind yellow, green in front of blue, white on red, black behind blue.

5. blue black red black blue green yellow green white; green on blue, yellow behind black, white on red, yellow in front of black, white behind blue, white on green, blue in front of yellow, red in front of green, black on white.

6. yellow white blue red blue green white black yellow; black on yellow, green behind white, red in front of blue, white on red, black behind blue, yellow in front of green, green in front of white, blue behind black, red on yellow.

7. white red green blue yellow green blue black red; black on white, blue behind red, black behind green, red in front of blue, black on yellow, white in front of green, yellow on blue, white on black, green behind red.

8. red blue green yellow red green black yellow blue; yellow on red, red behind blue, white on green, black behind yellow, white in front of red, blue in front of green, white on black, red in front of yellow, black behind blue.

9. yellow green blue green white yellow black white red; black on yellow, black in front of green, white on blue, red behind green, red on white, blue in front of yellow, green behind black, yellow on white, blue behind red.

10. black yellow black white red green white yellow green; white on black, blue behind yellow, red on black, blue in front of white, green on red, yellow on green, blue behind white, red on yellow, white in front of green.

Auditory Exercise 2

Summary of the exercise

1. Read a color combination once.
2. The learner builds the combination from memory.

3. Read the color combination again, so that the learner may compare and correct.
4. Read the follow-up combination, which at the start is the same as the previous one, but with a number of blocks added to the end.
5. Again the learner builds from memory.
6. Read the same color combination again, so that the learner may compare and correct.
7. Read the second follow-up combination, again once only.
8. The learner builds from memory.
9. Read the same color combination again, so that the learner may compare and correct.

Full description

The tutor must let the learner sit opposite herself at a table. The box with blocks is in front of the learner on the table, a small distance away from him so that there is a clear space right in front of him on the table.

The color combinations that one needs for this exercise follow immediately after the description of the exercise.

The tutor reads, for example, the first combination with six blocks to the learner, slowly and clearly: *white, red, blue; black on white, blue behind red, white on blue*. However, unlike in *Auditory exercise 1*, the combination must now be read *once only*, while the learner listens with his *eyes closed*. Then she allows the learner time to build the combination with the blocks. Then the tutor reads the combination once more, for him to check whether he has it right. He must correct any errors, and then *all the blocks are put back into the box*. Then the tutor reads the follow-up combination with ten blocks, again once only: *white, red, blue, green, red; black on white, blue behind red, white on blue, yellow in front of green, green on red*.

Notice that the first six blocks of this combination with ten blocks are exactly the same as the combination with six blocks that was previously read to the learner. Again the learner is given time to build the combination, and then the tutor rereads it, for the learner to check for correctness. After the correction of any possible errors, the blocks are put back into the box. The tutor now finally reads the follow-up combination with fourteen blocks, again once only: *white, red, blue, green, red, yellow, black; black on white, blue behind red, white on blue, yellow in front of green, green on red, white behind yellow, blue behind black.*

Again one should take note of the fact that the first ten blocks of this combination are exactly the same as those of the previous combination. This means that in *Auditory exercise 2* the same combination is read three times to the learner, but with every reading a number of new blocks are added.

The learner builds the combination, and then the tutor reads again to allow corrections. This ends the exercise.

When the exercise is done again, whether immediately or on another day, combination number 2 will be read to the learner, etc. As soon as the combinations from *six to fourteen blocks* become too easy, one progresses to those with *eight to sixteen* blocks, et cetera.

Color combinations for Auditory exercise 2

6 to 14 blocks

1. *6 blocks:* white, red, blue; black on white, blue behind red, white on blue.
   10 blocks: white, red, blue, green, red; black on white, blue behind red, white on blue, yellow in front of green, green on red.
   14 blocks: white, red, blue, green, red, yellow, black; black on white, blue behind red, white on blue, yellow in front of green, green on red, white behind yellow, blue behind black.

2. *6 blocks:* black, white, yellow; white in front of black, green on white, blue behind yellow.
   10 blocks: black, white, yellow, red, white; white in front of black, green on white, blue behind yellow, black behind red, yellow in front of white.
   14 blocks: black, white, yellow, red, white, green, blue; white in front of black, green on white, blue behind yellow, black behind red, yellow in front of white, black on green, white behind blue.

3. *6 blocks:* black, red, yellow; green behind black, white on red, blue behind yellow.
   10 blocks: black, red, yellow, white, black; green behind black, white on red, blue behind yellow, red behind white, green in front of black.

14 blocks: black, red, yellow, white, black, red, blue; green behind black, white on red, blue behind yellow, red behind white, green in front of black, red on red, white behind blue.

4. *6 blocks:* blue, white, black; yellow on blue, green behind white, red on black.
10 blocks: blue, white, black, green, blue; yellow on blue, green behind white, red on black, white on green, yellow in front of blue.
14 blocks: blue, white, black, green, blue, white, red; yellow on blue, green behind white, red on black, white on green, yellow in front of blue, white behind white, green on red.

5. *6 blocks:* yellow, red, green; blue in front of yellow, white on red, yellow behind green.
10 blocks: yellow, red, green, white, black; blue in front of yellow, white on red, yellow behind green, yellow in front of white, red behind black.
14 blocks: yellow, red, green, white, black, blue, white; blue in front of yellow, white on red, yellow behind green, yellow in front of white, red behind black, white on blue, green in front of white.

8 to 16 blocks

1. *8 blocks:* black, green, red, green; red on black, blue behind green, green on red, white in front of green.
12 blocks: black, green, red, green, blue, white; red on black, blue behind green, green on red, white in front of green, black on blue, yellow on white.
16 blocks: black, green, red, green, blue, white, red, green; red on black, blue behind green, green on red, white in front of green, black on blue, yellow on white, green behind red, yellow in front of green.

2. *8 blocks:* yellow, red, white, blue; white behind yellow, black in front of red, red behind white, green on blue.
12 blocks: yellow, red, white, blue, black, green; white behind yellow, black in front of red, red behind white, green on blue, yellow behind black, blue behind green.

16 blocks: yellow, red, white, blue, black, green, white, blue; white behind yellow, black in front of red, red behind white, green on blue, yellow behind black, blue behind green, red in front of white, blue on blue.

3. *8 blocks:* yellow, white, blue, blue; black in front of yellow, red on white, blue in front of blue, yellow behind blue.
12 blocks: yellow, white, blue, blue, black, red; black in front of yellow, red on white, blue in front of blue, yellow behind blue, white in front of black, green in front of red.
16 blocks: yellow, white, blue, blue, black, red, black, blue; black in front of yellow, red on white, blue in front of blue, yellow behind blue, white in front of black, green in front of red, blue on black, green behind blue.

4. *8 blocks:* green, yellow, blue, red; white on green, black behind yellow, red on blue, green in front of red.
12 blocks: green, yellow, blue, red, white, black; white on green, black behind yellow, red on blue, green in front of red, yellow on white, blue on black.
16 blocks: green, yellow, blue, red, white, black, white, red; white on green, black behind yellow, red on blue, green in front of red, yellow on white, blue on black, red behind white, blue in front of red.

5. *8 blocks:* red, green, blue, white; blue on red, yellow in front of green, black on blue, red behind white.
12 blocks: red, green, blue, white, black, green; blue on red, yellow in front of green, black on blue, red behind white, yellow on black, blue in front of green.
16 blocks: red, green, blue, white, black, green, red, white; blue on red, yellow in front of green, black on blue, red behind white, yellow on black, blue in front of green, black behind red, green on white.

10 to 18 blocks

1. *10 blocks:* green, yellow, blue, red, white; white on green, black behind yellow, red on blue, green in front of red, yellow on white.
14 blocks: green, yellow, blue, red, white, black, white; white on green,

black behind yellow, red on blue, green in front of red, yellow on white, blue on black, red behind white.

18 blocks: green, yellow, blue, red, white, black, white, red, green; white on green, black behind yellow, red on blue, green in front of red, yellow on white, blue on black, red behind white, blue in front of red, yellow on green.

2. *10 blocks:* yellow, red, white, blue, black; white behind yellow, black in front of red, red behind white, green on blue, yellow behind black.

   14 blocks: yellow, red, white, blue, black, green, white; white behind yellow, black in front of red, red behind white, green on blue, yellow behind black, blue behind green, red in front of white.

   18 blocks: yellow, red, white, blue, black, green, white, blue, yellow; white behind yellow, black in front of red, red behind white, green on blue, yellow behind black, blue behind green, red in front of white, blue on blue, green behind yellow.

3. *10 blocks:* blue, green, black, red, yellow; black behind blue, yellow in front of green, green behind black, white on red, blue behind yellow.

   14 blocks: blue, green, black, red, yellow, white, black; black behind blue, yellow in front of green, green behind black, white on red, blue behind yellow, red behind white, green in front of black.

   18 blocks: blue, green, black, red, yellow, white, black, red, blue; black behind blue, yellow in front of green, green behind black, white on red, blue behind yellow, red behind white, green in front of black, red on red, white behind blue.

4. *10 blocks:* red, yellow, blue, white, black; blue on red, black in front of yellow, yellow on blue, green behind white, red on black.

   14 blocks: red, yellow, blue, white, black, green, blue; blue on red, black in front of yellow, yellow on blue, green behind white, red on black, white on green, yellow in front of blue.

   18 blocks: red, yellow, blue, white, black, green, blue, white, red; blue on red, black in front of yellow, yellow on blue, green behind white, red on black, white on green, yellow in front of blue, white behind white, green on red.

5. *10 blocks:* black, white, green, yellow, red; green in front of black, red on white, white in front of green, blue behind yellow, black in front of red.

14 blocks: black, white, green, yellow, red, blue, green; green in front of black, red on white, white in front of green, blue behind yellow, black in front of red, yellow in front of blue, white on green.

18 blocks: black, white, green, yellow, red, blue, green, yellow, black; green in front of black, red on white, white in front of green, blue behind yellow, black in front of red, yellow in front of blue, white on green, yellow behind yellow, blue in front of black.

12 to 24 blocks

1. *12 blocks:* red, yellow, blue, black, green, white; blue on red, green in front of yellow, white behind blue, yellow on black, red in front of green, black behind white.

18 blocks: red, yellow, blue, black, green, white, red, blue, yellow; blue on red, green in front of yellow, white behind blue, yellow on black, red in front of green, black behind white, black on red, green behind blue, red in front of yellow.

24 blocks: red, yellow, blue, black, green, white, red, blue, yellow, red, white, black; blue on red, green in front of yellow, white behind blue, yellow on black, red in front of green, black behind white, black on red, green behind blue, red in front of yellow, white on red, blue behind white, green on black.

2. *12 blocks:* yellow, green, red, white, black, blue; red behind yellow, black in front of green, blue on red, green behind white, yellow in front of black, white on blue.

18 blocks: yellow, green, red, white, black, blue, yellow, red, green; red behind yellow, black in front of green, blue on red, green behind white, yellow in front of black, white on blue, white behind yellow, black on red, yellow in front of green.

24 blocks: yellow, green, red, white, black, blue, yellow, red, green, yellow, blue, white; red behind yellow, black in front of green, blue on red, green behind white, yellow in front of black, white on blue, white behind yellow, black on red, yellow in front of green, blue behind yellow, red on blue, black behind white.

3. *12 blocks:* green, black, yellow, blue, white, red; yellow behind green, white on black, red in front of yellow, black behind blue, green on white, blue in front of red.

   18 blocks: green, black, yellow, blue, white, red, green, yellow, black; yellow behind green, white on black, red in front of yellow, black behind blue, green on white, blue in front of red, blue behind green, white in front of yellow, green on black.

   24 blocks: green, black, yellow, blue, white, red, green, yellow, black, green, red, blue; yellow behind green, white on black, red in front of yellow, black behind blue, green on white, blue in front of red, blue behind green, white in front of yellow, green on black, red behind green, yellow in front of red, white behind blue.

4. *12 blocks:* black, white, green, red, blue, yellow; green on black, blue in front of white, yellow behind green, white on red, black in front of blue, red behind yellow.

   18 blocks: black, white, green, red, blue, yellow, black, green, white; green on black, blue in front of white, yellow behind green, white on red, black in front of blue, red behind yellow, red on black, blue behind green, black in front of white.

   24 blocks: black, white, green, red, blue, yellow, black, green, white, black, yellow, red; green on black, blue in front of white, yellow behind green, white on red, black in front of blue, red behind yellow, red on black, blue behind green, black in front of white, yellow on black, green behind yellow, blue on red.

5. *12 blocks:* white, blue, black, yellow, red, green; black in front of white, red on blue, green behind black, blue in front of yellow, white on red, yellow behind green.

   18 blocks: white, blue, black, yellow, red, green, white, black, blue; black in front of white, red on blue, green behind black, blue in front of yellow, white on red, yellow behind green, yellow in front of white, red behind black, white on blue.

   24 blocks: white, blue, black, yellow, red, green, white, black, blue, white, green, yellow; black in front of white, red on blue, green behind black, blue in front of yellow, white on red, yellow behind green, yellow in front of white, red behind black, white on blue, green in front of white, black behind green, red in front of yellow.

14 to 26 blocks

1. *14 blocks:* green, yellow, blue, red, white, black, white; white on green, black behind yellow, red on blue, green in front of red, yellow on white, blue on black, red behind white.
   20 blocks: green, yellow, blue, red, white, black, white, red, green, black; white on green, black behind yellow, red on blue, green in front of red, yellow on white, blue on black, red behind white, blue in front of red, yellow on green, white on black.
   26 blocks: green, yellow, blue, red, white, black, white, red, green, black, red, blue, yellow; white on green, black behind yellow, red on blue, green in front of red, yellow on white, blue on black, red behind white, blue in front of red, yellow on green, white on black, green behind red, white in front of blue, red on yellow.

2. *14 blocks:* yellow, blue, green, white, black, red, black; black behind yellow, red in front of blue, white behind green, yellow on white, blue behind black, green behind red, white in front of black.
   20 blocks: yellow, blue, green, white, black, red, black, white, yellow, red; black behind yellow, red in front of blue, white behind green, yellow on white, blue behind black, green behind red, white in front of black, green on white, blue behind yellow, black behind red.
   26 blocks: yellow, blue, green, white, black, red, black, white, yellow, red, white, green, blue; black behind yellow, red in front of blue, white behind green, yellow on white, blue behind black, green behind red, white in front of black, green on white, blue behind yellow, black behind red, yellow in front of white, black on green, white behind blue.

3. *14 blocks:* blue, green, yellow, black, red, white, red; red in front of blue, white on green, black in front of yellow, blue behind black, green in front of red, yellow in front of white, black on red.
   20 blocks: blue, green, yellow, black, red, white, red, black, blue, white; red in front of blue, white on green, black in front of yellow, blue behind

201

black, green in front of red, yellow in front of white, black on red, yellow behind black, green in front of blue, red in front of white.

26 blocks: blue, green, yellow, black, red, white, red, black, blue, white, black, yellow, green; red in front of blue, white on green, black in front of yellow, blue behind black, green in front of red, yellow in front of white, black on red, yellow behind black, green in front of blue, red in front of white, blue on black, red behind yellow, black in front of green.

4. *14 blocks:* blue, yellow, black, white, red, green, red; red in front of blue, green on yellow, white in front of black, blue behind white, yellow in front of red, black in front of green, white on red.

20 blocks: blue, yellow, black, white, red, green, red, blue, white, yellow; red in front of blue, green on yellow, white in front of black, blue behind white, yellow in front of red, black in front of green, white on red, green behind blue, black on white, red on yellow.

26 blocks: blue, yellow, black, white, red, green, red, blue, white, yellow, black, green, red; red in front of blue, green on yellow, white in front of black, blue behind white, yellow in front of red, black in front of green, white on red, green behind blue, black on white, red on yellow, blue behind black, yellow on green, white in front of red.

5. *14 blocks:* green, black, white, red, blue, yellow, blue; blue in front of green, yellow on black, red in front of white, green behind red, black in front of blue, white in front of yellow, red on blue.

20 blocks: green, black, white, red, blue, yellow, blue, red, green, yellow; blue in front of green, yellow on black, red in front of white, green behind red, black in front of blue, white in front of yellow, red on blue, white behind red, black in front of green, blue in front of yellow.

26 blocks: green, black, white, red, blue, yellow, blue, red, green, yellow, red, white, black; blue in front of green, yellow on black, red in front of white, green behind red, black in front of blue, white in front of yellow, red on blue, white behind red, black in front of green, blue in front of yellow, green on red, blue behind white, red in front of black.

16 to 32 blocks

1. *16 blocks:* green, yellow, blue, red, yellow, black, white, red; white on

green, red behind yellow, green on blue, black in front of red, blue on yellow, green behind black, red behind white, blue in front of red.

24 blocks: green, yellow, blue, red, yellow, black, white, red, green, black, blue, yellow; white on green, red behind yellow, green on blue, black in front of red, blue on yellow, green behind black, red behind white, blue in front of red, yellow on green, white on black, green in front of blue, black on yellow.

32 blocks: green, yellow, blue, red, yellow, black, white, red, green, black, blue, yellow, red, green, blue, white; white on green, red behind yellow, green on blue, black in front of red, blue on yellow, green behind black, red behind white, blue in front of red, yellow on green, white on black, green in front of blue, black on yellow, white behind red, yellow on green, red in front of blue, green on white.

2. *16 blocks:* white, black, red, green, black, blue, yellow, green; yellow in front of white, green on black, white in front of red, blue behind green, red in front of black, white on blue, green on yellow, red behind green.

   24 blocks: white, black, red, green, black, blue, yellow, green, white, blue, red, black; yellow in front of white, green on black, white in front of red, blue behind green, red in front of black, white on blue, green on yellow, red behind green, black in front of white, yellow in front of blue, white behind red, blue in front of black.

   32 blocks: white, black, red, green, black, blue, yellow, green, white, blue, red, black, green, white, red, yellow; yellow in front of white, green on black, white in front of red, blue behind green, red in front of black, white on blue, green on yellow, red behind green, black in front of white, yellow in front of blue, white behind red, blue in front of black, yellow on green, black in front of white, green behind red, white in front of yellow.

3. *16 blocks:* yellow, blue, green, white, blue, red, black, white; black behind yellow, white in front of blue, yellow behind green, red on white, green behind blue, yellow in front of red, white in front of black, green on white.

   24 blocks: yellow, blue, green, white, blue, red, black, white, yellow, red, green, blue; black behind yellow, white in front of blue, yellow behind green, red on white, green behind blue, yellow in front of red, white in front of black, green on white, blue behind yellow, black behind red, yellow on green, red behind blue.

32 blocks: yellow, blue, green, white, blue, red, black, white, yellow, red, green, blue, white, yellow, green, black; black behind yellow, white in front of blue, yellow behind green, red on white, green behind blue, yellow in front of red, white in front of black, green on white, blue behind yellow, black behind red, yellow on green, red behind blue, black in front of white, blue behind yellow, white on green, yellow behind black.

4. *16 blocks:* black, red, white, yellow, red, green, blue, yellow; blue in front of black, yellow behind red, black in front of white, green on yellow, white in front of red, black behind green, yellow behind blue, white on yellow.

24 blocks: black, red, white, yellow, red, green, blue, yellow, black, green, white, red; blue in front of black, yellow behind red, black in front of white, green on yellow, white in front of red, black behind green, yellow behind blue, white on yellow, red in front of black, blue in front of green, black on white, green in front of red.

32 blocks: black, red, white, yellow, red, green, blue, yellow, black, green, white, red, yellow, black, white, blue; blue in front of black, yellow behind red, black in front of white, green on yellow, white in front of red, black behind green, yellow behind blue, white on yellow, red in front of black, blue in front of green, black on white, green in front of red, blue behind yellow, red in front of black, yellow on white, black in front of blue.

5. *16 blocks:* white, red, blue, green, red, yellow, black, blue; black on white, blue behind red, white on blue, yellow in front of green, green on red, white behind yellow, blue behind black, green in front of blue.

24 blocks: white, red, blue, green, red, yellow, black, blue, white, yellow, green, red; black on white, blue behind red, white on blue, yellow in front of green, green on red, white behind yellow, blue behind black, green in front of blue, red on white, black on yellow, white in front of green, yellow on red.

32 blocks: white, red, blue, green, red, yellow, black, blue, white, yellow, green, red, blue, white, green, black; black on white, blue behind red, white on blue, yellow in front of green, green on red, white behind yellow, blue behind black, green in front of blue, red on white, black on yellow, white in front of green, yellow on red, black behind blue, red on white, blue in front of green, white on black.

20 to 40 blocks

1. *20 blocks:* green, yellow, blue, red, white, black, white, red, green, black; white on green, black behind yellow, red on blue, green in front of red, yellow on white, blue on black, red behind white, blue in front of red, yellow on green, white on black.

   30 blocks: green, yellow, blue, red, white, black, white, red, green, black, red, blue, yellow, white, black; white on green, black behind yellow, red on blue, green in front of red, yellow on white, blue on black, red behind white, blue in front of red, yellow on green, white on black, green behind red, white in front of blue, red on yellow, green in front of white, red behind black.

   40 blocks: green, yellow, blue, red, white, black, white, red, green, black, red, blue, yellow, white, black, green, yellow, blue, white, green; white on green, black behind yellow, red on blue, green in front of red, yellow on white, blue on black, red behind white, blue in front of red, yellow on green, white on black, green behind red, white in front of blue, red on yellow, green in front of white, red behind black, white on green, red in front of yellow, black behind blue, yellow on white, red in front of green.

2. *20 blocks:* yellow, blue, white, green, black, red, black, green, yellow, red; black in front of yellow, red on blue, green in front of white, yellow behind green, blue in front of black, white in front of red, green on black, white behind green, blue in front of yellow, black in front of red.

   30 blocks: yellow, blue, white, green, black, red, black, green, yellow, red, green, white, blue, black, red; black in front of yellow, red on blue, green in front of white, yellow behind green, blue in front of black, white in front of red, green on black, white behind green, blue in front of yellow, black in front of red, yellow on green, black behind white, green in front of blue, yellow behind black, green on red.

   40 blocks: yellow, blue, white, green, black, red, black, green, yellow, red, green, white, blue, black, red, yellow, blue, white, black, yellow; black in front of yellow, red on blue, green in front of white, yellow behind green, blue in front of black, white in front of red, green on black, white behind green, blue in front of yellow, black in front of red, yellow on green, black behind white, green in front of blue, yellow behind black, green on red, black in front of yellow, green behind blue, red on white, blue in front of black, green behind yellow.

3. *20 blocks:* blue, white, black, yellow, red, green, red, yellow, blue, green; red behind blue, green in front of white, yellow behind black, blue on yellow, white behind red, black behind green, yellow in front of red, black on yellow, white behind blue, red behind green.

30 blocks: blue, white, black, yellow, red, green, red, yellow, blue, green, yellow, black, white, red, green; red behind blue, green in front of white, yellow behind black, blue on yellow, white behind red, black behind green, yellow in front of red, black on yellow, white behind blue, red behind green, blue in front of yellow, red on black, yellow behind white, blue on red, yellow in front of green.

40 blocks: blue, white, black, yellow, red, green, red, yellow, blue, green, yellow, black, white, red, green, blue, white, black, red, blue; red behind blue, green in front of white, yellow behind black, blue on yellow, white behind red, black behind green, yellow in front of red, black on yellow, white behind blue, red behind green, blue in front of yellow, red on black, yellow behind white, blue on red, yellow in front of green, red behind blue, yellow on white, green in front of black, white behind red, yellow on blue.

4. *20 blocks:* white, black, red, blue, green, yellow, green, blue, white, yellow; green on white, yellow behind black, blue on red, white in front of blue, black on green, red on yellow, blue behind green, red in front of blue, black on white, green on yellow.

30 blocks: white, black, red, blue, green, yellow, green, blue, white, yellow, blue, red, black, green, yellow; green on white, yellow behind black, blue on red, white in front of blue, black on green, red on yellow, blue behind green, red in front of blue, black on white, green on yellow, white behind blue, green in front of red, blue on black, white in front of green, blue behind yellow.

40 blocks: white, black, red, blue, green, yellow, green, blue, white, yellow, blue, red, black, green, yellow, white, black, red, green, white; green on white, yellow behind black, blue on red, white in front of blue, black on green, red on yellow, blue behind green, red in front of blue, black on white, green on yellow, white behind blue, green in front of red, blue on black, white in front of green, blue behind yellow, green on white, blue in front of black, yellow behind red, black on green, blue in front of white.

5. *20 blocks:* black, red, green, white, yellow, blue, yellow, white, black, blue; yellow in front of black, blue on red, white in front of green, black behind white, red in front of yellow, green in front of blue, white on yellow, green behind white, red in front of black, yellow in front of blue.

30 blocks: black, red, green, white, yellow, blue, yellow, white, black, blue, white, green, red, yellow, blue; yellow in front of black, blue on red, white in front of green, black behind white, red in front of yellow, green in front of blue, white on yellow, green behind white, red in front of black, yellow in front of blue, black on white, yellow behind green, white in front of red, black behind yellow, white on blue.

40 blocks: black, red, green, white, yellow, blue, yellow, white, black, blue, white, green, red, yellow, blue, black, red, green, yellow, black; yellow in front of black, blue on red, white in front of green, black behind white, red in front of yellow, green in front of blue, white on yellow, green behind white, red in front of black, yellow in front of blue, black on white, yellow behind green, white in front of red, black behind yellow, white on blue, yellow in front of black, white behind red, blue on green, red in front of yellow, white behind black.

16.

Logical Thinking Exercise 1

Foundational reading skills mainly exercised in this variation are:

- concentration;
- auditory and visual discrimination of foreground-background;
- auditory and visual discrimination of position in space;
- auditory and visual discrimination of color;
- visual analysis of position in space;
- visual synthesis of position in space;
- integration;
- closure;
- imagination.

For this exercise the tutor again has to sit opposite the learner at a table. She must then let the learner arrange a sequence of colors with an underlying logic according to the examples given below, leaving one or more gaps at the end of the sequence, which the learner must fill in by discovering the logic behind it.

When doing this exercise, the tutor reads aloud the sequence of blocks according to one of the examples, so that the learner can arrange them in front of himself, and then, when she gets to the question mark(s), she asks him to complete the sequence by adding as many blocks as there are question marks in the example.

An example should make this clear. The tutor reads aloud the following sequence of blocks, so that the learner can arrange them from (his) left to right on the table in front of him: green yellow green yellow green yellow green. *See figure 14.*

Read slowly, so that the learner has sufficient time to put each color in

Figure 14

front of him. Then the tutor says to the learner, "If you had to add one more block to the sequence, which color would you choose?"

The learner should be able to see that it is a yellow block that is missing. This is, of course, an extremely simple example, but it is possible to devise sequences that are so complicated that they would present a very tough challenge even to highly intelligent learners.

To do this exercise with a learner, one starts with the simple example given above—which is also the first one in Group A below—so that the learner will understand how the exercise works. If the learner succeeds with this first example of Group A, the tutor gives him one or two more from the same group. It is important to make sure that the learner has really grasped the logical principle underlying the examples of Group A before moving on to Group B, which is slightly more difficult. Follow the same procedure if the learner succeeds with the example of Group B.

All the examples in each group are based on more or less the same principle. If the tutor therefore succeeds in discovering the principle underlying the first example in a group, she can accept that the same principle will also apply for the others in that group. It is important to let the learner discover this principle himself. As soon as he has achieved that, it should be fairly easy for him to also work out the answers to the further examples in the same group.

If the learner fails to solve an example, it is important not to simply give the answer, but to let him continue trying. The tutor can then through leading questions try to bring the learner on the right track, but it is of no value whatsoever simply to give the right answer to the learner. For this reason it is also very important that the tutor must thoroughly understand all the examples of this exercise. It will therefore be necessary for her to work through them ahead of the learner.

It is also important to regularly return to groups that had already been worked out. The tutor will find that, if she returns to previously worked out examples after some time, the learner will often again struggle with them.

In the examples below, the groups are arranged more or less in order of difficulty.

Examples of Logical Thinking exercise 1

In the examples below, the following abbreviations are used to represent the colors: g = green, y = yellow, r = red, b = blue, w = white, B = black. The answers are in brackets, right next to the question mark(s).

Group A
1. g y g y g y g ? (y)
2. B y B y B y B ? (y)
3. b g b g b g b ? (g)
4. w r w r w r w ? (r)
5. w B w B w B w ? (B)

Group B
1. r g y r g y r ? ·? (g y)
2. w r B w r B w ? ? (r B)
3. b y g b y g b ? ? (y g)
4. y B w y B w y ? ? (B w)
5. B b w B b w B ? ? (b w)

Group C
1. y g w B y g ? ? (w B)
2. g w r b g w ? ? (r b)
3. b g y r b g ? ? (y r)
4. w B y b w B ? ? (y b)
5. r w b y r w ? ? (b y)

210

Group D

1. r w B y g r w B ? ? (y g)
2. b w g B y b w g ? ? (B y)
3. y r g B w y r g ? ? (B w)
4. B y g r b B y g ? ? (r b)
5. g w r y b g w r ? ? (y b)

Group E

1. y g w b B r y g w ? ? ? (b B r)
2. r w b B y g r w b ? ? ? (B y g)
3. B r y w b g B r y ? ? ? (w b g)
4. B y r w b g B y r ? ? ? (w b g)
5. g y b B w r g y b ? ? ? (B w r)

Group F

1. y b w r g B B g r ? ? ? (w b y)
2. r g B y b w w b y ? ? ? (B g r)
3. g b w r B y y B r ? ? ? (w b g)
4. b B y r w g g w r ? ? ? (y B b)
5. r b g B y b b y B ? ? ? (g b r)

Group G

1. B y g w r B B y y g g ? ? ? ? (w w r r)
2. w B g b y w w B B g g ? ? ? ? (b b y y)
3. g y b w r B g g y y b b ? ? ? ? ? ? (w w r r B B)
4. b B y w g r b b B B y y ? ? ? ? ? ? (w w g g r r)
5. y r B g w b y y r r B B ? ? ? ? ? ? (g g w w b b)

Group H

1. B b b y y y g ? ? ? (g g g)
2. r w w b b b y ? ? ? (y y y)
3. w g g r r r b ? ? ? (b b b)
4. b B B y y y w ? ? ? (w w w)
5. g y y b b b r ? ? ? (r r r)

Group I

1. g r r b y y w B B g g r b b ? ? ? ? (y w w B)
2. B B y r r b w w g B y y r ? ? ? ? ? ? (b b w g g)

211

3. y w w B g g b r r y y w B B ? ? ? ? (g b b r)
4. g g r B B y b b w g r r B ? ? ? ? ? (y y b w w)

Group J

1. B y r r g g w b B B y y r ? ? ? ? ? (g w w b b)
2. b b y y g B r r w w b y g g ? ? ? ? (B B r w)
3. g w B B r r y b g g w w B ? ? ? ? ? (r y y b b)
4. b b B B g y r r w w b B g g ? ? ? ? (y y r w)

Group K

1. B b g y b r B w B b g y b ? ? ? (r B w)
2. b y B b g y r B y b y B b g y ? ? ? (r B y)
3. r g y w B b r w g y b B r g y w B b r w g ? ? ? (y b B)
4. b y B w r B g r w b y B b y B w r B g r w ? ? ? (b y B)
5. w B r y b r B b w B w B r y b r B ? ? ? (b w B)

Group L

1. r B y g r y g w w g y r g ? ? ? (y B r)
2. b b w r g w B r g g r B w g r ? ? ? (w b b)
3. b w g y b B r g y w B B w y g r B b y ? ? ? (g w b)
4. r w b y B b y B w r B g g B r w B y b B y ? ? ? (b w r)
5. B y w b y r r b B B B B b r r y b ? ? ? (w y B)

Group M

1. g y y b r r b y y g r g b w B ? ? ? ? ? (B w b g r)
2. b r y r g g r y r b r B w b B ? ? ? ? ? (B b w B r)
3. g B g r w w r g B g b y r w g ? ? ? ? ? (g w r y b)
4. w g g B r r B g g w y w B b r ? ? ? ? ? (r b B w y)
5. y w B b r r b B w y g g w r y ? ? ? ? ? (y r w g g)

Group N

1. b w r g y r w b g r r y B y g b w g ? ? ? ? ? ? (y B b g g w)
2. B w g b r y w B b g y r r w g B y g ? ? ? ? ? ? (w r B g g y)
3. b g w b r B g b b w B r y g g y r w ? ? ? ? ? ? (g y y g w r)
4. g b b w r b b g w b b r y B w g B r ? ? ? ? ? ? (B y g w r B)
5. g r w g b w r g g w w b b r B y y g ? ? ? ? ? ? (r b y B g y)

Group O

1. g b B g y w r w r w y w B g ? ? (g b)
2. r w b g w b y B y B w b b g ? ? (r w)
3. B y b r b w y g y g b w b r ? ? (B y)
4. y g b y w b B w B w w b b y ? ? (y g)
5. r b b w g B y B y B g B b w ? ? (r b)

Group P

1. y g B w b w w r g y w B w b ? ? (r w)
2. r g w B y y b g g r B w y y ? ? (g b)
3. r g B r y g w B b y g r r B g y ? ? ? ? (B w y b)
4. B g r y g w B b y g g B y r w g ? ? ? ? (b B g y)
5. w g B w y b r y g r g w w B b y ? ? ? ? (y r r g)

Group Q

1. b g y r w B g b y r w B g b r y w B ? ? ? ? ? ? (g b r y B w)
2. r b y B w b b r y B w b b r B y w b ? ? ? ? ? ? (b r B y b w)
3. r w y r w g w r y r w g w r r y w g ? ? ? ? ? ? (w r r y g w)
4. b w w b w B w b w b w B w b b w w B ? ? ? ? ? ? (w b b w B w)
5. b r r b g w w g r b r b g w w g r b b r g w w g r b b r w g w g ? ? ? ? ? ? ? ? (r b b r w g g w)

Group R

1. g r w b g r b y g r w y ? ? (g r)
2. B g w y B g r b B g w r ? ? (B g)
3. r w b y g B b y w g b y B w ? ? (b y)
4. r w g B y b w r B y g r B ? ? (B y)
5. w w w r B g y b r B y b w ? ? (r B)

Group S

1. B y r b w y g r w b B g y b w y r B ? ? (w b)
2. g y b B y r y w y B b g r B y y w b ? ? (y B)
3. y B r y w y g b w y r r w y w B g g ? ? (w y)
4. r r b b g y w g g b w b b b g B w y ? ? (g b)
5. r w r r y y b B y r w w b r y g B y ? ? (y r)

213

Group T

1. y b w r g B r w y b w r g ? ? ? ? ? (B r w y b)
2. w B y r b g r y w B y r b ? ? ? ? ? (g r y w B)
3. r w y B r g B y r w y B r ? ? ? ? ? (g B y r w)
4. g y y b b g b y g y y b b ? ? ? ? ? (g b y g y)
5. r r r g g y g r r r r g g ? ? ? ? ? (y g r r r)

Group U

1. w b g y r b B r y g B w g y r w ? ? ? ? ? ? (b r y g b B)
2. B w r b y w g y b r g B r b y B ? ? ? ? ? ? (w y b r w g)
3. B w B w r w b r w B b B B w r B ? ? ? ? ? ? (w r w B w b)
4. g b b B r b y r B b y g b B r g ? ? ? ? ? ? (b r B b b y)
5. g y g r r y r r r g r g g r r g ? ? ? ? ? ? (y r r g y r)

Group V

1. B w y b r w B b y r B w b r y w B r b y ? ? ? ? ? (B w r y b)
2. g y B w b y g w B b g y w b B y g b w B ? ? ? ? ? (g y b B w)
3. B r r y b r B y r b B r y b r r B b y r ? ? ? ? ? (B r b r y)
4. w g g r w g w r g w w g r w g g w w r g ? ? ? ? ? (w g w g r)
5. r g r g y g r g r y r g g y r g r y g r ? ? ? ? ? (r g y r g)

Group W

1. r w g g y r w g y g r w y g g r y w g g ? ? ? ? ? (y r w g g)
2. B b y r w B b y w r B b w y r B w b y r ? ? ? ? ? (w B b y r)
3. g g y w r g g w y r g w g y r ? ? ? ? ? (w g g y r)
4. b w b w r g b w b r w g b w r b w g ? ? ? ? ? ? (b r w b w g)
5. B B y y g r g B B y y r g g B B y r y g g ? ? ? ? ? ? ? (B B r y y g g)

Group X

1. b B r w g b r B w g b r w B g ? ? ? ? ? (b r w g B)
2. r B B y y B r B y y B B r y y ? ? ? ? ? (B B y r y)
3. g g r y b g r g y b g r y g b ? ? ? ? ? (g r y b g)
4. y g g r w g y g r w g g y r w ? ? ? ? ? (g g r y w)
5. w w r b y w w r b y w r w b y w r b w y ? ? ? ? ? (w r b y w)

214

Group Y

1. w r y B g b r y w B g b r y B ? ? ? (g w b)
2. r g y b w B g y r b w B g y b ? ? ? (w r B)
3. g g y b w r B g y g b w r B g y b w g r B ? ? ? ? ? ? ? ? (g y b w r B g)
4. y y y r r g g y y y r r g g y y r r y g g ? ? ? ? ? ? ? (y y r r g g y)
5. w b w b w b w b w w b w b w b w b w w b w ? ? ? ? ? ? ? (b w b w b w w)

Group Z

1. b y r g y r g b r g b y ? ? ? ? (g b y r)
2. g b y r w b y r w g y r w g b ? ? ? ? ? (r w g b y)
3. w g y r B b g y r B b w y r B b w g ? ? ? ? ? ? (r B b w g y)
4. y r w b B g w b B g y r B g ? ? ? ? (y r w b)
5. w r b B y g b B y g w r y g ? ? ? ? (w r b B)

Group A2

1. g r y b B w g r y b B g r y b g ? ? ? ? ? (r y g r g)
2. w b B y g r w b B y g w b B y w ? ? ? ? ? (b B w b w)
3. r y r b r w r y r b r r y r b r ? ? ? ? ? (y r r y r)
4. w w g w y y w w g w y w w g w w ? ? ? ? ? (w g w w w)
5. g y g y b r g y g y b g y g y g ? ? ? ? ? (y g g y g)

Group B2

1. g B y r b w B y r b w y r b w r ? ? ? ? ? (b w b w w)
2. B w g b r y w g b r y g b r y b ? ? ? ? ? (r y r y y)
3. g r b y y g r b y y g b y y g y ? ? ? ? ? (y g y g g)
4. b r b w r w r b w r w b w r w w ? ? ? ? ? (r w r w w)
5. w y y g y y y y g y y y g y y g ? ? ? ? ? (y y y y y)

Group C2

1. w B b r y g w b r y g w r y g w ? ? ? ? ? (y g w g w)
2. y g B b g r y B b g r y b g r y ? ? ? ? ? (g r y r y)
3. b r w w r b b w w r b b w r b b ? ? ? ? ? (r b b b b)
4. y y y g g g y y g g g y g g g y ? ? ? ? ? (g g y g y)

215

Group D2

1. b y B g w r b y g w r b y w r b ? ? ? ? (y r b y)
2. g w r y r y g w y r y g w r y g ? ? ? ? (w y g w)
3. b g g B w w b g B w w b g w w b ? ? ? ? (g w b g)
4. y y b w y g y y w y g y y y g y ? ? ? ? (y g y y)

Group E2

1. w g y r b B w g y b B w g y B ? ? ? (w g y)
2. r w y B b g r w y b g r w y g ? ? ? (r w y)
3. b y r g B w b y r B w b y r w ? ? ? (b y r)

Group F2

1. b b B r w g y B B r w g y r r w g y ? ? ? ? ? ? ? (w w g y g g y)
2. B B y g r b w y y g r b w g g r b w ? ? ? ? ? ? ? (r r b w b w)
3. g g w y b y r w w y b y r y y b y r ? ? ? ? ? ? ? (b b y r y y r)

Group G2

1. b w w r b y g w r r b y g r b b y g ? ? ? ? (b y y g)
2. B g g y w r b g y y w r b y w w r b ? ? ? ? (w r r b)
3. b B B y r w g B y y r w g y r r w g ? ? ? ? (r w w g)

Group H2

1. g y b r w B B g y b r w w g y b r r g y b ? ? ? ? ? ? (b g y y g g)
2. b w r y B g g b w r y B B b w r y y b w r ? ? ? ? ? ? (r b w w b b)
3. y r B g w b b y r B g w w y r B g g y r B ? ? ? ? ? ? (B y r r y y)

Group I2

1. B r y g w w b B r y g g w B r y y y g ? ? ? ? ? ? ? (B r r y B B r)
2. b y g w r r B b y g w w r b y g g w ? ? ? ? ? ? ? (b y y g b b y)

216

3. w b r g y y B w b r g g y w b r r g ? ? ? ? ? ? ? (w b b r w w b)

Group J2
1. g w r r b y B w r b b y B r b y y B ? ? ? ? (b y B B)
2. B g w w y r b g w y y r b w y r r b ? ? ? ? (y r b b)
3. w B y y r b g B y r r b g y r b b g ? ? ? ? (r b g g)

Group K2
1. g r b w B y g r g b w r B y b g r w b w B ? ? ? (B y y)
2. b B r y w g b B b r y B w g r b B y r y w ? ? ? (w g g)
3. w r y b g B w r w y b r g B y w r b y b g ? ? ? (g B B)

Group L2
1. r y B g w b r r y y B g B w b g r y w B g ? ? ? (b w b)
2. g w y b B r g g w w y b y B r b g w B y b ? ? ? (r B r)
3. b B w r y g b b B B w r w y g r b B y w r ? ? ? (g y g)

Group M2
1. r g r w b g y B w r g b w b y ? ? ? (y B B)
2. w B w y g B r b y w B g y g r ? ? ? (r b b)
3. y b y r B b g w r y b B r B g ? ? ? (g w w)

Group N2
1. r r w w b B b y g B r w y b B ? ? ? (g y g)
2. b b B B g w g r y w b B r g w ? ? ? (y r y)
3. B B y y w r w b g r B y b w r ? ? ? (g b g)

17.

Directional, Coordination and Balance Exercises

Arrows Exercise

You need the arrows chart for this exercise. The arrows point in four directions: up, down, left and right. The steps below can be worked through with the arrows chart. It is important that the learner should learn to do these exercises at a relaxed and leisurely pace at first. Do not let him rush through them. Only when he really starts getting comfortable with the exercise should one aim at attaining greater speed. One should continue with Step 1 until the learner can read the whole chart without hesitations or mistakes before advancing to Step 2.

Step 1

The tutor must paste the arrows chart on the wall, so that the learner can look at it. The learner must stand upright, with his clenched fists held at the shoulders. Now the learner must "read" the arrows one after the other, simultaneously announcing the direction in which each arrow is pointing and pushing out his fists in the direction so announced. This means that if the learner starts "reading" the arrows, he will shoot out the left fist towards the left, while simultaneously saying aloud, "Left!" *See figure 15.*

He must immediately bring his left fist back to the shoulder, ready to "read" the next arrow. This means that he will shoot out the left fist again, saying, "Left!" Again he must bring the left fist back to the shoulder immediately. Then he must "read" the third arrow. He must shoot out the right fist to the right and say, "Right!" The right fist is also brought back to the shoulder

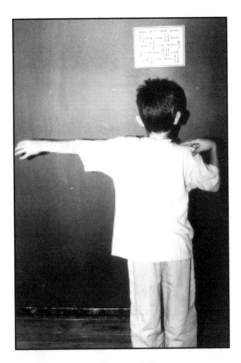

Figure 15

immediately, and then the direction of the next arrow is announced. The left fist is again pushed out, while the learner says, "Left!" To "read" the next arrow, the learner must shoot out both fists above the head, simultaneously announcing, "Up!" Both fists are brought back to the shoulders, ready to "read" the next arrow, which is "Down!" In this way the learner must read through the whole arrows chart, from top to bottom. The tutor must turn the chart around through 180 degrees before letting the learner read it again.

In this way the learner must with the fists show the direction in which each arrow is pointing, while simultaneously announcing the direction. Left and right are shown with one fist only, but up and down with both. The tutor must check that the learner does everything correctly.

This exercise may seem very simple, even childish. It is, however, extremely important. If the learner can "read" through the whole arrows chart without making any mistakes, the tutor must not think that he does not need this exercise. All the skills that underlie reading, of which position in space is one, must be drummed in so securely that the learner can apply them in reading situations without having to think of them at all.

Step 2

The learner must "march" on the spot while reading the arrows. He announces and shows the direction of each arrow, synchronizing it with each step of the *left* foot. The fists are held at the shoulders. For left and right one arm at a time is extended, for up and down both. Let the learner read through the whole arrows chart while he synchronizes with the steps of the left foot. *See figure 16.*

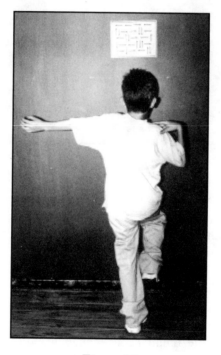

Figure 16

Step 3

This is exactly the same as Step 2, except that the learner must synchronize with steps of the *right* foot.

Spatial Exercise

For this exercise the tutor should ask the learner to remove five blocks of five different colors from his box, close the box and *turn the box upside down*. She could then give the following instruction:

"Take a green block, and put it in front of the box." The learner must put the green block in front of the box.

"Take a blue block, and put it behind the box." The learner must put the blue block behind the box. *See figure 17.*

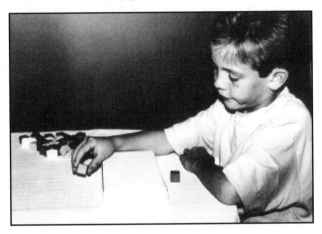

Figure 17

"Take a black block, and put it to the left of the box."

"Take a white block, and put it to the right of the box."

"Take a red block, and put it on top of the box."

That is the end of the exercise. It is a very simple, but a very important exercise. Do not think that the exercise is unnecessary if the learner gives the correct answers every time. The idea of the exercise is to drill basic concepts and orientations. Therefore, please continue to do the exercise for the full time that it appears in the program.

Important note 1: Make sure that you know where "in front" and where "behind' is. Many people, even adults, are uncertain or inconsistent about these spatial terms. The important thing to remember is that, when an object does not have its own front and back sides, one always interprets space from inside one's own body. In order to put the blue block behind the box, the blue block will be further away from the learner than the box. In order to put the green block in front of the box, the green block will be between the learner and the box.

If you have any doubt in your mind about these spatial terms, go to a wall. Put anything behind the wall. Whatever you have put behind the wall will be hidden behind the wall and will therefore not be visible to you. It will be further away from you than the wall.

Important note 2: In order not to confuse the learner about these spatial terms, it is recommended that the tutor sometimes stand behind the learner when doing this exercise, and sometimes in front of him. Wherever the tutor is standing, the answers must still be the same!

Important note 3: When doing this exercise, the box must sometimes be put in a horizontal position in front of the learner, like this:

Sometimes, again, the box must be put vertically in front of the learner, like this:

Beanbags Exercises

To do the Beanbags exercises, the tutor must first buy or make two beanbags. Cut two pieces of cloth, about 9 by 4 inches (24 X 10 centimeters). Fold each piece double, and then sew two sides together, so that two little bags of 4½ by 4 inches (12 X 10 centimeters) will have been formed. Then fill the bags with something like dried beans, maize, corn or rice before sewing up the open side. Note that the bags should not be filled too tight.

Beanbags exercise 1

The tutor and learner stand facing each other, about 7 to 10 feet (2 to 3 meters) apart. The tutor has one of the beanbags in her hands. She throws the beanbag at the learner, who must catch it with both hands. Then the learner throws the bag back at the tutor. He must take turns with the left and right hands; one throw must be performed with the left, and the next with the right hand.

Beanbags exercise 2

The tutor and learner stand facing each other, about 7 to 10 feet (2 to 3 meters) apart. The tutor has both the beanbags in her hands, one in each hand. She first nominates the hand with which the learner must catch, e.g. "Right!" and then throws one of the beanbags at the learner, who must catch it with the nominated hand. Then the learner throws the bag back at the tutor with the same hand. The tutor throws the bag at the learner again, this time nominating the other hand. The learner must catch with the hand so nominated.

Beanbags exercise 3

The tutor and learner stand facing each other, about 7 to 10 feet (2 to 3 meters) apart. The tutor has both the beanbags in her hands, one in each hand. She throws one of the beanbags at the learner, who must catch it with the hand on the same side as the hand with which the tutor threw. Then the tutor also throws the other bag at the learner, while the learner simultaneously throws the bag in his hand back at the tutor. The tutor and learner continue to throw the two beanbags simultaneously at each other.

Beanbags exercise 4

The tutor and learner stand facing each other, about 7 to 10 feet (2 to 3 meters) apart. The tutor has both the beanbags in her hands, one in each hand. She throws both the beanbags simultaneously at the learner, who must catch both, one in each hand. Then the learner throws both bags back at the tutor, who must also catch them both, one in each hand. The tutor and learner continue to throw the two beanbags simultaneously at each other.

Paper Crumpling Exercises

Paper Crumpling exercise 1

For this exercise, one needs an old telephone directory, or sheets of any other paper that is as soft as, and about the same size as, a page of a telephone directory.

The tutor tears a page from the directory, and gives it to the learner. He must then crumple the piece of paper into a tight ball. It is very important, however, that he must strictly use one hand only for this task. The learner may also not press his hand against his body. *See Figure 18.*

Figure 18

Then the tutor tears another page from the directory, and lets the learner crumple this also, but this time with the other hand.

The learner must crumple three sheets of paper with each hand at every practice session.

Paper Crumpling exercise 2

For this exercise one uses scrap paper of $8^1/_2$ by 11 inches (A4-size). The tutor gives the learner one sheet of paper in each hand. He must then simultaneously crumple both papers into tight balls. It is very important that each hand must strictly do its own work. The learner should sit with his hands wide apart, so that one hand cannot offer any help to the other. The learner may also not press his hands against his body or on any object, like a table. The learner should crumple three sheets of paper per hand per session.

Important note: If the learner finds it hard to crumple the stiffer paper with both hand simultaneously, one can temporarily allow him to crumple one sheet at a time, until his hands have become stronger. Then let him crumple two sheets of paper simultaneously.

Balance Exercises

Balance exercise 1

For this exercise one needs about twenty boxes, like shoeboxes. Arrange the boxes in two rows, so that the learner can step in them. Let him walk in the two rows of boxes, stepping into each box in turn.

Balance exercise 2

Only two boxes are needed for this exercise. Put the two boxes side by side on the floor. The learner puts one foot into each box. The tutor stands behind the learner. He then lifts up one foot, and the tutor pushes the box under this foot forward with her own foot. The learner steps into this box, and then lifts his other foot for the tutor to push this other box forward. The tutor continues pushing alternate boxes forward, so that the learner can walk forward, stepping in the two boxes. *See figure 19.*

Figure 19

Balance exercise 3

Again one needs two boxes only for this exercise. The learner steps into both boxes, and then lifts one foot off the floor, balancing only on the other. He then bends down and moves one box forward, so that he can step into it. He then lifts the other foot, bends down, and moves the other box forward. *See figure 20.*

Figure 20

18.

Mathematical Exercises

Counting Exercises

Counting exercise 2

The learner sits at a table opposite the tutor. He must now carry out the instructions that follow.

The tutor will start by asking the learner to arrange a row of blocks, say ten, on the table directly in front of him, leaving a space of roughly an inch (a few centimeters) between each block.

The learner now has to put his right arm on the table, with the forearm directly in front of his body and parallel to the edge of the table. This will mean that the elbow will be at an angle of about 90 degrees. The right arm must be kept in this position for the duration of the exercise. He must put the index finger of the left hand on the first block on the left of the row, saying, "One!" Then he puts the finger on the second block, saying, "Two!" *See figure 21.*

Figure 21

227

In this way the learner continues counting all the blocks. When he arrives at the tenth block, he must continue by counting backwards to one again. If there were any hesitations anywhere in this counting up and down, the tutor must let the learner count again, up and down.

As soon as he can count the ten blocks fluently and without any hesitation—several successive sessions may be required to achieve this—the tutor may instruct the learner to add an extra block either to the left or the right of the existing row, and then the counting continues, now with one block more. He must continue counting with the left hand for the whole session, the right arm still resting on the table in front of him. At the next session he must switch hands. Then the right hand counts and the left arm must rest on the table. He must now put the index finger of the right hand on the first block on the left of the row, saying, "One!"

Please note that the learner's forearm must be on the table, directly in front of him. In this way, while he is counting up and down, he is continually crossing the middle line.

As the learner makes progress, at successive lessons the tutor can let him arrange longer and longer rows of blocks, up to a maximum of 30 blocks.

As soon as this maximum of 30 has been reached, one can continue the exercise by following the steps of *Counting exercise 3*, as set out below. This means that, as soon as the learner can count fluently and without mistakes or hesitations from 1 to 30 and back, one would let them go to the next step in the counting exercise, i.e. 11 to 40 and back. When he puts his finger on the first block on the left to start counting, he would then not say, "one," but "eleven," et cetera. If the learner experiences any difficulties counting from 11 to 40 and back, it may mean that the tutor was in too much of a hurry to continue to a following step and that the previous step had not been drilled adequately. However, if the learner shows only slight hesitations when counting between 31 and 40, the tutor could let him arrange only 21 blocks in front of himself so that he will initially only count from 11 to 31 and back. She could then gradually extend the row of blocks up to 40, as the learner makes progress. As soon as he is able to count fluently from 11 to 40 and back, the tutor can advance to the next step, which is from 21 to 50 and back. In this way she can work through all the steps of counting in ones. To count in twos, the learner must imagine that each block in the row in front of him represents two blocks. Later, when counting in threes, he must imagine that each block represents three blocks.

Counting exercise 3

The tutor must instruct the learner to fold his hands together and to put them on the table in front of him. (Note that the blocks are not used for *Counting exercise 3*.) Then she must instruct him to count from 1 to 30 and back. This is the first step of this counting exercise, as given below.

Every step of *Counting exercise 3* must be done over and over, until the learner can do it fluently and without hesitation. Only when the learner is able to count fluently and without any hesitation from 1 to 30 and back does one continue to the next step, which is to count from 11 to 40 and back.

The different steps of the exercise are set out below. Only when the learner has become completely fluent and automatic on one step may one continue to the next. It is also very important to do regular revision of previous steps.

Counting in ones
Count from 1 to 30 and back.
Count from 11 to 40 and back.
Count from 21 to 50 and back.
Count from 31 to 60 and back.
Count from 41 to 70 and back.
Count from 51 to 80 and back.
Count from 61 to 90 and back.
Count from 71 to 100 and back.

Counting in twos
Count from 2 to 60 and back.
Count from 12 to 70 and back.
Count from 22 to 80 and back.
Count from 32 to 90 and back.
Count from 42 to 100 and back.
Count from 52 to 110 and back.
Count from 62 to 120 and back.
Count from 72 to 130 and back.
Count from 82 to 140 and back.
Count from 1 to 59 and back.
Count from 11 to 69 and back.

Count from 21 to 79 and back.
Count from 31 to 89 and back.
Count from 41 to 99 and back.
Count from 51 to 109 and back.
Count from 61 to 119 and back.
Count from 71 to 129 and back.
Count from 81 to 139 and back.

Counting in threes
Count from 3 to 99 and back.
Count from 21 to 117 and back.
Count from 39 to 135 and back.
Count from 2 to 98 and back.
Count from 20 to 116 and back.
Count from 38 to 134 and back.
Count from 1 to 97 and back.
Count from 19 to 115 and back.
Count from 37 to 133 and back.

Counting in fours
Count from 4 to 120 and back.
Count from 24 to 140 and back.
Count from 44 to 160 and back.
Count from 3 to 119 and back.
Count from 23 to 139 and back.
Count from 43 to 159 and back.
Count from 2 to 118 and back.
Count from 22 to 138 and back.
Count from 42 to 158 and back.
Count from 1 to 117 and back.
Count from 21 to 137 and back.
Count from 41 to 157 and back.

Counting in fives
Count from 5 to 150 and back.
Count from 25 to 170 and back.

Count from 45 to 190 and back.
Count from 4 to 149 and back.
Count from 24 to 169 and back.
Count from 44 to 189 and back.
Count from 3 to 148 and back.
Count from 23 to 168 and back.
Count from 43 to 188 and back.
Count from 2 to 147 and back.
Count from 22 to 167 and back.
Count from 42 to 187 and back.
Count from 1 to 146 and back.
Count from 21 to 166 and back.
Count from 41 to 186 and back.

The tutor can herself work out further steps.

Tables Exercise

The purpose of this exercise is to teach the learner the mathematical tables.

Again the tutor and learner should sit opposite each other at a table. The tutor takes two blocks, and puts them in front of the learner and says, "I give you two blocks. How many blocks have you got?" The learner must answer, "Two." The tutor takes two more blocks, and puts them to the left (from her point of view) of the other pair, and says, "I give you two more blocks. Twice I have given you two blocks. How many blocks have you got?" The learner answers, "Four." The tutor again takes two blocks and puts them to the left of the others, and says, "I give you two more blocks. Three times I have given you two blocks. How many blocks have you got?" The learner answers, "Six."

The purpose of the fairly elaborate questions and answers is to make sure that the learner understands the meaning of multiplication. When the tutor is quite sure that the learner really understands what multiplication is, she can simplify by just saying "One times two" when she puts the first pair of blocks in front of the learner on the table, and "Two times two" when she puts the second pair in front of him, et cetera.

In this way the tutor continues adding blocks to those already on the table, asking the appropriate questions, and the learner giving the appropriate answers. However, if the learner gives a wrong answer, or is very hesitant about an answer, the tutor stops adding blocks, and then takes away two blocks at a time.

For example, let us say that at six times two blocks the learner gave a wrong answer, or was very hesitant, the tutor will first let the learner count all twelve blocks, so that he will know that the correct answer is twelve, and will then remove two blocks, saying, "Five times two?" After the answer, "Ten," she removes two more blocks and says, "Four times two?" In this way she continues until again there are only two blocks, and then she starts adding again. She continues adding until she arrives at a place where the learner gets stuck, and then she removes again.

In this way the tutor goes up and down, drilling the learner on the two times table, up to twenty-five times two. When there are no longer enough blocks to continue adding blocks, one just pretends, and asks the questions. When the learner has become fluent on this procedure, the tutor starts to question the learner at random on the two times table: "What is six times two? Eighteen times two? Five times two? Seventeen times two? Nine times two? Twenty-four times two?" et cetera.

If the learner is completely fluent on the two times table, the tutor starts teaching him the three times table in exactly the same way.

19.

Reading Exercises

One sometimes finds that a person's reading ability is satisfactory, but that he battles with spelling. It is therefore believed that the reading exercises are irrelevant in remediating a spelling problem. This is not the case. Spelling is our active knowledge of the written word, while reading is our passive knowledge. In the same way that a person's active vocabulary can only be improved *via* the passive, our active knowledge of the written word can also only be improved *via* the passive. Of course, there must be enough repetition of the same words. In fact, a "pyramid of repetition" must be built.

If however, the learner continues to make stubborn spelling mistakes by the time you have completed level three of the program (there are always the odd case or two), the following exercise can be used to rectify the problem:

The tutor says, "d. Now repeat the letter after me." The learner says *d*.
The tutor says, "i. Now start from the beginning." The learner says *d i*.
The tutor says *f.* The learner says *d i f.*
The tutor says *f.* The learner says *d i f f.*
The tutor says *i.* The learner says *d i f f i.*
The tutor says *c.* The learner says *d i f f i c.*
The tutor says *u.* The learner says *d i f f i c u.*
The tutor says *l.* The learner says *d i f f i c u l.*
The tutor says *t.* The learner says *d i f f i c u l t.*
The tutor says, "What word did we spell?"
The learner says, "difficult."
The tutor says, "Now write the word for me."

Repeat this regularly until the learner can spell the word *difficult*. Use the same method to teach the spelling of other words.

Reading Exercise 1

For this exercise the tutor must use the *yellow* word cards.

The tutor takes any six of the word cards in her hand. She must make sure that none of these six words start with a capital letter. The words with capital letters must be left until all the other yellow word cards have been dealt with. The tutor and learner sit at opposite sides of a table. The tutor holds the word cards ready in her hand and then puts two words down on the table—one on top of the other—in front of the learner in quick succession and then immediately covers both words with her hand. It is important that the action of putting the word cards on the table and covering them with one's hand should be a very quick one. If fact, one should always strive to do it faster.

With her hand covering the word cards, the tutor waits for the learner to say both words. She then puts the next two words in front of him in the same way, and waits for him to say both words, followed by the fifth and sixth word cards.

If the learner was unable to read any of the words, or if he read any of the words hesitantly or incorrectly, she must put the word or words in question aside so that they can be drilled later. She puts one word at a time in front of the learner and asks, "What word is this?" She drills them over and over until he can read all six words fluently.

As soon as the learner is able to read the first six words correctly and without hesitation, two more words are added and the process starts all over again. As soon as the learner can read these eight words well, then two more are added. As soon as the learner can read these ten words well, two more are added again, et cetera. Whenever the learner is unable to read any of the words, or if he reads any of the words hesitantly or incorrectly, she puts the word or words in question aside so that they can be drilled. Two new words should only be added if the learner could read all the words in the pile fluently and without hesitation.

As soon as there are too many words to deal with in one lesson, then divide the word cards into two sections. In one lesson, only one of the sections is used. The two sections must be alternated on a daily basis. When the number of words in each of the two sections becomes too many again, one can divide them into three sections. However, one should never have more than three sections.

It is very important that one should not discard word cards, but should continue drilling words over and over.

Only when the learner is able to read all the yellow word cards without any hesitation, is he ready to read the first chapter of the reading book (or chapter one of *Rainbow Dreams*). If he reads this chapter fluently and without hesitation, he is ready to continue to level two of the program. If, however, he still stumbles and hesitates, work on the yellow word cards must continue.

Reading Exercise 2

This exercise is exactly the same as *Reading exercise 1*, except that now the tutor uses the *white* word cards.

Only when the learner is able to read all the white word cards without any hesitation, is he ready to read chapter two of the reading book (or chapter two of *Rainbow Dreams*). If he reads this chapter fluently and without hesitation, he is ready to continue to level three of the program. If, however, he still stumbles and hesitates, work on the white word cards must continue.

Reading Exercise 3

This exercise is exactly the same as *Reading exercise 1*, except that now the tutor uses the *blue* word cards.

Only when the learner is able to read all the blue word cards without any hesitation, is he ready to read chapter three of the reading book (or chapter three of *Rainbow Dreams*). If he reads this chapter fluently and without hesitation, he is ready to continue to level four of the program. If, however, he still stumbles and hesitates, work on the blue word cards must continue.

Reading Exercise 4

As soon as the learner is able to read all the word cards fluently and without hesitation, one can move on to the *word lists*. (If the tutor is making use of *Rainbow Dreams*, she must open the book at the word lists that precede chapter four, and put the book in front of the learner.) The words are printed in three columns. She must instruct the learner to put the index finger of his right hand (or left, whichever is most convenient to the learner) under the first word of the left-hand column. He must read the word aloud, and then he must move his finger down to the second word, saying also this word aloud. In this way the learner must move his finger down the column from word to word, reading each one aloud. When he arrives at the bottom of the first column, he must move his finger up to the beginning of the second column, and then read the second column, and after that also the third column, in the same way.

Every time this exercise is done, it is important that the tutor change the order in which the word list is read, otherwise the learner will quickly memorize the words in sequence, and he will be reciting and not really reading the words. Sometimes she must let the learner read the columns from top to bottom, as explained above, but she must vary this every time, as follows:

- Read the words horizontally, from left to right, and not vertically in columns, starting at the top. The finger then moves horizontally, from column to column.
- Read the words horizontally, from right to left, starting at the top.
- Read the words horizontally, from left to right, starting at the bottom.
- Read the words horizontally, from right to left, starting at the bottom.
- Read the first column from top to bottom, the second from bottom to top, and the third from top to bottom.
- Read the first column from bottom to top, the second from top to bottom, and the third from bottom to top.

Only when the learner is able to read through the whole word list of the fourth chapter without any hesitation, is he ready to read the text itself. If he reads the text fluently and without hesitation, he is ready to continue to chapter five. If, however, he still stumbles and hesitates, he must be taken back to the word list.

The fifth chapter must be learned in the same way.

20.

Dyslexia Program

This program is aimed at improving the reading ability of schoolchildren—or adults—as quickly and as effortlessly as possible.

A very important principle, that must always be considered in the application of this program, is that *the more time one spends with the learner on this program and the longer one perseveres, the better the results that can be expected.* One could compare this to physical training exercises. A person, who embarks on a program of physical exercise and who spends one hour every day and continues for a long period, can certainly expect much better results than the person who devotes fifteen minutes per day to exercise and stops after only three months. Success at any venture is invariably commensurate to the amount of time and effort expended.

Two very important considerations, before starting the *Audiblox 2000* program, is therefore:

1. How serious is the learner's reading problem?
2. How much time do the tutor and the learner have at their disposal to devote to the *Audiblox 2000* program?

In the case of a severe reading problem, at least one lesson per day, five days per week, is required. Practical experience has shown that in most cases this is the amount of time required to solve the reading problem of a severely dyslexic person in a reasonable time.

A possibility that should be considered in the case of a child—or adult—with a severe reading problem is that vacation time may be used for a one-week or two-week "crash" course. During such a crash course, the same lesson of sixty minutes can be repeated over and over, as many times as possible—up to five times per day—with intermittent rest periods of fifteen minutes and a lunch break of half an hour. This delivers excellent results in most cases. After this crash course, the normal program must be continued, spending as much time as possible on the program.

However, if it is the tutor's considered opinion that the learner's reading problem is not too severe, then two to three sessions per week will probably be sufficient. Furthermore, if the problem is not too serious and there are severe time constraints, so that only half an hour per day is available, then the program can be adapted to fit in with the time on hand. In such a case it is recommended that *Sequencing exercise 3* and the *Reading exercises* be done on Day 1 and all the remaining exercises on Day 2, *Sequencing exercise 3* and the *Reading exercises* again on Day 3 and the remaining exercises on Day 4, and *Sequencing exercise 3* and the *Reading exercises* again on Day 5, et cetera.

Lastly, it is important that the program should not be interrupted. Make sure that the learner receives the prescribed number of lessons per week.

Level 1

This program is to be followed until the learner is able to read all the yellow word cards without any hesitation. He must also be able to read the first chapter of the reading book (or chapter one of *Rainbow Dreams*) without hesitations and without any errors.

Important note on the Pattern exercises: Start with *Pattern exercise 1*. As soon as the learner succeeds in correctly reproducing a pattern with ten blocks, move on to *Pattern exercise 2*.

Important note on *Sequencing exercise 3*: Whenever two or more lessons are done on the same day, as in the suggested crash course, one continues with the *same* row, making the row longer and longer. In the first lesson, one should start with a new row. When doing the second (or third or fourth or fifth) lesson, one continues with the *same* row, making this same row longer and longer.

Important note: When following this program with high school students or adults, the Beanbags exercises and Balance exercises can be omitted, and *Counting exercise 2* can be replaced by *Counting exercise 3*.

The following program should be followed:

Day 1: *Sequencing exercise 3 for 17 minutes;*
Arrows exercise step 1 for 2 minutes;
Pattern exercise 1 (or 2) for 17 minutes;
Spatial exercise for 1 minute;
Reading exercise 1 for 15 minutes;
Counting exercise 2 for 5 minutes;
Paper Crumpling exercise 1.

Day 2: *Sequencing exercise 3 for 17 minutes;*
Arrows exercise step 1 for 2 minutes;
Pattern exercise 1 (or 2) for 17 minutes;
Spatial exercise for 1 minute;
Reading exercise 1 for 15 minutes;
Counting exercise 3 for 5 minutes;
Paper Crumpling exercise 1.

Day 3: Repeat the program of Day 1.

Day 4: Repeat the program of Day 2.

Day 5: Repeat the program of Day 1.

Level 2

This program is to be followed until the learner is able to read all the white word cards without any hesitation. He must also be able to read chapter two of the reading book (or chapter two of *Rainbow Dreams*) without hesitations and without any errors.

Important note on *Counting exercise 3*: Days 1 and 3 must be used to master a new step. Day 5 must always be used to revise steps that had already been mastered.

The following program should be followed:

Day 1: *Sequencing exercise 3 for 15 minutes;*
Arrows exercise step 2 for 2 minutes;
Pattern exercise 1 (or 2) for 16 minutes;

Spatial exercise for 1 minute;
Reading exercise 1 for 5 minutes;
Reading exercise 2 for 10 minutes;
Counting exercise 3 for 5 minutes;
Paper Crumpling exercise 2;
Balance exercise 1 for 3 minutes.

Day 2: *Sequencing exercise 3* for 17 minutes;
Arrows exercise step 1 for 2 minutes;
Auditory exercise 1 for 17 minutes;
Spatial exercise for 1 minute;
Reading exercise 1 for 10 minutes;
Reading exercise 2 for 5 minutes;
Counting exercise 2 for 5 minutes;
Beanbags exercise 1 for 3 minutes.

Day 3: Repeat the program of Day 1. Remember that in *Counting exercise 3* the new step, that you are working on at present, must be exercised.

Day 4: Repeat the program of Day 2.

Day 5: Repeat the program of Day 1. Remember that in *Counting exercise 3* steps that you have already worked on must be revised.

Level 3

This program is to be followed until the learner is able to read all the blue word cards without hesitation. He must also be able to read chapter three of the reading book (or chapter three of *Rainbow Dreams*) without hesitations and without any errors.

Important note on *Counting exercise 3*: Days 1 and 3 must be used to master a new step. Day 5 must always be used to revise steps that had already been mastered.

The following program should be followed:

Day 1: *Sequencing exercise 3* for 17 minutes;
Arrows exercise step 3 for 2 minutes;

Pattern exercise 2 for 17 minutes;
Spatial exercise for 1 minute;
Reading exercise 1 for 5 minutes;
Reading exercise 2 for 5 minutes;
Reading exercise 3 for 5 minutes;
Counting exercise 3 for 5 minutes;
Beanbags exercise 2 for 3 minutes.

Day 2: *Sequencing exercise 3* for 15 minutes;
Arrows exercise step 2 for 2 minutes;
Auditory exercise 1 for 16 minutes;
Spatial exercise for 1 minute;
Reading exercise 1 for 5 minutes;
Reading exercise 2 for 5 minutes;
Reading exercise 3 for 5 minutes;
Counting exercise 2 for 5 minutes;
Beanbags exercise 3 for 3 minutes;
Balance exercise 2 for 3 minutes.

Day 3: *Sequencing exercise 3* for 17 minutes;
Arrows exercise step 1 for 2 minutes;
Pattern exercise 2 for 17 minutes;
Spatial exercise for 1 minute;
Reading exercise 1 for 5 minutes;
Reading exercise 2 for 5 minutes;
Reading exercise 3 for 5 minutes;
Counting exercise 3 for 5 minutes;
Paper Crumpling exercise 2.

Day 4: *Sequencing exercise 3* for 15 minutes;
Arrows exercise step 2 for 2 minutes;
Auditory exercise 2 for 16 minutes;
Spatial exercise for 1 minute;
Reading exercise 1 for 5 minutes;
Reading exercise 2 for 5 minutes;
Reading exercise 3 for 5 minutes;

Counting exercise 2 for 5 minutes;
Beanbags exercise 2 for 3 minutes;
Balance exercise 2 for 3 minutes.

Day 5: *Sequencing exercise 3* for 17 minutes;
Arrows exercise step 3 for 2 minutes;
Pattern exercise 2 for 17 minutes;
Spatial exercise for 1 minute;
Reading exercise 1 for 5 minutes;
Reading exercise 2 for 5 minutes;
Reading exercise 3 for 5 minutes;
Counting exercise 3 for 5 minutes;
Beanbags exercise 3 for 3 minutes.

Level 4

This program is to be followed until the learner is able to read all the word lists without hesitation. He must also be able to read chapters four and five of the reading book (or chapter four and five of *Rainbow Dreams*) without hesitations and without any errors.

Important note on *Counting exercise 3*: Days 1, 3 and 5 must be used to master a new step. Days 2 and 4 must be used to revise steps that had already been mastered.

The following program should be followed:

Day 1: *Sequencing exercise 3* for 15 minutes;
Arrows exercise step 3 for 2 minutes;
Pattern exercise 2 for 14 minutes;
Spatial exercise for 1 minute;
Reading exercise 4 for 15 minutes;
Counting exercise 3 for 5 minutes;
Logical thinking exercise 1 for 5 minutes;
Beanbags exercise 3 for 3 minutes.

Day 2: *Sequencing exercise 3* for 13 minutes;
Arrows exercise step 2 for 2 minutes;

Auditory exercise 2 for 13 minutes;
Spatial exercise for 1 minute;
Reading exercise 1 for 5 minutes;
Reading exercise 2 for 5 minutes;
Reading exercise 3 for 5 minutes;
Counting exercise 3 for 5 minutes;
Tables exercise for 5 minutes;
Beanbags exercise 4 for 3 minutes;
Balance exercise 3 for 3 minutes.

Day 3: Follow program for Day 1.

Day 4: Follow program for Day 2.

Day 5: Follow program for Day 1.

21.

Frequently Asked Questions

Q: *From your experience, how long does it take generally before one starts seeing results when following the Audiblox program, and how long must one work with one's child before his problem will have been solved completely?*

A: In order to achieve *any* results it is important that the following pitfalls be avoided:

- Instead of taking pains to ensure that the exercises are done exactly right, many people, in their haste to get started, rush through the descriptions of the exercises. Rather start a week later, but make sure that you are doing everything exactly right. Read the descriptions of the relevant exercises several times, and if you have the demonstration video, watch the demonstrations of the relevant exercises carefully.

- After having had their children assessed, parents often simultaneously follow a variety of programs, each program intended to address a different aspect of the child's problem. Fifteen minutes per day are then spent on this program, twenty minutes on that program, ten minutes on yet another program, and so on. In this way, *Audiblox* is often also squeezed somewhere into the schedule. One should be wary of such an approach. Although not all programs can be written off as a mere waste of time—some certainly do offer good possibilities of application— following too many programs at once, especially in the initial stages, can prevent a "pyramid of repetition" from being constructed. Without building this "pyramid of repetition" *first*, it will not be possible to address a child's—or an adult's—reading problem in an effective manner.

When the above-mentioned pitfalls have been avoided, the speed of improvement is generally dependent on a number of factors. A few are:

- The giftedness of the learner: The more gifted a learner, the faster his progress will be.
- The severity of the learning problem: The more severe the learning problem, the more work will be required to help the learner to "catch-up."
- The time spent on the program: Success is commensurate to the amount of time and effort expended on the program.
- The presence of a language problem: In the case of a language problem, especially if the problem is severe, progress is usually slower in the initial stages than in cases where a language problem is absent.

It must be noted that improvement is seldom gradual. When improvement becomes noticeable, it is usually sudden. Parents and teachers often say that it was as if a "miracle had happened." The following letter, posted on an LD bulletin board on the Internet, is an example of what one can expect to see when improvement becomes noticeable:

I have a dyslexic boy who is now ten. He is going into Grade Five. He usually ends his year with a fail in reading and writing. Since Grade Two the school has wanted him to repeat his year and I have refused, promising to try to help him myself. We have been through many different programs (at school and at home), with very little results.

We began *Audiblox* about six weeks before Grade Four ended. His concentration has greatly improved; he actually listens to what the teacher is saying; less clowning in class. He can now actually pick up a book and read on his own, something he never did before. The principal called me to tell me that for the first time my son passed all his courses! He got a C in reading and a B in writing!

The average time one usually has to wait for this change to occur is about three months. It can, however, be as soon as six weeks, as the example above illustrates, or it can take as long as six months. It should be noted that the mother, who posted the letter above, worked diligently for a half-hour per day, six days per week.

If a crash course is followed, as explained in chapter 20, results usually show much sooner than three months.

After this initial—and usually clearly visible—intellectual jump, it frequently happens that the learner finds himself on a plateau again. After a few weeks or months, there is often another leap forward. This pattern can repeat itself many times.

One must make sure that a learner's problem has been solved completely before discontinuing the program. The minimum time that is required to achieve this is about one year, but it can take as long as two, and in rare cases even more. Once it has become clear that the erstwhile learning problem is now definitely something of the past, it is highly advisable to continue for at least a few months more. If one discontinues the program before the foundational skills of reading have been thoroughly automatized, there is the danger of a relapse. On the other hand, once the foundational skills have been automatized and the learner is clearly no longer behind in his reading, spelling and writing, the problem will not return if the program is discontinued. However, it must be made clear that, the longer one continues the program, the greater will be the value that the learner will derive from it.

Q: *My son has been diagnosed with a nonverbal learning disability. He has a variety of academic difficulties, including problems with reading comprehension, mathematics and science. Will Audiblox address his problems?*

A: Yes. In fact, in most cases it is easier and quicker to solve a nonverbal learning problem than a verbal learning problem. *Audiblox* addresses the *cause* of the nonverbal learning problem, i.e. the inadequate development of foundational learning skills such as visual perception and visual memory.

Mathematics is a subject that consists of two aspects:

- *Knowledge.* There is much in math that one simply has to know and that one therefore has to learn, for example many terms, definitions, symbols, theorems and axioms. These are all things that the learner must *know*, and not things that he must know how *to do.*
- *Skills.* There are, on the other hand, many things in mathematics that the learner must learn to *do,* like, for example, the skills of counting, of adding and subtracting, of multiplication and of division. Furthermore, one of the most important skills for math is logical thinking, which makes problem solving possible.

Many of the basic knowledge and skills mentioned above, that relate to mathematics, are taught and exercised in the *Audiblox* program, like for example counting, adding and subtracting, and multiplication tables. In addition, the skill of logical thinking is also taught. In the case of a younger learner, this should in most cases be sufficient to solve his math problem adequately. However, in the case of an older learner, merely following the *Audiblox* program may not be sufficient. The older learner has so far been unable to acquire the math skills adequately and to learn the knowledge that has been presented to him. Through the *Audiblox* exercises, he will certainly acquire the skills required for math, but he may also have fallen behind as far as the knowledge aspect of math is concerned. It may therefore be advisable to send him for extra math classes also, so that he may catch up on the knowledge aspect.

Q: *Besides being dyslexic, my son has also been diagnosed as ADHD. We really have a hard time getting him to cooperate with his teachers. He often does not respond to verbal instructions, fidgets constantly, and cannot stay seated. He wants his needs met immediately and is quite insistent if this does not happen. Will Audiblox address these problems?*

A: No, *Audiblox* will not address any of the problems you mentioned. It is advised that you read the book *The Myth of ADHD and Other Learning Disabilities. Parenting without Ritalin.* The book is available from Huntington House Publishers, Lafayette, Louisiana, U.S.A. Their telephone number is 337-237-7049 and their website address www.huntingtonhousebooks.com. The book acknowledges the symptoms of ADHD, but denies that ADHD is a psychiatric illness, and explains how symptoms such as the above can be alleviated.

Q: *Our son has a language problem. I am trying to imagine how we will be able to fit in three hours per day for him to listen to the stories on tape. It just doesn't seem possible.*

A: Remember that it was stated that it is not necessary for the child to sit still and listen to the stories all the time. A background of language must be created for the child. He may, therefore, continue with his other daily activities against this background. The stories can therefore be played, for example, while he is getting ready for school in the mornings, while you are driving him to and from school, while he is playing with the dog, or watching TV, or sitting at the dinner table. It can also be played during the first hour after he has gone to bed. In certain cases it may not be possible to use a walkman. A normal tape player can then be used. When one uses a walkman and one wishes to set the sound volume on the tape player, one should make sure that the words are clearly audible, but it should not be too loud, since this may cause a headache.

There may be days on which you will not be able to fit in the full three hours, but try the best you can.

Q: *I understand that you offer a service of customizing the Audiblox program to address the person's specific needs.*

A: A customized program can speed-up the results tremendously and is highly recommended—and sometimes necessary—in cases of severe and multiple learning problems. This service can easily be provided via e-mail. Visit the website www.audiblox2000.com for details.

However, if your program is not being customized, it is advised that you follow the program prescribed in chapter 20 to the letter.

Q: *I am a first-grade teacher, and would like to know more about implementing the Audiblox program in my classroom.*

A: It is recommended that you make use of the *Schoolblox* program. *Schoolblox* was designed to be used as part of the nursery school program and/or as part of the junior primary/elementary school program.

The teacher uses a large, rectangular board, called a PERSEPTO, while each learner has an *Audiblox Learner* set and a workbook. Introductory training is provided by means of a training manual and video. For more advanced training one must attend a training course. Visit the website www.audiblox2000.com for details.

Q: *From what age can one use the Audiblox program? I have a two-year-old and a four-year-old, and would like to prevent them from having reading problems when they go to school.*

A: *Audiblox* can be used from about three years and upwards. Until that age, language is the most important intellectual aspect to take care of. Parents should talk to their little ones from the day they are born, as much and as often as possible, often repeating the same words, the same phrases, and the same language structures over and over. It is also important to read to one's children often—especially to read the *same* story many times over—and to teach them rhymes and songs. When a child is about three years of age one can introduce the *Audiblox* program. The program below can be followed.

Preschool Level a

Because the attention span of a preschool child is still short, it is important to start with a short program of only ten minutes.

Important note on *Sequencing exercise 3*: One should start *Sequencing exercise 3* with only *two* blocks, add only *one* block every time the child has the row correct, and add none when he has it wrong, i.e. ②/1/0.

A description of *Counting exercise 1* follows directly after the program. Remember to start counting from one to three and back and to gradually add more blocks as the child progresses. This program is to be followed until the child can count fluently from one to five and back.

Day 1:   *Spatial exercise* for 1 minute;
         Sequencing exercise 3 for 7 minutes;
         Arrows exercise step 1 for 2 minutes.

Day 2:   *Pattern exercise 1* for 5 minutes;
         Arrows exercise step 1 for 2 minutes;
         Counting exercise 1 for 3 minutes.

Day 3:   Repeat the program of Day 1.

Day 4:   Repeat the program of Day 2.

Day 5:   Repeat the program of Day 1.

Preschool Level b

This program will require the child to concentrate for twenty minutes. Start *Sequencing exercise 3* with three blocks now, add one every time the child has the row correct, and add none when he has it wrong, i.e. ③/1/0. When doing *Counting exercise 1*, the child must now be ready to start learning to count from one to six and back.

This program is to be followed until the child can in one session get to fourteen blocks with *Sequencing exercise 3,* i.e. in seven minutes.

Day 1: *Spatial exercise* for 1 minute;
Sequencing exercise 3 for 7 minutes;
Arrows exercise step 1 for 2 minutes;
Counting exercise 1 for 4 minutes;
Pattern exercise 1 for 6 minutes.

Day2-5: Repeat the program of Day 1.

As soon as the child is able to get to fourteen blocks in a session with *Sequencing exercise 3*—i.e. in seven minutes—he is ready to advance to Preschool Level c.

Preschool Level c

The child must remain on this level until he has succeeded in doing a pattern with ten blocks correctly in *Pattern exercise 1*. Start *Sequencing exercise 3* with three blocks, but add two every time the child has the row correct, and add none when he has it wrong, i.e. ③/2/0.

Day 1: *Spatial exercise* for 1 minute;
Sequencing exercise 3 for 10 minutes;
Arrows exercise step 1 for 2 minutes;
Pattern exercise 1 for 10 minutes;
Reading exercise 1 for 7 minutes.

Day 2: *Counting exercise 1* for 4 minutes;
Sequencing exercise 3 for 9 minutes;
Arrows exercise step 1 for 2 minutes;
Pattern exercise 1 for 9 minutes;
Reading exercise 1 for 6 minutes.

Day 3: Repeat the program of Day 1.

Day 4: Repeat the program of Day 2.

Day 5:   Repeat the program of Day 1.

Preschool Level 8

Day 1:   *Spatial exercise* for 1 minute;
         Sequencing exercise 3 for 12 minutes;
         Arrows exercise step 1 for 2 minutes;
         Paper Crumpling exercise 1;
         Pattern exercise 1 for 12 minutes;
         Reading exercise 1 for 8 minutes;
         Beanbags exercise 1 for 4 minutes.

Day 2:   *Counting exercise 1* for 5 minutes;
         Sequencing exercise 3 for 11 minutes;
         Arrows exercise step 1 for 2 minutes;
         Paper Crumpling exercise 1;
         Auditory exercise 1 for 10 minutes;
         Reading exercise 1 for 8 minutes;
         Balance exercise 1 for 3 minutes.

Day 3:   Repeat the program of Day 1

Day 4:   Repeat the program of Day 2

Day 5:   Repeat the program of Day 1

The child must remain on this level until he is able to do a row of 25 blocks correctly in *Sequencing exercise 3* in a session of twelve minutes. As soon as he has achieved this, he may be put on the first level of the Dyslexia Program (see chapter 20).

Important Note: When the child advances to the Dyslexia Program, instead of doing the *Pattern exercise* on Day 2, the time allocated to the *Pattern exercise* should be divided as follows:

Beanbags exercise 1 for 4 minutes
Auditory exercise 1 for 10 minutes
Balance exercise 1 for 3 minutes

- As soon as the child has made sufficient progress on *Beanbags exercise 1,* the tutor must move him up to *Beanbags exercise 2.*
- As soon as he has made sufficient progress on *Beanbags exercise 2,* the tutor must move him up to *Beanbags exercise 3,* et cetera.
- In the same way the child must be promoted from *Balance exercise 1* to *Balance exercise 2,* et cetera.

It is very important, however, *not* to move too soon from one level of an exercise to the next, more difficult level. Remember that these exercises address skills that need to be *automatized.*

Counting Exercise 1

The child sits at a table opposite the tutor. He must now carry out the instructions that follow. The tutor will start by asking the child to put a block of any color, for example "yellow," on the table directly in front of him. Then the tutor may say, "I want you to take a green block from your box and put it to the *left* of the other one." The child must put the green block to the left (his own left) of the yellow block, leaving a space of about the width of his hand between the two blocks. Then the tutor may continue by saying, "Now find a red one and put it to the *right* of those two blocks." Again he must leave a space of about the width of his hand between the yellow block and the red one.

The child has now arranged a row of three blocks on the table in front of him. He now has to put his right arm on the table, with the forearm directly in front of his body and parallel to the edge of the table. This will mean that the elbow will be at an angle of about 90 degrees. The right arm must be kept in this position for the duration of the exercise. He must put the index finger of the left hand on the first block on the left of the row, saying, "One!" Then he puts the finger on the second block, saying, "Two!" In this way the child continues counting all the blocks. When he arrives at the third block, he must continue by counting backwards to one again. If there were any hesitations anywhere in this counting up and down, the tutor must let the child count again, up and down. He must continue counting with the left hand for the whole session, the right arm still resting on the table in front of him. At the next session he must switch hands. Then the right hand counts and the left arm must rest on the table. Please note that the child's forearm must be directly in front of the child on the table.

As soon as he can count the three blocks fluently and without any hesitation—several successive sessions may be required to achieve this—the tutor may instruct the child to add an extra block either to the left or the right of the existing row, and then the counting continues, now with one block more.

As soon as the child is able to count four blocks without any mistakes or hesitations, one can add another block. In this way the tutor can continue adding more and more blocks, up to a maximum of ten. When the child is able to count ten blocks up and down fluently and without any hesitation, he is ready to go to *Counting exercise 2*.

Auditory Exercise 1

The preschool child may not be able to do *Auditory exercise 1* with four blocks already. For his benefit color combinations of two blocks and three blocks are added below.

2 blocks
1. yellow blue
2. green white
3. white yellow
4. black red
5. blue black
6. red white
7. blue yellow
8. green red
9. yellow red
10. white blue

3 blocks
1. blue red black
2. red yellow green
3. yellow green blue
4. black white blue

5. white blue red
6. green blue yellow
7. blue yellow white
8. yellow red blue
9. blue white green
10. red white green